THE MOVIE BOOK

BOOK

by Steven H. Scheuer

A Ridge Press Book/Playboy Press

A Ridge Press Book/Playboy Press

Special thanks to
Richard Koszarski, my research associate, for his invaluable
assistance in preparation of the manuscript.
Mary Corliss, a knowledgeable and resourceful picture editor, who
managed to locate many new stills from venerable old films.

Editor-in-Chief: Jerry Mason
Editor: Adolph Suehsdorf
Art Director: Albert Squillace
Managing Editor: Moira Duggan
Associate Editor: Mimi Gold
Associate Editor: Barbara Hoffbeck
Associate Editor: Madelyn Larsen
Associate Editor: Kathleen Murray
Art Associate: David Namias
Art Production: Doris Mullane

Published simultaneously in the United States and Canada by Playboy Press,
Chicago, Illinois. Printed in the United States of America.
Library of Congress Catalog Card Number: 74-82056.
ISBN: 87223-413-4. First Edition.

Playboy and Rabbit Head design are trademarks of Playboy, 919 North
Michigan Avenue, Chicago, Illinois 60611 (U.S.A.). Reg. U.S. Pat. Off.,
marca registrada, marque déposée.

Dedication
In loving memory of Charlie Cook
and for Jimbo, who
first encouraged me to study
the art of film.

CONTENTS

INTROD

UCTION

The first history of the film was published in 1895 by one of Mr. Edison's assistants. At fifty-five pages, it was a short history.

Eighty years have passed since then, and the story of the motion picture has grown somewhat more complicated. Not only is there an industry to consider, but an art as well, with a living history that grows richer and more complex day by day.

Of course, so dynamic a medium has been the subject of many histories, large and small. By the 1930's and 40's a whole range of critics were attempting to cast the movies into a variety of political, psychological, or aesthetic molds. This produced a long series of lopsided views which attempted to analyze every aspect of this developing art with the aid of a single yardstick. Revisionist historians of more recent years have done much to redress the balance, but they also have special causes to plead.

I don't claim, of course, that this is the first objective history of the movies. In boiling down their complicated story to these few hundred pages, I have had to do a great deal of picking and choosing, deciding, ultimately, on the basis of my own selective judgments. But I do feel that the format of this film-history book is a special one that allows a rather involved story to be told clearly and concisely. An introductory section which spells out the main evolution of the film drama is followed by a much more eclectic account of the growth of the movies, a study of those genres that made up the greater part of Hollywood history. The standard approach to film history, the year-by-year or country-by-country approach, is useful but limited. One loses the trees for the forest. But the fluctuating fortunes of the western or the horror film, for example, are barometers that can help us understand the development of the film world as a whole. The changing fortunes of film genres reflect shifting audience tastes, of course, but on a more subtle level they also reveal the evolving fashions of filmmaking itself. Early filmmakers lacked sophisticated studio facilities, so they made a lot of westerns. The coming of sound brought on an invasion of musical films. These examples are obvious, but they serve to indicate the organic relationship between genre films and the larger state of the art. This investigation of film genres is a peculiarly modern concern, for earlier writers expressed little but scorn for them. Today, though, their place as the master threads in the larger fabric of film history is quite clear, and by tracing their fortunes the rambling growth pattern of the motion picture suddenly becomes more clear.

In addition, throughout this broader investigation I

have stopped to consider other major factors in the movie story —the influence of directors like Griffith and John Ford, the studio system, television, and the impact of those foreign films that actually made it to American shores. Films cannot be understood without some grasp of the process of their creation, and I have tried to make this a story of filmmaking as well as a story of films. In this book I am much more interested in providing a structure for the reader to flesh out with his own viewing experience, than in piling up a mountain of critical comments on one title after another. When I stop to analyze particular films or filmmakers, it is to clarify the much larger context of which I find them representative.

Although it may seem surprising, the present historical moment is the best yet for getting a balanced overview of film history. The intensive researches of film scholars over the past decade have illuminated many dark corners completely overlooked by earlier writers. Recent strides in film-archive work and restoration have so stuffed museums and private collections that a critic has more older films available for reappraisal than at any time previously. Today we are able to review landmark achievements by directors from Antonioni to Zinnemann, and to study at firsthand films that critics like James Agee were forced to ignore as lost forever. This book is based quite closely on such an active reappraisal of film history, and for this reason I feel that the comments on the classical period of the movies are of special interest. They establish a context against which the turbulent world of the modern cinema begins to make a lot of sense.

But, for all this talk, we must never forget that the language of film is a language of images. The hundreds of rare stills reprinted here are not present just for their nostalgic value. Rather, they supplement and amplify the text, explaining at a glance what might not have been possible in any number of words. Most have never been seen since their first appearance; they have been culled from private collections, studio holdings, and museum vaults throughout the world.

Have I written the definitive history of film? Hardly. That task would easily fill several huge multivolume encyclopedias and would require many thousands of pages. What I have tried to do is present a way of looking at film history, of organizing the nearly one million titles that make up the body of this twentieth-century art. That was quite enough of a chore right there, but it still reserves for you, the reader, the pleasure of making the important discoveries. **—S.H.S.**

New York City June, 1974

At the close of the nineteenth century the moving picture was an idea whose time had come. Photography had advanced to a stage where even hobbyist experimentation was widespread and exposure time had been cut to a fraction of a second. The Zoetrope, or "wheel of life," had firmly established itself as an appealing parlor toy, and a spectator could peer through the slits of its revolving drum to glimpse an instant of endlessly repeated cartoon motion. For decades the inventive impulse of man labored to add movement to the images which were so integral a part of Victorian entertainments. Audiences flocked to magic-lantern lectures and looked at dioramas, and even the most modest home boasted a picture album and a stereopticon. By 1876 the phonograph had captured living sound, but the link that would perfect motion photography was still missing: a medium to transport the hundreds of images required to duplicate movement. Patent records of the period list scores of Rube Goldberg devices designed to fool the eye: enormous spinning glass discs or intricately slotted metal drums, all ingenious, but in the end all hopelessly impractical. That transparent celluloid film could be this medium was apparent almost simultaneously to inventors all over the world who were working on the problem. The web of creation is too confused to ever untangle, but it might be pointed out that the moving picture was quite definitely not the invention of Thomas Alva Edison. That history should remember Edison as the cinema's creator is a tribute more to his abilities as a showman than to his skill as an inventor. Against Edison's better judgment, one of his assistants, W. K. L. Dickson, perfected the basic Kinetoscope device largely from the earlier researches of the English photographer Eadweard Muybridge and the Frenchman Étienne Marey, but Edison's own attitude toward the work was laissez-faire at best. His true place of honor in the history of the cinema comes from his successful merchandising of the device, and the commercial history of the medium could well be dated from America's first copyrighted motion picture, **Edison Kinetoscopic Record of a Sneeze, January 7, 1893,** registered at the Copyright Office by Dickson two days later. Edison's idea was to exploit the device as a peep-show attraction, reasoning that projection to large audiences would quickly wear out its novelty. But public interest was so deep-rooted that others developed the projection principle before him. Latham's Eidoloscope was exhibited in America in 1895, and the Lumières gave the first European projection that December.

The introduction of theatrical projection was the final element necessary for the creation of "the movies," as distinct from the peep shows and parlor toys which had come before. The shared audience experience, the mystique of darkness, and the enforced concentration on the luminous, larger-than-life image dazzled turn-of-the-century audiences who, certainly at first, would watch anything put before them. But gradually they grew weary of trains arriving at stations, waves breaking on the shore, or a cavalry on parade. Vaudeville houses moved their film programs from the front of the bill to the "chaser" position, to clear the house at the end of each show. By 1900 the novelty

14

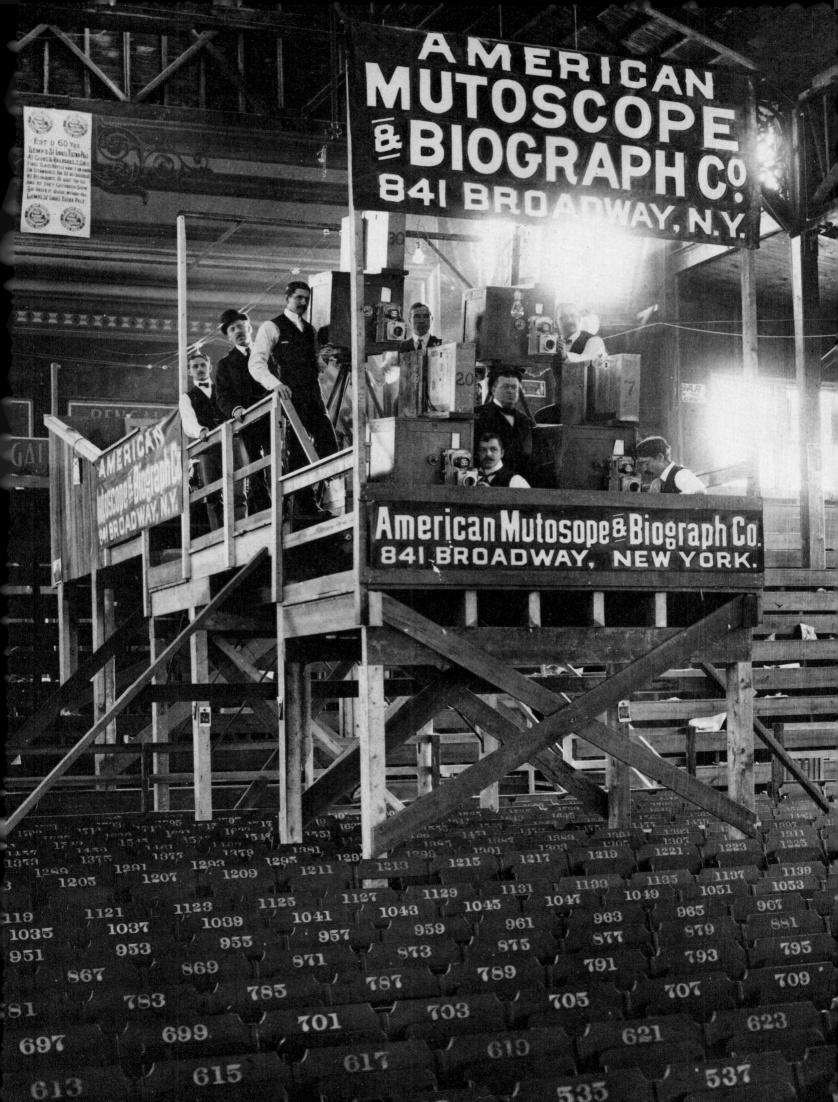

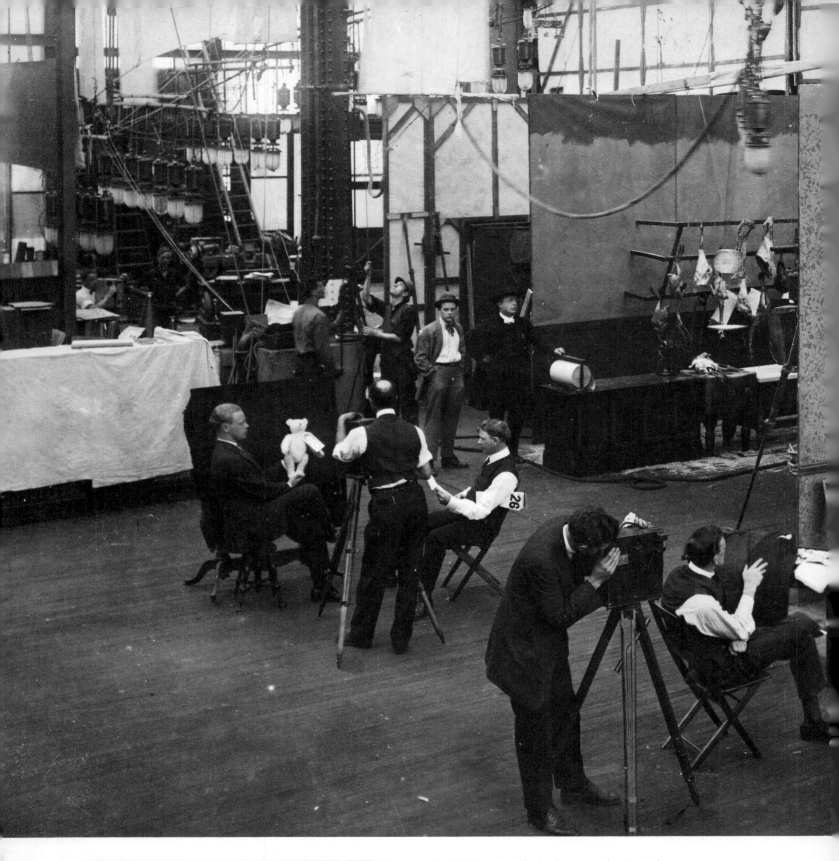

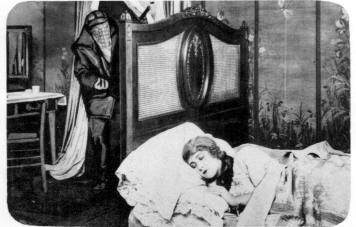

By 1912 the story film had come to dominate the screen, and the elements of film grammar were already well established. Above, the Edison studio in action, with different "units" shooting side by side in typically theatrical settings. The first efforts at expanding the scope of the film came from Italy. In films like **Quo Vadis?** (1912, r), they made good use of huge casts and extravagant settings, supplying what no theater production could ever offer. D. W. Griffith built on this element of spectacle in **The Birth of a Nation** (1915, top r), combining it with a superior command of film technique. Notice in this enlargement how he alters the shape of the image for dramatic effect. And, of course, also in at the beginning was the serial. Here's Pearl White (l) in episode One of **The Exploits of Elaine** (1915).

had worn off and the moving picture as an entertainment form was in danger of disappearing. But even as had happened a decade before, a new idea swept suddenly through the major film-producing centers. The Williamson Company in England, Georges Méliès and Alice Blaché in France, and Edwin S. Porter in America began simultaneous production of story films. Although it certainly was not the first film narrative, Porter's **The Great Train Robbery,** copyrighted by the Edison Company on December 1, 1903, epitomized this new wave of filmmaking. Porter broke the film down into comparatively brief shots, intelligently alternated interiors and exteriors, panned his camera to capture moving action, incorporated some primitive matte work, and even offered a highly melodramatic close-up of the gang leader firing point-blank at the audience. The film was sensationally successful and remained for years a staple of the burgeoning storefront nickelodeon trade.

Within a dozen years film grew from a novelty arcade attraction to a major American industry. Edison was quickly joined by a series of competitors who sprang up as far west as Chicago, and whose equipment varied but slightly from his own. Foreign films flooded the market as well—Italian Cines, Méliès and Pathé in France, Hepworth in England, and the Danish Nordisk company—all competing for time on American screens. To bring order (and profit) out of this chaos, the major international patent holders formed the Motion Picture Patents Company in 1908, attempting to control all production and exhibition through exercise of patent rights. Theater owners were forced to cough up a weekly "license fee," and producers not in the club were branded as illegal "independents" and harassed by goon squads. "Independent" directors like Allan Dwan and Cecil B. De Mille often appeared on location fully armed to protect themselves against Patents Company snipers. The trust was eventually busted in the federal courts, but it had long since lost the war with the independents as far as audiences were concerned. Artistically and economically conservative, the trust refused to accept the coming of feature films or the establishment of the star system, two gambles which paid off heavily for the independents. Of the original nine members of the Patents Company, only Vitagraph struggled into the twenties; the new Hollywood was only for those with the courage to be innovative.

Before the final wreck of the Patents Company, the chief director at Biograph finally threw up his hands and quit. D. W. Griffith had begun directing there in 1908, and by 1913 he had hundreds of short films to his credit. During this period he had taken the basic vocabulary of the film, bits and pieces introduced by Porter and others years earlier, and welded it into a cinematic grammar, an expressive flow of shots capable of generating joy, sorrow, pity, fear, or exultation. With his cameraman Billy Bitzer, Griffith had demonstrated in film the potentialities of an art form, but he chafed under the restrictions of the conservative Biograph management. He needed longer running times to develop the complex emotional schemes which interested him. And he needed

Some directors with artistic pretensions began exploring more sophisticated aspects of film storytelling. Left: Cecil B. De Mille tried to make **The Whispering Chorus** (1918), with Raymond Hatton, his most "artistic" work. He may have tried too hard. Right: Mary Pickford played a double role in **Stella Maris** (1918), one of Marshall Neilan's best films. This forgotten pioneer was among the most important of the early directors. Below: D. W. Griffith's **Intolerance** (1916) has long been considered the artistic peak of the early silent film. Four stories were told simultaneously, and Robert Harron and Mae Marsh appeared in the modern story.

One of the earliest experiments in film stylization was Maurice Tourneur's **Prunella** (opposite, top). Jules Raucourt and Marguerite Clark starred in the 1918 fantasy, which was designed by Ben Carré. But audiences rejected it in favor of the real world. Bottom: Griffith's **True Heart Susie** (1919), the finest of his romantic pastorals, with Robert Harron, Clarine Seymour, and Lillian Gish. The arrival in 1922 of Robert Flaherty's **Nanook of the North** (above) opened an entirely new field for filmic exploration, that of the documentary.

vast amounts of money to capture on a grand scale the dreams he had for the cinema. Deserting the sinking ship, he moved to Mutual, where he gathered his forces before beginning his most ambitious project. When Griffith released **The Birth of a Nation** in 1915, the motion picture abruptly came of age. Technically the film was a wonder in the scope of its production and in the ingenuity of its stylistic devices, but even more important were the emotions it unleashed. The film stirred its audiences with artfully crafted pathos and undreamed-of excitement, but it stirred uglier emotions as well. The sight of the Ku Klux Klan riding to the rescue of embattled white womanhood touched off race riots in many cities and led to the banning of the film in several places. The censors hacked away at the prints and excised the most objectionable material, but their very ardor proved Griffith's main point. With this one film he demonstrated conclusively the medium's power to stir the heart and mind, and brought instant recognition to what was still largely regarded as a cheap plaything. Moved chiefly by this storm of liberal protest, Griffith marshaled even greater forces and retaliated with the vast panorama of **Intolerance.** Holding four distinct narratives in carefully balanced counterpoint, the film showed how self-appointed (and self-serving) "uplifters" throughout history hypocritically destroy true love and happiness in the name of religion, patriotism, or justice. Thematically as well as technically, it shot completely over the heads of critics and audiences alike, many of whom accused it of having no plot. Griffith personally assumed the debts of this box-office disaster and spent years repaying his creditors, never again attempting so extravagant an experiment. Instead he turned to intimate character studies, like **Broken Blossoms,** the story of a gentle Chinese man (Richard Barthelmess) and his love for a white girl (Lillian Gish) set against the background of London's Limehouse. On a more personal level, a series of pastoral dramas and romances recaptured the countryside of Griffith's youth, and in masterpieces like **True Heart Susie** and **A Romance of Happy Valley** we are given a rare insight into this extremely private corner of Griffith's world. These films were joined by a pastoral cycle which nostalgically evoked a rural America that was even then quite obviously slipping away. Films like King Vidor's **The Jack Knife Man** and Henry King's **Tol'able David** dealt with uncomplicated conflicts and emotions set against unspoiled American landscapes. For a time extremely popular, the genre had completely disappeared by the beginning of the urbanized thirties. Griffith himself did not survive the decade. His ambitious drama of the Revolutionary War, **America,** was not successful, and the downbeat **Isn't Life Wonderful?** was rejected by audiences. Only **Way Down East** kept him financially solvent, for a time, as audiences found irresistible the rescue of Lillian Gish from the brink of an icy waterfall. With **Orphans of the Storm,** Griffith demonstrated for the last time the artistic vision that had placed him at the head of the industry for a dozen years. Soon he lost his own studio and was hired by Paramount to direct vehicles for Don Alvarado and W. C. Fields. By 1931 he was through.

Right: Swedish director Victor Sjöström meets the grim reaper in his film **The Phantom Carriage** (1920). He later returned to acting in films like **Wild Strawberries.** Critics complained that while the Europeans were producing art, Hollywood was wasting its time on things like **The Sheik** (1921, below), with Valentino. But at least one Hollywood director never wallowed in entertainment for its own sake. Stroheim's **Greed** (far right) shocked audiences with its brutality and realism in 1924. Here, Gibson Gowland has just murdered Zasu Pitts on Christmas Eve.

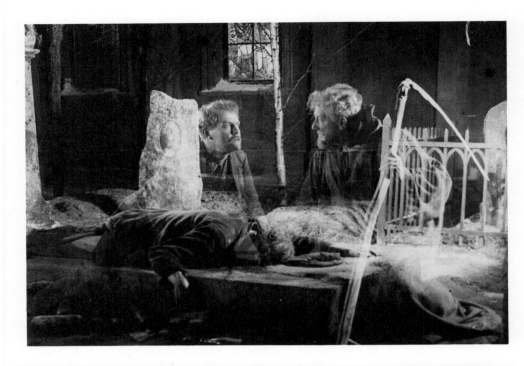

Cecil B. De Mille passed through a crisis similar to Griffith's, but was shrewd enough to dump his artistic ambitions when they got in the way of commercial success. Directing his first film in 1913, De Mille quickly produced a string of box-office successes, including a notable **Carmen** with Geraldine Farrar. But his artistic credentials were also strongly established in his first years as a director. **The Cheat** (1915), a stylish and erotic melodrama featuring Sessue Hayakawa and Fannie Ward, displayed a continental sophistication completely lacking in Griffith's work and created a major sensation. De Mille's artistic pretentions grew more and more apparent, and he frequently experimented with complex lighting effects which he called "Rembrandt lighting." He poured all of his energies into **The Whispering Chorus** (1918), a grim and fatalistic tale of a man haunted by inner furies, but it failed miserably at the box office and De Mille vowed never to repeat that mistake. He quickly switched to a series of titillating comedies and melodramas, such as **The Affairs of Anatol** and **The Golden Bed,** which make up the bulk of his twenties releases. They provided a peek into a wealthy, often "decadent" high-society life, and always ended with an inescapably moral conclusion. The poor girl found she really didn't like those people on the other side of the tracks, or the rich wife received a well-deserved comeuppance. De Mille was slow to enter the spectacle field since his **Joan the Woman,** with Farrar terribly miscast as the Maid, flopped in 1916. But in 1923 he parted the Red Sea for the first **Ten Commandments** and the De Mille epic formula was born. Balanced between a modern and a biblical story, the effect of this film was rather diffuse, but in **King of Kings** he produced one of the finest silent-period films, an intelligent and extremely handsome production, and one which informs much of his later work.

In **Sunset Boulevard,** Erich von Stroheim says that there were three directors who showed promise in the early days: D. W. Griffith, Cecil B. De Mille, and Max von Mayerling. Of course, Stroheim is talking about himself, although his own career as a director did not begin quite so early. Stroheim gained his first important film experience with Griffith, beginning as an extra, and later serving as a technical adviser as well. His portrayal of a Hun in **Hearts of the World** led to a series of such roles, most notably in **The Heart of Humanity,** where he may be seen tossing a baby out a window while attempting to rape a Red Cross nurse. He directed himself in **Blind Husbands** (1919), playing an unscrupulous seducer loose in the Tyrol, but it was **Foolish Wives** that cemented his reputation. Universal touted him as "$troheim, director of the first million-dollar picture." The eleven-month shooting schedule and construction of elaborately realistic settings ran the budget to unheard-of heights, but Stroheim felt that he, the artist, should not have to worry about such things as money. Although **Foolish Wives** was profitable, Universal found his extravagance too chancy and threw him off his next film, **Merry-Go-Round.** This turned out to be an historic move, as it established the primacy of producing companies over directors, who prior to this time had operated with wide freedom. Stroheim

Cecil B. De Mille produced the
first version of **The Ten
Commandments** in 1923 and
successfully combined sex and religion,
a formula he followed for years to
come. Here, Estelle Taylor leads
the worship of the Golden Calf.

went immediately to Goldwyn, for whom he directed **Greed,** a massive transposition of Frank Norris's naturalistic novel **McTeague.** Taken from him and hacked to a fraction of its length, **Greed** was rejected by a public totally unprepared for its intense sordidness and savagery. But Stroheim quickly rebounded with a critically and commercially successful version of **The Merry Widow,** featuring Mae Murray and John Gilbert, and then began preparing his masterpiece, **The Wedding March.** A delicate story of star-crossed lovers, it is set against the crumbling glitter of pre-war Vienna. This film also was taken from him and released in truncated form, then quickly lost in the wave of sound pictures. His **Queen Kelly** was shelved after a half-million dollars had been spent. Stroheim's career seemed at an end. Finally, Fox allowed him to direct a cheap talkie, **Walking Down Broadway,** which was completed amicably and under budget. But studio executives pounced on the film for alleged aberrations, ordered it reshot, and dumped Stroheim. It was the last film he directed. Stroheim's major contribution lies in the psychological complexity and maturity of his work and in his characteristic visual style, unblinking and realistic on the one hand, but dreamily stylized and romantic when necessary. Unlike De Mille, he lacked the flexibility, or desire, to compromise with the growing studio system. And like his mentor Griffith, his career was forcibly ended by an ungrateful and thoughtless industry.

The one filmmaker of the time most responsible for the growth of the industry was Thomas H. Ince. Ince had started as an actor at Biograph during Griffith's tenure, but quickly moved west, where he was associated with such companies as Universal and Kay Bee. There he wrote, produced, directed, and edited dozens of short films, gaining a thorough knowledge of the filmmaking process. When he opened his own studios at Inceville, he put into operation an efficiency plan for the production of films from carefully prepared scenarios. Work was divided among various specialized departments, all overseen by a chief producer who supervised closely a large number of productions being shot simultaneously all over the lot. In its most excessive form this procedure came to be thought of as the Hollywood factory system, but Ince was able to avoid the trap of a mass-produced look and emphasize the benefits of collaboration. Seen today, his films are notable for their simplicity and realism. He made stars of William S. Hart and Charles Ray by giving their productions an unprecedented feeling of authenticity. Among his more interesting productions are **The Wrath of the Gods,** a spectacular drama featuring Hayakawa, **Civilization,** one of a group of antiwar films, and **The Italian,** a study of immigrants on New York's lower East Side, which seems a precursor of neorealism. Unfortunately, Ince's career was abruptly cut short when he died under mysterious circumstances in 1924.

Ince had been one of the guests on a November cruise of the "Oneida," William Randolph Hearst's floating pleasure palace. This particular trip turned into one of the more excessive Hollywood extravaganzas of the

25

Preceding pages: Douglas
Fairbanks in **The Black Pirate** (1926),
Hollywood's first all-Technicolor
feature. Right: Margaret Livingston
and George O'Brien in F. W.
Murnau's **Sunrise** (1927). Fox imported
Murnau to produce some real
European art films in America,
and this was the finest example.
The late silent directors were
greatly influenced by the German
camera style, and its traces
turned up in such films as Clarence
Brown's **A Woman of Affairs**
(1929, above), with John
Gilbert and Greta Garbo.

Prohibition era, and after two days at sea Ince was taken ashore at San Diego. It
was said that he was suffering from "acute indigestion." Shrouded in secrecy,
Ince—or his body—was rushed to Los Angeles, where his death was an-
nounced as the result of heart failure brought on by the earlier indigestion. His
body was quickly cremated, allegedly at Hearst's bidding, but the cloud which
covered his last days only brought on a flurry of wild rumors. One speculation
was that Ince was already dead when taken off the yacht, supposedly shot by
Hearst himself. Already somewhat miffed at a suspected liaison between his
mistress, Marion Davies, and comedian Charlie Chaplin, also a guest on the
cruise, it was claimed that Hearst had surprised Marion with Tom Ince and lost
control of the situation. This was all constructed out of leak and conjecture, as
none of the supposed witnesses ever testified to such goings-on, among them,
Louella Parsons, who quickly thereafter became chief Hollywood columnist (for
life!) of the entire Hearst syndicate. What made Ince's death even more suspi-
cious was that it followed a whole series of grand Hollywood scandals, including the Arbuckle case (more about this later); a growing exposure of heavy drug
traffic in Hollywood which had culminated in the death of matinee idol Wallace
Reid; and the murder of prominent director William Desmond Taylor. Taylor
had been shot to death in his apartment on a February night in 1922, and the
police investigation immediately overturned a couple of rocks. Arriving on the
night of the murder, they were greeted by some Paramount executives burning
the director's private papers, but the conflagration proved incomplete. It was
soon discovered that Taylor had been carrying on a series of affairs with, among
others, Mack Sennett comedienne Mabel Normand and top Paramount star
Mary Miles Minter, both of whom were immediately tried in the headlines
across the country. Each was suspected of being the mysterious figure seen
running from the scene of the crime, described as being dressed like a man, but
running like a woman! Tabloids screamed that Taylor was the focal point of a
Hollywood sex-and-drugs cult and embellished their claims with lurid "evidence." The two stars faded in the evening sky, joining a host of lesser lights who
also were the victims of the scandals of the early twenties. Those were the days
when Will Hays, President Harding's dour Postmaster General, was hired in an
attempt to salvage Hollywood's reputation, but it was a decade before the "Hays
Office" clamped down with the full force of industry-sanctioned censorship.

The producers were obviously wary about giving Hays such
powers and would have preferred to keep him only as a figurehead. But the
increasingly raunchy tone of Hollywood releases eventually forced their hand.
Stroheim alone could have brought on a wave of blue-nose repression in
twenties America. One reason Stroheim's films appeared in such a fragmented,
mutilated form was their scissoring by the censors that did exist in those days.
His vaunted realism even extended—or perhaps one should say particularly
extended—into the notorious orgy sequences that run through many of his films.
For the brothel scenes in **The Wedding March,** Stroheim imported real prosti-

tutes from Madame Francine's, a particularly extravagant bordello that was long a favorite of his. The whole ambience of a Viennese whorehouse was re-created in almost exact detail and shot in bleary-eyed, eighteen-hour sessions behind locked studio doors. Booze flowed freely and the crew was told to shoot everything, including some highjinks with the whores and a couple of burros. What happened to this footage is not known. Suffice it to say that only a very convincing few minutes of this episode remains in the film. Stroheim brought the girls from Madame Francine's back in **Queen Kelly,** a film that went somewhat deeper into sadism than his earlier work. One can still see flashes of the mad queen's whip collection in some of the shots, but most of this material didn't see the light of day. The central episode of **Queen Kelly** was to have been a scene showing Gloria Swanson, just out of a convent school, being forced into a marriage with a degenerate African planter (played by one of Stroheim's favorites, Tully Marshall). All of this happens over her dead aunt's bier in an upstairs room of the aunt's brothel in Dar Es Salaam. As Marshall chased Swanson around the bed while shooting this scene, he grabbed her hand and dribbled saliva over it. "Why did you do that!" screamed Gloria, as she tore herself from Marshall's grasp. "Von Stroheim told me to," he answered, and Swanson walked off the set to make her famous "there's a madman in charge" call to Joseph P. Kennedy, the film's financial backer. It was the last day of shooting and the film remained incomplete, Swanson and Kennedy taking a half-million dollar loss because of their decision to throw in the towel.

By the mid-twenties Hollywood was in full swing, having discovered and perfected the sure-fire formula of romantic escapism. Castles towered over Hollywood back lots as Douglas Fairbanks took the lead in the production of swashbuckling spectacles. In **The Mark of Zorro, Robin Hood, The Thief of Bagdad,** and **The Black Pirate,** Fairbanks successfully evaded the problems of the twentieth century and audiences clamored for more. On a less athletic plane, another form of swashbuckling was provided by Rudolph Valentino, who in **The Sheik** and **Monsieur Beaucaire** created a cult that still exists fifty years after his death. Valentino came to prominence in **The Four Horsemen of the Apocalypse** and **Blood and Sand,** but was not always served as well in later vehicles. Unlike Fairbanks, he did not have complete control over his films and occasionally was presented in something as silly as **The Young Rajah.** Rivaling Fairbanks and Valentino in popularity, Lon Chaney marked a very different type of twenties star. For years he had worked himself up through extra and bit parts, reaching the peak of his career in Universal's **The Hunchback of Notre Dame** and **The Phantom of the Opera.** Today, however, his performances for Tod Browning in such offbeat MGM releases as **The Unholy Three, The Unknown,** and **West of Zanzibar** project a disquieting sense of the macabre.

The Unknown was probably the most disturbing of these, a circus tale which featured Chaney as Alonzo the Armless, whose act consisted of hurling knives at Joan Crawford with his feet. Joan is romantically pursued by

Stroheim turned more heavily to romanticism after the **Greed** debacle, and his masterpiece, **The Wedding March,** finally appeared in 1928, two years after shooting began.

All the apple blossoms in this garden were artificial, handmade of paper or wax, and individually fastened to the branches. Hal Mohr was responsible for the much-admired photography. Here Von romances Fay Wray underneath a watchful crucifix, a standard obsession of his.

Another two examples of the peak of silent-film art
in 1928. Left: Raoul Walsh and Gloria Swanson
in Walsh's **Sadie Thompson,** her best film and
his first masterwork. Above: Fun en masse in King
Vidor's **The Crowd,** a film heavily influenced by
German films, with James Murray and Eleanor Boardman.

Maria Falconetti in Dreyer's **The Passion of Joan of Arc** (1928), one of the last great works of the silent screen. It was ignored by audiences in favor of talking pictures. Composed largely of intense close-ups, this is one of the few times in the film that we see Joan in a long shot.

Strongman Norman Kerry, but she recoils from his touch, loathing the embrace of a man's arms. She seems drawn to Chaney, but he finds himself unable to reciprocate, since he is only faking his armlessness. For years he has lived with his arms strapped tightly to his side because he is a murderer being sought by the police and can easily be identified by the double thumbs on each of his hands. His passion for Joan finally becomes uncontrollable and he has his arms amputated, but of course when he returns she proudly tells him that she has overcome her earlier phobia and has made it with the Strongman. Chaney's close-up here and in similar moments of supreme irony contain his most chilling bits of acting, and leave the viewer's memory permanently scarred with a distinctly unpleasant, Browningesque image.

The twenties were not all Hollywood nonsense, however. Robert Flaherty's **Nanook of the North,** a documentary of the daily struggle for existence of the Eskimo, surprised everyone by becoming a worldwide success. But an attempt to follow it up with a South Seas picture, **Moana,** was just as surprising a failure. It was the drama in Nanook's life which accounted for that film's popularity, but in **Moana** the natives played all day and picked fruit off the trees. Audiences were more interested in entertainment than anthropology. Karl Brown's **Stark Love,** shot in the Blue Ridge Mountains with a cast of mountain people, was important in bringing documentary techniques to the fiction film, but its example was not immediately followed. Films like Stroheim's **Greed,** or **The Salvation Hunters,** the first work of Josef von Sternberg, were occasionally produced and widely discussed, but audiences preferred romances on a larger scale. At the time of its appearance, **The Covered Wagon** was hailed around the world as a landmark, but its story of the crossing of the Plains seems heavy-handed today and is distinctly inferior to John Ford's **The**

Iron Horse and **Three Bad Men,** which came soon after. Probably the perfect balance of commercial and artistic considerations in the mid-twenties was struck by King Vidor's **The Big Parade,** which examined the Great War from the perspective of the individual soldier. Produced at some distance from the Armistice, it was a far cry from the anti-Hun tracts of the war years, but not yet as cynical in its perceptions as the antiwar films of the early thirties—**All Quiet on the Western Front** and **Journey's End,** for example. **The Big Parade** helped establish MGM as a major power in the twenties, but perhaps more typical an image of the Lion's roar was provided in **Ben Hur,** a financial boondoggle which took years to make and went through various casts and directors before appearing in 1926. Perhaps the dominant image of Hollywood in the twenties is supplied by this film, as Ramon Novarro and Francis X. Bushman race their chariots past piled-up wrecks and speeding camera cars, riding not just for a prize of gold but for a place in Hollywood history.

By the mid-twenties European films, whose cut of the American market had been wiped out by the war, were once again growing in popularity. Germany quickly provided a series of stylish dramas which were generally too grim for American audiences. **The Cabinet of Dr. Caligari** was booed off the screen at New York's Capitol Theatre, but registered on critics as a profound experiment in bringing "modern art" to the movies. Actually, a certain amount of experimental work had already been done on film, notably in Italy, France, and Russia, and French director Maurice Tourneur had produced **The Blue Bird** and **Prunella** in this country in 1918, both based on the avant-garde theater work of Gordon Craig. Yet Hollywood consistently looked to Europe for its "art." Producers were fascinated with German director F. W. Murnau's **The Last Laugh,** and, although it failed dismally in the American market, its director was quickly imported to produce ready-made "art films" for William Fox. Unquestionably the greatest success of all the German films was **Variety,** a triangle drama which featured Emil Jannings as one of a group of aerialists. But the real star of this film was the camera: flying cameras, multiple superimpositions, exaggerated close-ups, and a whole panoply of stylized devices were displayed in the film and quickly copied in Hollywood. Just to make sure they were getting it down right, the Americans imported most of the German film industry, producers, directors, stars, and cameramen—an action which effectively transformed the visual style of the American cinema from the late twenties on. Less widely shown, but equally discussed in critical circles, were Swedish and Russian films. Mauritz Stiller's **Arne's Treasure** and Victor Sjöström's (Seastrom, in his Hollywood days) **The Phantom Carriage** were widely acclaimed by critics, although they were two years old by the time they finally appeared in New York. Hollywood snapped up both these directors, too, as well as Stiller's protégée, Greta Garbo. The refinements in editing technique pioneered by the Soviet films seem to have been largely misunderstood or overlooked by even the more perceptive critics of the time, but Sergei Eisenstein's **The Battleship**

Potemkin and **Ten Days That Shook the World** and Vsevolod Pudovkin's **Storm Over Asia** were all hailed for their "realism." By 1930 even Eisenstein was in Hollywood, working under contract to Paramount on a script of Theodore Dreiser's **An American Tragedy.** The effect of this transfusion of European talent into Hollywood was considerable, and a truly international style developed by 1927-28. Murnau's **Sunrise,** Paul Leni's **The Man Who Laughs,** and Victor Sjöström's **The Wind** greatly influenced the best work of the native American directors. The European influence can be clearly seen in King Vidor's **The Crowd,** Frank Borzage's **Street Angel,** John Ford's **Four Sons,** and many of the early works of Josef von Sternberg. But the fluid, expressive style of these films was never to reach its full potential. In 1927 sound had arrived.

Work on the sound film may have culminated with Al Jolson's appearance in **The Jazz Singer,** but it certainly did not begin there. Edison, for one, had his staff experiment with moving pictures only as an adjunct to the already-proven phonograph device. He envisioned all the great operas stored in home libraries on some form of sound/film system and worked toward this end for twenty years. But his Kinetophone device failed to overcome the twin problems of synchronization and amplification, and had a very limited commercial career. The same difficulties plagued European inventors. At the Paris Exposition of 1900, one could see "talking" films of Sarah Bernhardt and Benoit Coquelin at the Phono-Cinéma-Théâtre of Clément Maurice, but keeping the film and the record in "sync" was a nearly impossible task. Before World War I, such films had been made of Eva Tanguay, Yvette Guilbert, Sir Harry Lauder, Anna Held, and many others, but the projects could never overcome their technical limitations. The modern sound-on-film process can be traced back to Eugene Lauste's first successful optical sound track in 1910, but his equipment still lacked sufficient amplification. Only with Lee de Forest's Phonofilm system, successfully demonstrated in 1923, did sound film become a practical reality. Seen today, his films of vaudeville routines and news events (he recorded President Coolidge in 1923) seem quite satisfactory, but audiences were not too excited. Showmanship was missing, and this was provided by the Warner Brothers and Vitaphone. With their company kept solvent only on the profits of Rin-Tin-Tin pictures, the Warners took a gamble and invested in the sound-on-disc system being developed by Western Electric. (In 1926 it still appeared that the problems of synchronization could be more easily solved than the audio problems of sound-on-film recording.) In August they premiered the Vitaphone system at the Warner Theatre in New York. The program consisted of a silent film with a music-and-sound-effects score, John Barrymore in **Don Juan,** and a series of shorts featuring such luminaries as Mischa Elman, Giovanni Martinelli, Marion Talley, and movie czar Will Hays. There was no mad rush. Filmed speeches and specialty numbers held no magic for audiences. The real importance of **The Jazz Singer's** premiere the following year was that sound only then became integrated into

the whole dramatic mystique of the movies, and when Jolson spoke his few minutes of dialogue the talkies became irresistible. The Warners were caught off guard by the sudden success, and it wasn't until 1928 that they released the first all-talking feature, **The Lights of New York.** Meanwhile, Fox had been developing the Movietone process, a sound-on-film process based on the Phonofilm and the German Tri-Ergon patents. The adaptability of this process was quickly demonstrated in 1927 with the advent of the Fox Movietone News, and soon the clumsier Vitaphone disc system was pushed from the market. It was at this time that William Fox moved to secure a monopoly on sound-on-film equipment, basing his claim on the primacy of the Tri-Ergon patents. If successful, this would have given him effective control of the entire industry, but his shaky financial pyramid tumbled in the stock-market crash, and he was out-maneuvered in Washington by the cagey Louis B. Mayer, who pulled strings to bring on a Justice Department antitrust investigation of Fox's operations.

The transition to sound in 1928-29 was inevitably chaotic, and one of its more unusual products was the part-talking film, basically a silent film with talking sequences jammed into it to pep up its chances at the box office. These were contemptuously referred to as "goat-gland operations," and such films as **Lonesome, The Four Devils,** and **The Mysterious Island** emerged in this bastardized form. Filmmakers soon found that by gaining sound they had lost movement, since the noisy cameras had to be locked up in sound-proof "iceboxes" and operated from a fixed position. The possibilities of editing sound tracks were also unknown. To circumvent all these problems, film technique

Mastery over the sound film was
gained by the more creative directors.
Josef von Sternberg made **The Blue
Angel** (1930, above) with Emil
Jannings and a new discovery,
Marlene Dietrich. Fritz Lang's
M (1932) brought Peter Lorre to the
screen (r) as the child murderer
who whistles "In the Hall
of the Mountain King." These two
films demonstrated many of the
possibilities of off-screen
sound and voice-over narration.

returned to that of the theater. A ten-minute sequence would be rehearsed and played out intact, but shot simultaneously from many different camera positions. In the cutting room the editor chose at will between various close, medium, and long shots. This was basically the same technique adopted by live television twenty years later. These limitations quickly changed the structure of films; instead of containing many short scenes, as in the novel, films were now composed of fewer but longer scenes, as in the theater. Courtroom dramas, for example, became momentarily popular. Stage plays and players were bought up wholesale, and so were stage directors. Paramount operated a studio in Astoria, Queens, to allow its new theater imports to moonlight, shooting film by day and playing the legitimate stage at night. In this way, we have records of many memorable stage productions of the twenties, such as the Marx Brothers in **The Cocoanuts** and Jeanne Eagels in **The Letter.** This canned theater, much of it drawing-room melodrama of little visual interest, soon lost its impact on audiences. Most of the theater people went back to Broadway having made only minor contributions to the film. But a few, like John Cromwell, George Cukor, and Rouben Mamoulian, stayed and helped transform Hollywood. Mamoulian's case is perhaps the most interesting. A highly respected director for the Theatre Guild, with such productions as **Porgy** and **R.U.R.** to his credit, Mamoulian was familiar with the most advanced international trends in theater and cinema. He knew the work of the Soviet directors, was apparently familiar with Eisenstein's and Pudovkin's theories of the proper use of the sound film, and was the first director to put these theories to practical use. The Soviet principle of montage was based on juxtaposition of shots. If one shot of given dramatic value is selectively juxtaposed with a second, a third and entirely distinct value may be formed in the viewer's mind—a synthesis of the two shots on screen. This was the principal on which the Soviet silent films were constructed, and it was proposed that the sound film allow a juxtaposition between image and sound as well, with similar results. The sound technicians in Hollywood, who completely ruled the sets at this time, would have none of this. Sound and image must not be juxtaposed, but linked. We must hear exactly what we see, and even background music on the track was frowned upon. If required, a character unobtrusively turned on a radio or opened the door to an off-screen ballroom. Mamoulian's first film was **Applause,** the story of a fading burlesque star featuring Helen Morgan. From the start, his grasp of the possibilities of sound film was astonishing. He had to convince his crew that it was practical for the camera to follow two characters as they talked, or that it was even possible to mix the inputs of two mikes simultaneously. Today **Applause,** Tay Garnett's **Her Man,** and John Cromwell's **The Dance of Life** appear among the few worthwhile films of 1929-30, but audiences and critics of the time preferred nonstop talkathons like **Disraeli** and **Madame X.** In his next film, **City Streets,** Mamoulian used the sound track to convey the thoughts of a character for the first time, developing the purely filmic potential of the interior monologue. In **Dr. Jekyll**

and Mr. Hyde, he created synthetic sound to accompany Fredric March's transformations, mixing a variety of sounds together with the magnified beat of his own heart to create an artificial "sound stew." The audacious use of the camera in this highly stylized tale marked a high point of the early horror genre, but Mamoulian's next film was his masterpiece, **Love Me Tonight.** Using the musical genre to its fullest, Mamoulian freely associated sound and image throughout the film. Starting with the "Morning Song of Paris," he introduces a city of sounds and orchestrates these sounds into an urban symphony. Melodies travel across the countryside to unite the hero and heroine, and we never see anyone singing the title song at all. It just appears over a split-screen shot of Maurice Chevalier and Jeanette MacDonald, uniting them as in a dream.

In the stylish films of Paramount, life as a wonderful dream was pretty much studio policy. That was their profile, and audiences knew what to expect when they saw the stars rising over the Paramount mountain. Paramount, MGM, and RKO-Radio pretty much cornered the dream market in thirties Hollywood, but Warner Brothers had the monopoly on real life. Largely at the urging of production chief Darryl F. Zanuck, Warner's Depression-era films centered on the lives of the urban working class. James Cagney and Joan Blondell, Warren William and Bette Davis, the whole Warner stock company radiated a new form of city-bred street-smarts which captivated those audiences for whom a movie ticket was the only affordable entertainment. The cycle started by building on the gangster genre, already growing in popularity but lacking a gut impact to compare with the daily headlines. Warners added the guts by combining speed and violence, spicing **Little Caesar** and **The Public Enemy** with rapid-fire dialogue and shocking, seemingly gratuitous violence. Other studios followed suit quickly: Paul Muni in **Scarface,** Spencer Tracy in **Quick Millions,** even Gary Cooper in **City Streets,** were all on the other side of the law. The new gangster film not only probed the roots of lawlessness but also clinically exposed graft and corruption throughout society. Law, justice, patriotism, and even capitalism fell under cynical scrutiny. "The state lied!!" gasped Paul Muni in **I Am a Fugitive from a Chain Gang,** but audiences knew he was making a fatal mistake when he placed his life in the hands of politicians and the criminal-justice system. **Blood Money,** one of the few films directed by the remarkable Rowland Brown, exposed the bail-bond racket, while **The Mouthpiece** attacked the legal profession. Con men became heroes in **The Half-Naked Truth** and **Blonde Crazy.** The whole political structure came under attack. In **The Dark Horse,** back-room politicians were shown to pull the strings for dim-witted office seekers. **Okay, America** had mob leader Edward Arnold blackmailing the President of the United States, while in **Gabriel Over the White House** a black sedan sprays the front of the White House with machine-gun fire. Frank Capra saw the spirit of Populism as the only force capable of defeating the bosses who seemed to have the country by the throat. In **Mr. Deeds Goes to Town, Mr. Smith Goes to Washington,** and especially **Meet John**

A good example of a film that exuberantly embraced the possibilities of sound was Lewis Milestone's **The Front Page**. The rapid pacing and overlapping dialogue it pioneered were later adopted by directors like Welles and Hawks. Here, Mary Brian watches helplessly as Adolphe Menjou barks orders into the phone and Pat O'Brien burns the keys off his typewriter. The playful, dizzying speed of this film seemed astonishing in 1931, but few people have seen it recently because its producer, Howard Hughes, has withheld it from distribution.

The schism between dream and reality in thirties cinema became apparent in the early part of the decade. In Sternberg's Dietrich films, a sophisticated, often bizarre eroticism flourished in a Paramount dream world. Left: Marlene in **Blonde Venus** (1932). Below left: With Sam Jaffe in **The Scarlet Empress** (1934). Far removed was the Warner Brothers social-comment cycle, especially Mervyn LeRoy's **I Am a Fugitive From a Chain Gang** (1932, below), with Paul Muni.

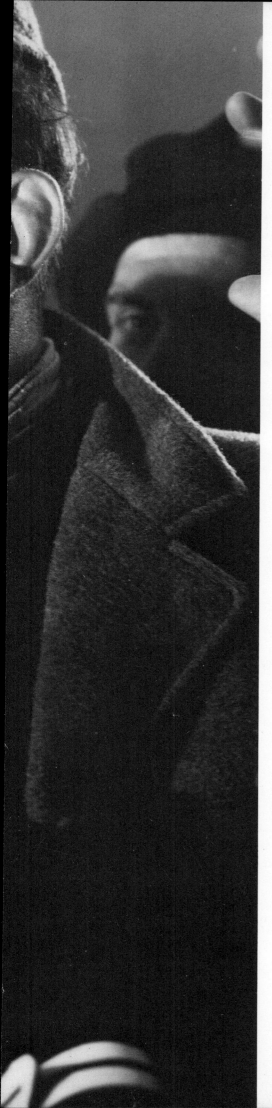

Doe, he pictured the whole capitalist system as the tool of sinister big-business interests (Edward Arnold again). Only a return to the social and religious heritage of the country could save the Republic. King Vidor's solution to the problem was to move his unemployed city dwellers onto a farm commune in **Our Daily Bread.** But not everyone saw "the people" in such innocent terms. Fritz Lang's **Fury,** for one, pictured them as a mindless mob capable of instant incitement to lynch law. By the late thirties this negativism had withered under the barrage of various pressure groups who saw it as un-American. Positive values were stressed, but one had to go into the past to find them. A string of biographies of noteworthy statesman and scientists provided suitable models; Paul Muni in various disguises played the title role in **Louis Pasteur, The Life of Emile Zola,** and **Juarez.**

It was not only the social criticism of current films which roused pressure-group ire but their increasingly frank sexual content as well. The year 1934 was a watershed year, dividing Hollywood into pre-Code and post-Code epochs. Largely through the organization of the Legion of Decency, a tough censorship code was forced on filmmakers, who were fined and denied a Code seal if they transgressed. The fine was minor, but almost no theater would show a film without a seal, at least until the fifties. What is largely forgotten today is that while the Code dampened any presentation of sexual conduct, it also took the edge off the worst of the racist stereotypes of the day. But censorship is censorship. No longer could Hollywood produce films like **The Story of Temple Drake, Call Her Savage,** or **Design for Living,** adult presentations of primarily sexual material. A number of screen personalities, particularly Mae West and Betty Boop, had to undergo drastic image changes, while more wholesome stars like Shirley Temple rose to great popularity. The best evidence of the reactionary character of this movement may be seen in the post-Code reissues of pre-Code hits. **King Kong** was censored on reissue to eliminate sex and violence, cuts which have only recently been restored on existing prints. Audiences today still miss the reissue cuts in **Love Me Tonight,** including a double-entendre song and Myrna Loy singing "Mimi"—banned because her navel could be seen through her negligee.

By the end of the thirties the dream factory had pretty well triumphed over the shaky school of realism. As never before or since, Hollywood turned to period melodramas and adaptations of classical (and-not-so-classical) books and plays. Ancient-history spectacles, like De Mille's **The Sign of the Cross** or **Cleopatra,** were few and far between, but the nineteenth century was covered in minute detail. Hollywood warehouses were bursting with antique costumes and artifacts, meticulously reconstructed or assembled from all over the world by studio art departments. When much of this material was auctioned off by Fox and MGM in the seventies, the last traces of this grand age of Hollywood illusion were scattered to the winds. Judy Garland's ruby slippers were gone, the stars were gone, even the studios were pretty much

In 1935, John Ford's **The Informer** was the year's surprise hit. Cheaply produced, and released without much publicity, it soon developed a wide following and won Oscars for Ford, Max Steiner (music), Dudley Nichols (script), and Victor McLaglen (actor).

gone. A department store rises from the ruins of the Fox Western Avenue lot, where Will Rogers and Shirley Temple did their stuff for John Ford and Frank Borzage. Not only the buildings have vanished, but the spirit was well, that particular form of creative energy responsible for Cathy and Heathcliff on the moors in **Wuthering Heights,** or the grand-scale showmanship of **The Great Ziegfeld.** It was folly to remake **Mutiny on the Bounty, Lost Horizon,** and **Goodbye, Mr. Chips,** because these stories are not for all seasons. They belong to a romantic age that painted on broad canvases; our own romanticism lies much farther down the scale. **Love Story** was emotionally extravagant for the seventies. The best films of the thirties have never lost their following, and audiences will still come, even if only as far as the nearest television, to see Errol Flynn romp through **Captain Blood** and **The Adventures of Robin Hood,** or to bask in the bravura performances of Bette Davis in **Jezebel,** Garbo in **Anna Karenina,** or Katharine Hepburn in **Little Women. Gone With the Wind,** not the best or even the most entertaining of Hollywood extravaganzas, still draws audiences because it has something rare to offer: that extraordinary magic which even Hollywood distilled on rare occasions.

Of course, a good part of the escapist fare of the thirties was not played in period costume. **Red Dust, The Front Page, Only Angels Have Wings, Dinner at Eight, Imitation of Life,** or **Private Lives** are so redolent of the thirties that they have become the standard by which we look at that decade. Yet they reflect it only in a very special way, like a magic mirror that shows us not what we are but what we might be. Although the value of these films is more than apparent today—not that their kind has disappeared—critics of the time found that films which were not loaded to the gunwales with transparent social content were somehow beneath notice. Perhaps the greatest thirties director, Josef von Sternberg, was also the one who suffered most strongly from the socio-political bias of critics of the day. He was most closely associated with Marlene Dietrich, whom he made a star in **The Blue Angel** and developed in a half-dozen films of rare luster and visual grace. Sternberg was concerned with textures and light, and incorporated actors in his compositions as just another prop to be moved about at will. Performances he created synthetically through a careful assemblage of bits and pieces of image and sound. He exploited the dynamism of a star personality like Dietrich by building his films around her instantly identifiable "image." This manipulation of the star personality prefigured Hitchcock's use of James Stewart and Cary Grant, or Ford's use of John Wayne. But instead of seeing the cool and brilliant studies of personalities in collision, which Sternberg offered in **Morocco** or **Shanghai Express,** his critics accused him of debasing his talent with flashy Dietrich vehicles. Reacting against the studied eroticism of **Blonde Venus,** they labeled him a purveyor of "cheesecake." In 1934, one of the country's most respected film journals declared: "In Sternberg we have a director who concentrates on surface effects, who emphasizes the externals of film mechanics in a most inarticulate manner

Costume films grew quite popular by mid-decade, and studios lavished great care on these "class" properties. Top left: Anita Louise as Titania in Max Reinhardt's **A Midsummer Night's Dream** (1935). Oscar-winning photography was by Hal Mohr. Top right: Paul Muni, in one of his classical biographical roles, in **The Story of Louis Pasteur** (1936), directed by William Dieterle. Bottom left: Charles Laughton and Binnie Barnes in Alexander Korda's **The Private Life of Henry VIII** (England, 1933). Bottom right: Robert Taylor and Greta Garbo in George Cukor's **Camille** (1936), arguably her best performance.

By the late thirties Hollywood's
prestige productions were much
heavier on content that on style.
Opposite, top: Frank Capra's **Lost
Horizon** (1937). This scene was
shot in a Los Angeles ice house.
Opposite, bottom: Luise Rainer and Paul
Muni in Sidney Franklin's **The
Good Earth** (1937). Above:
Bette Davis and Henry Fonda in
the scarlet-gown sequence of
William Wyler's **Jezebel** (1938).
Right: Merle Oberon, Laurence
Olivier, and David Niven in Wyler's
Wuthering Heights (1939).
Lush orchestrations were typical
of such films and these scores
were the work of, respectively,
Dimitri Tiomkin, Herbert Stothart,
Max Steiner, and Alfred Newman.

and represents his own delirious fancies as real life." This was the year that audiences began to desert Sternberg's increasingly baroque works, and the expensive failures of **The Scarlet Empress** and **The Devil Is a Woman** doomed his career. Today these films seem the high point of thirties style, but in 1934-35 audiences were being directed to **The Barretts of Wimpole Street** and **The House of Rothschild,** or discovering for themselves **David Harum** and **It Happened One Night.** If nothing else, Sternberg's fall from grace marks an early low point of critics as tastemakers.

In New York at least, critics had the opportunity to make amends by promoting the better foreign films which dribbled across the Atlantic at irregular intervals. The flow had stopped abruptly as sound came in, but the tiny art-theater circuit which spread outward from New York, and the few enterprising distributors who serviced it, gradually began to introduce a primitive titling system. At first, films had title cards jammed into them every few minutes, like Pabst's **Westfront 1918,** completely blotting out picture and sound and providing at best an inadequate summary of the dialogue. Then titles were superimposed at the bottom of the frame, the technique which persists today, but the early titling jobs on Fritz Lang's **M** or René Clair's **À Nous la Liberté** left a lot to be desired. But this work rapidly became quite professional and exact, and the chief pioneer in this movement was probably Herman G. Weinberg, who seems to have titled most of the great French and Italian films of the next thirty years. The success of his efforts might be reflected in the long-standing admonition to film students to avoid any print of **Children of Paradise** not titled by Weinberg. This was not merely a case of his version being longer, but infinitely more flavorful as well. What eventually was shown in America depended on various flukes of fate. Most of Jean Renoir remained unseen, although his **La Grande Illusion** did attract considersble attention here, largely due to interest in Stroheim's performance. **Carnival in Flanders, Harvest,** and **The Baker's Wife** were all quite successful. Some of Marcel Carné's moody work was shown, like **Port of Shadows** with Jean Gabin and Michele Morgan, and a few works by Julien Duvivier and René Clair. After 1934, when the strings of the Hays Code were drawn tighter, European films, especially the French, began to seem more and more licentious. This impression was usually underlined by an advertising campaign which promised what the American censors would never let the films deliver, and it was well into the sixties before the wholesale butchery of European films was ended. Hedy Lamarr in **Ecstasy** became one of the legends of the art-house circuit in the thirties. What never got shown at all was the experimental work of the French underground. Luis Buñuel's surrealist masterpiece, **L'Age d'Or,** and Jean Vigo's imaginative **Zéro de Conduite** were not shown for many years, although the best work of the Soviet filmmakers was usually available without much delay. The Cameo Theatre on Eighth Avenue in New York (now a sexploitation house) was the home of the Russian art cinema, and Eisenstein proudly had his picture taken in

Above: Robert Donat won an Oscar for his role in **Goodbye, Mr. Chips** (1939), edging out Clark Gable's Rhett Butler. Sam Wood directed and Greer Garson co-starred. Opposite: While the boys discuss flying the mail, Jean Arthur and Cary Grant have other things to think about in Howard Hawks's **Only Angels Have Wings.** The 1939 release was one of the best and most typical of Hawks's adventure films.

front of its marquee displaying his **Old and New (The General Line)** during his New York visit in 1930. Of course, English films generally managed to avoid the language barrier, and Hitchcock's **The 39 Steps** and **The Lady Vanishes** were popular enough to bring that director permanently to Hollywood in 1940. **The Private Life of Henry VIII** won an Oscar for Charles Laughton, and the film's success convinced Alexander Korda that he could crack the American market with expensive superproductions. But it took a few handsome failures like **Rembrandt** and **Things to Come** to convince him of the insularity of the American audience, an insularity which became total when war broke out in Europe.

It was in the forties that Hollywood captured its widest audience. Weekly attendance had risen steadily from 60 million in 1933 to 85 million during the war years. In the boom of 1946-48, attendance topped out at 90 million paid admissions a week. Customers were moving past the cash boxes as fast as the theaters could manage them. They flocked indiscriminately to practically everything, for while attendance was at its all-time high, the actual number of feature releases was at a record low. In this seller's market the studios could make money with anything, and anything made money. Only the forties could have supported in style the kitsch of Carmen Miranda and Maria Montez, a whole vulgar genre which was gleefully exhumed in the sixties as "camp." But this very guarantee of success permitted experimentation as well, and only the forties could allow the elaborate production of films like **Citizen Kane** and **How Green Was My Valley,** films that found an audience which they have not lost since, but films which might never have gone into production in any other period—though for widely differing reasons.

> **How Green Was My Valley** and **Citizen Kane** are prototypical studio films of the forties, and if we look at them more closely we can see the two divergent approaches which marked major Hollywood production. **How Green Was My Valley** was a classical Fox undertaking, a marshaling of the master talents from all over the lot for the benefit of one monumental work. It has been said that at its best the studio system resembled the medieval town with its separate craftsmen's guilds coming together to create a cathedral. If this is so, then **How Green Was My Valley** is the Chartres of Hollywood. Its director, John Ford, was then at the peak of a career a quarter-century old, twenty years of it associated with the Fox company. He had the enviable reputation of being able to combine commercial and artistic requirements, a fact demonstrated with staggering clarity during the two previous years when he directed **Stagecoach, Young Mr. Lincoln, Drums Along the Mohawk, The Grapes of Wrath, The Long Voyage Home,** and **Tobacco Road.** Yet he was also highly regarded for his ability to deliver these projects under studio requirements of budget and length. His reputation as a pragmatic studio veteran was uppermost in Darryl F. Zanuck's mind when he assigned Ford to direct this most costly release of Fox's 1941 season. Making so complex a film was like directing a military operation

Above: David O. Selznick's **Gone With the Wind** (1939) marked the high point of romanticism in thirties Hollywood. Vivien Leigh and Clark Gable starred in the screen classic. Opposite, above: Henry Fonda and John Carradine in John Ford's **The Grapes of Wrath** (1940), a film which marked the return of socially conscious material after an absence of some years. Below: Orson Welles in **Citizen Kane** (1941), a film that made full use of deep-focus photography, overlapping sound, and many other innovative techniques. Welles was only twenty-five when he wrote, directed, and starred in this revolutionary film.

and required a no-nonsense hand at the tiller. The rest of the "package" was assembled for similar reasons: Arthur Miller behind the camera, with twenty-five years experience as a top director of photography; Alfred Newman, who had been composing film scores since the coming of sound; Richard Day, an outstanding art director since Stroheim's **Foolish Wives;** Philip Dunne, a comparatively young screenwriter with such epic titles as **Suez** and **The Rains Came** to his credit; and perhaps the most important ingredient of all, Richard Llewellyn's best-selling novel, a solid property in the best Hollywood tradition.

By contrast, **Citizen Kane** was constructed from the ground up by much younger talent. Orson Welles himself had never made a feature film, and at the age of twenty-five had only a few sensational years in theater and radio behind him. He was brought to Hollywood as one of the more formidable infusions of New York theatrical blood, and RKO's hopes were high regarding this certified East Coast genius who viewed their studio as a giant plaything for his creative impulses. He was given Herman J. Mankiewicz to help develop the original screenplay and Gregg Toland as technical collaborator and cinematographer. Mankiewicz had an involved though largely undistinguished career, and the nature of his contribution to the script is still hotly debated, generally by antagonists of the auteur theory who gleefully point out that it was Mankiewicz who, as a child, owned a bicycle named "Rosebud." Toland was an innovative cameraman quite taken with a "pan-focus" system he had been developing for some years (particularly on some earlier Ford films, like **The Grapes of Wrath** and **The Long Voyage Home**). He made sure that Welles used it to best advantage in this film as well. The art direction was by Van Nest Polglase and Perry Ferguson, regulars of what was probably the best studio art department of the time, but the important musical score was composed by Bernard Herrmann, new to films. Just as the script was newly developed, so were the actors new to the screen, mostly Welles's old pals from the Mercury Theatre (in contrast, some of Ford's cast had experience dating back to D. W. Griffith). Welles was given complete autonomy and allowed to shoot what he wished, how he wished; the exact nature of the project was vague even to most of the people at the studio.

These two approaches, marshaling the best talents on the lot, and giving the genius a free hand, dated back at least to the days of Griffith and Ince, but quite possibly reached their high point right here. Ford produced a melancholy tale of social disintegration, the decline of a Welsh mining village and a mining family, told in a flashback which emphasized the fated slide to ruin. The style was classical and highly polished, impeccably acted and tastefully produced. Welles's film by comparison seemed revolutionary, expressionistic in its use of camera and sound, exaggerated, fragmented, more concerned with the nature of storytelling than with telling any particular story. The New York Film Critics named **Citizen Kane** the best film, and John Ford the best director, splitting their affections down the middle. In Hollywood, the story was some-

TEXAS
WISCONSIN
ABILENE
BENTON
Cleveland
FRANKFORT
WYOMING
RICHMOND
HUSETTS
F
N
ILLINO
NASHVI
NEW HAMPSHIRE

what different. **Kane** won an Oscar for best original screenplay, but **How Green Was My Valley** took best picture, director, black-and-white cinematography, art direction, and supporting actor.

There were seemingly two ways to make films in Hollywood, but really only one way. The genius route was littered with the unfilmed work of men like Griffith and Stroheim, and Welles soon found himself added to the list. His next film, **The Magnificent Ambersons,** was taken from him and cut (and partly reshot) by others. Then a complex South American project was aborted after much footage had been shot. Welles's career stumbled along intermittently afterwards. **The Stranger,** a competent thriller about a Nazi hiding in New England, was hardly worth his energies. Much more successful was **The Lady from Shanghai,** a truly Wellesian investigation of passion and corruption, and a love letter to wife Rita Hayworth, as well. The climactic fun-house sequence here only emphasized how Welles's talent and imagination were being wasted. In 1948 he spent twenty-three days shooting **Macbeth** for Republic Pictures, and in the fifties and sixties became a wanderer among the world's film capitals.

Ford's career kept on much as before. After a spell with the army, for whom he made the magnificent **The Battle of Midway,** he did **They Were Expendable,** a study of the struggle, defeat, and disintegration of a PT boat squadron, and went on to his great westerns, **My Darling Clementine** and the cavalry trilogy, westerns about the changing concepts of the West.

But while **How Green Was My Valley** and **Citizen Kane** may be shown as examples of two very different forms of studio filmmaking, they are closely linked on one major technical level, and this is the exploitation of deep-focus photography. This technique was largely a reaction against the unreality of thirties camera style, with its soft-focus backgrounds that provided halos for the stars' close-ups. With deep focus, objects both near and far could be registered clearly at the same time, the result of experimentation with lenses and lighting carried out mainly by Gregg Toland and Arthur Miller, and stylistically developed by directors Ford, Welles, and William Wyler. If, in the thirties, a director wished to indicate the significance of a mysterious box to a group of conspirators he would cut from the plotters to a close-up of the box, standard montage technique as it had developed since Griffith. But deep focus enabled the two to share the same frame, with an emphasis indicated through lighting and composition and not merely by a direct cut. The development of this style changed the whole atmosphere of American films almost immediately. Relationships could be indicated in a more subtle manner, and the continuity of each image did not have to be broken merely for the insertion of explanatory close-ups. The camera (work on the set) took precedence over the editing bench (post-production work). The most important early examples of this style may be found in Miller's **Tobacco Road** and **How Green Was My Valley** and in Toland's **The Grapes of Wrath, The Westerner, The Long Voyage Home, Citizen Kane,** and **The Little Foxes**—all films of 1940-41, and all directed by either Ford,

Preceding pages: The rally in the rain from Frank Capra's **Meet John Doe** (1941). Opposite, top: Sara Allgood and Donald Crisp with their family in John Ford's **How Green Was My Valley** (1941). Far left: Trevor Howard and Celia Johnson in David Lean's sentimental romance, **Brief Encounter** (1946). Center: Joan Crawford and Jack Carson in **Mildred Pierce,** her Oscar-winning performance, directed by Michael Curtiz (1945). Bottom: Otto Preminger's **Laura** (1944), with Dana Andrews and Gene Tierney. These are typical examples of wartime movie entertainment.

Welles, or Wyler.

There is a bitterness underlying most of the cinema of the forties which was new to the American screen and qualitatively distinct from the social consciousness of a decade earlier. The dramas, romances, adventure films, and even comedies of the thirties were twisted around and examined from a darker perspective. Instead of dealing with the building of relationships, dramas of the forties dealt with their failure. There were often vague psychological undercurrents at work, and neurosis as a plot device became a favorite tool of screenwriters. Romances of the period included such shadowed and shadowy masterworks as **Now, Voyager, Brief Encounter, Gilda,** and **Letter from an Unknown Woman,** tales of wrenching pain, breakup, or disillusionment, all lacking in the exhilarating, positive romanticism of such late-thirties work as **Love Affair.** Very often the heroine becomes murderously dominant, turning such films as **Leave Her to Heaven, Double Indemnity, The Lady from Shanghai,** and **Out of the Past** into tales of twisted passion. There is only a hazy area separating the romances of the period from the dark and introspective "films noir," and often the two are bound inextricably. "Film noir" emerged as a dominant style by the mid-forties, with its concerns for corruption and dissolution, stylized shadows and camera angles, and rain-swept nighttime cityscapes. Sometimes the sun is never seen at all in the more severe examples of the noir film.

The prevalence of this mood practically extinguished the cycle of period romanticism that had been growing in the thirties. Errol Flynn's **The Sea Hawk** was really the tail end of a line extending back to his **Captain Blood.** Henry King's **The Black Swan,** starring Tyrone Power, was presented as sheer fairy tale, its pirates acting like refugees from Captain Hook's crew, and its stunning Technicolor photography (by Leon Shamroy) shining darkly, like a Rembrandt oil. One reason for the demise of the spectacle was a solipsistic fear in Hollywood that large sets might be bombed by the Japanese, but even when it became apparent that the studios were not likely targets, the genre was not revived. **Forever Amber** owes its existence to the popularity of Kathleen Winsor's scandalous novel. It was not until De Mille released **Samson and Delilah** at the decade's end that the genre made a fittingly spectacular return.

The war on the home front was the subject of a few notable films, chief among them Selznick's **Since You Went Away** (1944), directed by John Cromwell. Above: Robert Walker and Jennifer Jones as the young lovers in wartime America. Right: Sam Goldwyn followed the troops home in **The Best Years of Our Lives** (1946), directed by William Wyler. Michael Hall, Teresa Wright, Myrna Loy, and Fredric March were the average American family. Opposite: Rita Hayworth and Glenn Ford in **Gilda** (1946), a classic "film noir," with its view that life is driven by turbulent passions.

But the mainstream of forties drama was small-scale, taking advantage of a rich assortment of character actors, some truly extraordinary stars, and material considerably more mature than that tackled in the late thirties. Stage adaptations like **Of Mice and Men, The Shanghai Gesture, The Letter,** and **The Little Foxes** were filled with a cinematic grace far beyond the theatricality of a few years earlier. As Hollywood once had filled up with German directors, now a whole school of French directors arrived, refugees from the European war who lent a certain continental presence. Jean Renoir's **Swamp Water** and **The Southerner** dealt with the backwaters of the American countryside in a manner reminiscent of the early pastorals, or of Renoir's own **Toni,** while René Clair directed such fashionably stylish exercises as **And Then There Were None** and **The Flame of New Orleans.** Julien Duvivier was also imported **(Tales of Manhattan),** as were such stars as Jean Gabin, Simone Simon, and even Stroheim, who had just established himself in Paris. Hitchcock, unlike the French directors, stayed permanently in the American studios. With **Rebecca,** and even more powerfully in **Shadow of a Doubt,** he demonstrated how easily he could exploit the technical advantages of Hollywood.

Yet the major theme was always the war. If not directly concerned with the fighting, the trials and traces of the war could be included in any number of ways. Standard thrillers were decked out in war garb by Fritz Lang and Hitchcock, in particular. In **Ministry of Fear** and **Man Hunt,** Lang offered the same sinister, pervasive forces he had been dealing with for twenty years, but here they were called Nazis. Hitchcock's **Saboteur** carried the same format as his earlier **The 39 Steps,** or the much later **North by Northwest:** the hero involved in a double chase across country by both the good guys and the bad guys. Here fifth-column work was the excuse. **Foreign Correspondent** concluded with Joel McCrea making an impassioned preparedness speech over the radio, although for most of the film the villains were handled no differently than in **The Lady Vanishes.** And **Lifeboat** was a technical exercise for which a lone Nazi came in quite handy. The war seemed to be very important as the background to **Casablanca,** but what emerged was a timeless, placeless tale of love, friendship, and sacrifice, probably better known today than at the time of its release.

The popular family drama was transplanted to England in William Wyler's **Mrs. Miniver,** but the genre was examined somewhat more closely in John Cromwell's **Since You Went Away.** This remarkable study of the home front remains perhaps the most evocative film of its era, superbly captured on film by Lee Garmes and Stanley Cortez. **The More the Merrier** turned the mundane problem of the housing shortage into bright comedy, while Minnelli's **The Clock** showed the tribulations of a young couple who meet, fall in love, and marry, all on a weekend pass. One could even see the shadow of the war cast obliquely into such films as **Wilson,** the brilliantly produced, but rather stuffy biography of the late President, or Charles Chaplin's **Monsieur Verdoux,** in

which the Bluebeard excuses his few murders as the work of an amateur when compared with that of the munitions makers.

The final wrap-up of the war went on for years. **The Best Years of Our Lives** provided the definitive Hollywood version, but returning GIs were all over the screen after 1945. Joseph Cotten explained about his **Love Letters** to Jennifer Jones, and John Hodiak tried to unravel the mystery of his own past in **Somewhere in the Night.**

The gimmick employed in this film—amnesia—indicates yet another characteristic trend in forties cinema, the preoccupation with mental disturbance and psychoanalysis. Psychiatrists were heroes in **Now, Voyager** and villains in **Shock.** Gregory Peck fell in love with his psychiatrist in **Spellbound,** while Herbert Lom parted **The Seventh Veil** for Ann Todd. Robert Ryan married Barbara Bel Geddes just to spite his analyst in Max Ophuls' brilliant **Caught,** and emotional disturbance was used more and more as an explanation for criminal behavior in films like **Rope.** This fixation even found its way into such genres as the musical **(Lady in the Dark),** but it was in the gangster film that it reached its zenith, with James Cagney curling up in Ma's lap to cure his migraines in **White Heat.** "Made it, Ma. Top of the world!" he shouts just before exploding along with half a chemical plant in the film's apocalyptic conclusion.

With the war's end, Hollywood endured a shock wave of changes that altered forever its basic structure. The development of deep-focus techniques at the start of the decade marked a move toward realism which accelerated greatly. The chief reason for this was the sudden influence of the documentary school. Directors like Wyler, Ford, Capra, and Huston had spent the war working on army documentaries and brought back a feeling for the dramatic value of natural locations and nonprofessional actors, as well as an appreciation of the lightweight equipment used by the documentarists. Producer Louis de Rochemont of "The March of Time" fame incorporated some of these elements in **The House on 92nd Street** (1945). Soon after this the first films of the Italian neo-realists began to arrive: Roberto Rossellini's **Open City** and **Paisan,** and Vittorio De Sica's **Shoe Shine** and **The Bicycle Thief** captured critical attention for their plain and unaffected style and their sense of physical authenticity. This seemed a great change from the hot-house studio presentations of Hollywood, where real locations had been abandoned when sound arrived. But soon American films like Jules Dassin's **The Naked City** and **The Set-Up** took advantage of location work, and filmmaking in America began its slow but steady crawl away from the Hollywood production centers.

Perhaps the most serious change of all was the result of legal action on the part of independent theater owners and the federal government. The studios had been under investigation for monopolistic booking practices since the twenties. Then a government suit, which culminated in the 1947 consent decrees, forced the movie production companies to divest themselves of

Preceding pages: Martha Raye and Charles Chaplin in **Monsieur Verdoux** (1947), Chaplin's "comedy of murders." Above: Orson Welles in the funhouse sequence from his love letter to Rita Hayworth, **The Lady from Shanghai** (1948). Opposite: The postwar foreign invasion. Top: Basil Sidney and Laurence Olivier in Olivier's **Hamlet** (1948). Below: James Mason and Kathleen Ryan in Carol Reed's **Odd Man Out** (1947, l). Lamberto Maggiorani in Vittorio De Sica's **The Bicycle Thief** (1948, center). And Martita Hunt and Anthony Wager in David Lean's **Great Expectations** (1947, r).

the movie theaters they owned. Since exhibitors were no longer forced by the movie-producing companies to accept a studio's entire output, which ranged from lavish releases with big stars to quick cheapies made for the B-picture market, films would presumably have to sell on their individual merits. It quickly became apparent that this meant commercial merit alone, with scant attention paid to the artistic qualities of the film in question. No longer could the profit-making portion of a studio's schedule support a few experimental "artistic" ventures, a standard Hollywood indulgence since the silent days. Now everything had to make money on its own. In retrospect, the results were predictable. Now, more than ever, films had to appeal to a mass audience.

But the mass audiences suddenly had disappeared. Television, beginning to vie for audiences in the East by 1949, quickly supplied the knockout blow in a lethal one-two combination. The average weekly attendance figure that hit 90 million in 1948 dropped to 70 million in 1949, and to 60 million in 1950. In a few more years, thanks almost entirely to the impact of nationwide network television, half the American film audience had gone home for good.

The 1950's saw an uncertain industry struggling to cope with severe internal changes and external pressures. Not only did films have to deal with a radical shift in the country's social fabric, they somehow had to cope as well with a technological revolution unparalleled since the coming of sound. As might be expected, the films of the fifties were fraught with tensions on every level, not the least of which was the basic split between the old Hollywood glamour and the new search for "realism" in style and subject matter. Seen from the sixties, these two elements appeared irreconcilable, and films of the period were damned as superheated, melodramatic gloss.

Only recently has it become clear that for the first time American filmmakers were confronting head-on problems of family life, the failed American dream, political paranoia, and the growing sense of nihilism beneath the surface of the postwar world. Suddenly every dramatic situation seemed to focus on the dissolution of the bourgeois family unit, which only a few years earlier, in films like **Since You Went Away,** or the Andy Hardy series, was celebrated as the cornerstone of the American way of life. This is probably most clear in the spate of films on alienated youth, a phenomenon that seems to have come as a sudden and unpleasant surprise. The inhabitants of **The Blackboard Jungle** possessed a streak of viciousness and cruelty that the Dead End Kids completely lacked, although in terms of pop sociology their deprivations were much the same. So who could explain why this new generation appeared to be going berserk? A few films investigated the causes of the breakdown, most notably Nicholas Ray's **Rebel Without a Cause,** which postulated the emasculated father as the weak link in the American family unit. As his parents argue back and forth from the corners of the CinemaScope screen, James Dean cries despairingly, "You're tearing me apart!" His only solution is to form, with Natalie Wood and Sal Mineo, a family unit based on mutual trust and understanding,

Some baroque moments from 1950,
a year of exceptional
polish and style. Left: Gloria
Swanson in Billy Wilder's **Sunset
Boulevard,** an extraordinary tombstone
for Hollywood's golden age.
Above: Bette Davis, Gary Merrill,
Anne Baxter, and George Sanders
with the coveted Sarah Siddons
Award in Joseph L. Mankiewicz's
All About Eve. Right: Anton Walbrook
and Simone Signoret in Max Ophuls'
La Ronde, a charming and graceful
romantic caprice which had
terrible censorship problems in America.

Dramatic highlights from some of the best Hollywood films of the early fifties. Top left: Robert Walker and Farley Granger after the carousel wreck in Hitchcock's **Strangers on a Train** (1951). Top right: Frank Sinatra watches Montgomery Clift give out with a blast in Fred Zinnemann's **From Here to Eternity** (1953). Bottom left: Marlon Brando as the leather-jacketed cyclist in Laslo Benedek's **The Wild One** (1953). Bottom right: Another of Brando's characteristic early roles, Stanley Kowalski, in Elia Kazan's film of **A Streetcar Named Desire** (1951). Vivien Leigh was Blanche Dubois in this classic version of the Tennessee Williams masterpiece.

the only structure which can combat the cosmic emptiness of "man alone."

Films like Sirk's **There's Always Tomorrow** and Ray's **Bigger Than Life** showed that the dramas of suburban middle-class living could be as engrossing as the grand-scale productions of an earlier Hollywood, and considerably more relevant. It seemed that the dramatic focus was moving away from the larger-than-life to the average and ordinary. **Marty,** written by Paddy Chayefsky, and its followers put the average man in the spotlight, but never was the common man quite so common. Today unpleasantly patronizing tones are evident in the work of this school, which consisted mainly of New York television people like Chayefsky and Sidney Lumet. In essence, the trend resembled late-nineteenth-century literary naturalism, which was in reaction to the flowery romanticism of an earlier day and which focused on the lives of ordinary working people, who were often seen as fated and driven by powerful outside forces. This deterministic streak marks much of fifties cinema as well. Turbulent emotions move the characters, and they act almost like puppets, moving inexorably to some preplanned destiny. In **A Place in the Sun,** Montgomery Clift is led to his fate by a confluence of social pressures and internal character weaknesses, which his conscious mind neither controls nor understands. Patty McCormack in **The Bad Seed** was driven by mysterious demonic powers and in the end had to be dealt with through heavenly intercession. This manipulation was sometimes presented in other guises, like Frank Sinatra's drug addiction in **The Man With the Golden Arm,** or the alcoholism rampant in so many post-**Lost Weekend** films. If people are constantly smoking in forties films, they are forever drinking in the fifties. Some films even investigated the way the entire country could be manipulated, like the little-appreciated Budd Schulberg-Elia Kazan **A Face in the Crowd,** which had Andy Griffith as a TV demagogue who becomes a political force of national dimension. The work of the newspaper world was similarly dissected in Billy Wilder's **Ace in the Hole,** a cynical story of a reporter who milks a cave-in tragedy for his own advantage. These tales of venality and corruption extended into many odd corners, and filmmakers delighted in exposing the clay feet of the public's former idols. Theatrical life was exposed in Joseph L. Mankiewicz's **All About Eve,** and Hollywood itself in Wilder's **Sunset Boulevard** and the even more trenchant **The Goddess** by Paddy Chayefsky and John Cromwell. Intellectuals were shown as dupes of international Communism in the puerile **My Son John.** In line from **Double Indemnity, Niagara** depicted a murderous tinge in American family life against a background of the nation's honeymoon paradise. A few filmmakers paid scant attention to these prevailing trends and went their own way, mostly old-timers like Henry King, with his small masterpiece **I'd Climb the Highest Mountain,** or John Ford, with **The Quiet Man** and the delicate **The Sun Shines Bright.** But even Ford, in **The Last Hurrah,** found it necessary to pay a formal good-bye to a way of life that was passing, not from the Old West but from fifties America.

The director who flourished most in this murky era was Alfred

A high point of mid-fifties cinema:
Grace Kelly and James Stewart
in Hitchcock's **Rear Window** (1954).
Each of the courtyard apartments
contains a mini-Hitchcock movie for
the immobilized photographer.

Hitchcock, whose style took full advantage of restructured audience attitudes to create a series of pure fifties masterpieces. James Stewart was Hitchcock's main vehicle for establishing instant rapport between audience and screen character. In **Rear Window, The Man Who Knew Too Much,** and **Vertigo,** three of Hitchcock's more brilliant works, the director made use of Stewart's uncanny ability to project a completely unforced and natural persona, which was still quite obviously that of a star. In **Rear Window,** he was laid up in his apartment voyeuristically studying the goings-on in the apartments across the courtyard. In this detached fashion Stewart seems to get involved in a murder, but far more interesting is the way in which his examination of others' lives forces him to examine his life and his relationship with Hitchcock's favorite actress, Grace Kelly.

A far more typical fifties situation is that of **The Man Who Knew Too Much,** the story of an average American family whose sweet little boy is kidnapped by international conspirators. Films of the period were bursting with little children in a hopeful fashion that has not been seen since, and even Hitchcock made use of this obsession. In what is perhaps his masterpiece, **Vertigo,** we have a Pygmalion-Galatea story grafted onto a murder mystery. The moral ambiguity of this film, its psychological complexities, and its exceptionally sophisticated interweaving of structure and content combine to give **Vertigo** a special place in the American cinema.

In one of his weaker efforts, **Dial M for Murder,** Hitchcock even dabbled in 3-D, the only major director to express an interest in this odd process. The success of **This Is Cinerama** in 1952 had prompted a rush to trick screen gimmicks, which seemed for a time to bolster flagging attendance. The Cinerama process was initially a three-projector system which utilized a curved, 146-degree screen to partially surround its audiences. The wider field enabled the eye's peripheral vision to suggest a depth not apparent with standard processes. At first successful, with travelogue-style roller-coaster rides and flights through the Grand Canyon, Cinerama by the sixties was forced to go the route of the story film.

Soon after the appearance of Cinerama, Arch Oboler released **Bwana Devil,** the first feature in the Natural Vision 3-D process. Although made independently on a shoestring budget, **Bwana Devil** was a sensation at the box office and set off a brief surge of 3-D features, at least one of which, **House of Wax,** easily landed on "Variety"'s list of all-time top-grossing films. But if Cinerama's main problem was its lack of a narrative line, 3-D had to contend with uncomfortable glasses and projection which was often sloppy enough to induce prodigious headaches and eyestrain.

Much more successful was Fox's CinemaScope process, which premiered with **The Robe** in 1953. CinemaScope could produce an image twice as wide as standard by utilizing available projection equipment and by adding an anamorphic lens to "unsqueeze" the image which had been optically compressed on the film. One rationale behind all these processes was increased "realism," although in practice this was not always the case. The wider screen slowed down the pace of films considerably as individual shots became longer, unbroken by close-ups or reaction shots. For a while, especially on such early 'Scope films as **How to Marry a Millionaire,** it seemed as though films were regressing to the proscenium staging of the theater. However, directors like Minnelli, Sirk, and Ray quickly learned to master the unwieldy new ratio. By and large, the early CinemaScope was optically substandard; it distorted the edges of the frame and produced an uncomfortable fish-eye effect during tracking movements. It was somewhat improved shortly thereafter, but could never compare with the clarity of VistaVision, a wide-film process which was unfortunately dropped by 1961. **Strategic Air Command, War and Peace,** and **The Searchers** were some of the best examples of VistaVision photography.

　　The trend toward the "real" in style and subject extended to the star system as well, and fifties stars characteristically reflect human weaknesses which seemed absent in the great stars of the past. James Dean created a new image of the inarticulate hero who was filled with emotions that could never find direct expression. Almost single-handedly, he established in **East of Eden** and **Rebel Without a Cause** not merely the existence of a generation gap but also the agonies which resulted from the love-hate relationship it grew from. In **Giant** his frustrated obsession for Elizabeth Taylor sublimated into the creation of a personal empire, a titanic version of the safe little world he tried to form with Mineo and Wood in **Rebel.** Dean's death in an automobile accident in 1955 should be remembered as more than just an event which precipitated an almost necrophiliac cult; it was a crippling blow to one of the most characteristic elements of fifties cinema.

　　On a somewhat older plane, Marlon Brando also incarnated a certain inarticulate quality, but one which was likely to come exploding out in physical action, as it did most notably in his Stanley Kowalski role in **A Streetcar Named Desire.** Stanley's basic distrust of the words Blanche hides behind is instinctive and justifiable, and the man of action destroys her flimsy rhetorical barriers. As Terry Molloy in **On the Waterfront,** he can hardly find words to share his frustration with his brother (Rod Steiger), but by the film's conclusion he again finds that action, in the form of beating up Lee J. Cobb, is the best means of expression when words have become inadequate. This persona descended into caricature in **The Wild One,** but Brando's fifties roles were varied enough to include Napoleon, Marc Antony, and Sky Masterson as well.

　　Less clearly defined was the career of Montgomery Clift, established in the late forties but not fully realized until his appearance as the fated hero of **A Place in the Sun.** His extremely low-keyed, often neurotic portrayals are evident in **From Here to Eternity, The Young Lions,** and **Lonelyhearts.** Remembered best today for his characterization of Prewitt in **From Here to Eternity**—an Oscar he lost while everyone else connected with the film was

The only film Charles Laughton ever directed was **The Night of the Hunter** (top), an uneasy blend of Griffith and German expressionism. Shelley Winters and Robert Mitchum starred (1955). Bottom left: Peter Ustinov and Martine Carol in Max Ophuls' last film, **Lola Montès** (France, 1955), once acclaimed by an American auteur critic as the greatest film of all time. Bottom right: Nicholas Ray's **Rebel Without a Cause** (1955), the best of the alienated-youth films of the period. With Sal Mineo, James Dean, and Natalie Wood.

Opposite top: Rock Hudson, Lauren Bacall, Robert Stack, and Dorothy Malone in one of Douglas Sirk's better melodramas, **Written on the Wind** (1957). Left: Burl Ives, James Dean, and Raymond Massey in Elia Kazan's **East of Eden** (1955), from the Steinbeck novel. Above: Gregory Peck hunts the white whale in John Huston's version of **Moby Dick** (1956), one of the fifties' most ambitious literary adaptations.

winning one—he performed most interestingly in **Suddenly, Last Summer** and **Wild River,** films which made good use of his qualities of loneliness and inner strength. Clift was teamed with Marilyn Monroe in her last film, **The Misfits** (also Clark Gable's last film), and the fragile persona which they shared created an interesting resonance in this otherwise overwritten failure.

Monroe's career in the fifties was a classic example of her star buildup. Her brief exposure in a series of films like **Clash by Night** led to the full treatment in **Niagara** and **How to Marry a Millionaire** (in which she is practically the only saving grace), and a carefully balanced host of others. Exploited throughout for her sexpot qualities, it became clear very early on that she was one of the screen's most gifted comediennes, bringing her own special charm to films like **The Seven-Year Itch, Bus Stop,** and **Some Like It Hot.** The dreamy vulnerability she projected redefined sexiness, which had hardened by the early fifties into the image of Jane Russell or Ava Gardner, and seems particularly fresh when seen today. Like Dean's death, Monroe's robbed the cinema of more than a star, rather a very special presence.

One cannot end a discussion of the films of the fifties without stopping to consider briefly its very characteristic genres, for this was the last great age of the genre movie. The western was perhaps the most transparently changed—the clean-cut heroes, goals, and ideals of an earlier day replaced by classic neuroses. The so-called "adult western" had appeared at the end of the

war and by now was operating in full force. The old western myths were examined, inverted, and discarded. The westerner was used as an allegorical figure, a wanderer over an earlier, unspoiled American landscape. Or he was seen as a victim of the forces around him, a man like you or me, prey to the same fears and inadequacies. This sort of revisionism was especially strong in the fantasy genre. Supernatural horror films, long a staple, now almost disappeared, being replaced by a classic science-fiction cycle. The period considered itself too pragmatic to waste much time with vampires and werewolves, but these basic elements were dressed in scientific garb and returned as interplanetary invaders **(The Thing).** Flying saucers went from the front pages right to the drive-in screens **(The War of the Worlds).** Nuclear testing caused strange and monstrous mutations **(Them!).** Deranged scientists used the new technology for unspeakable ends (**I Was a Teenage Frankenstein**—a great success because of its implicit parody of parental authority). Occasionally certain political or philosophic allegories snuck in, like Don Siegel's **Invasion of the Body Snatchers** or Jack Arnold's **The Incredible Shrinking Man,** but the general run was somewhere on the level of **Plan Nine from Outer Space,** a pastiche of flying saucers, grave robbing, and stock footage of an already-dead Bela Lugosi.

One classic genre which renewed itself for a last gasp was the spectacle, which had not been seen in any quantity since the silent period. De Mille's **Samson and Delilah** set the tone for this revival, and soon Hollywood was staggering under the weight of remakes of **Quo Vadis?, The Ten Commandments,** and **Ben Hur.** These three films, and many others, took advantage of the new trend toward location shooting, and soon Hollywood was sending vast crews to Spain, Egypt, and Italy. These giant films had one advantage: By their very scope they could offer audiences something unavailable at home on television. They made full use of the new visual processes and even extended them to such new sensations as stereophonic sound and Smell-O-Vision. It is noteworthy, though, that the period films did not escape to the turn of the century, as had been the fashion previously, but to the very dawn of Judeo-Christian civilization. There is no nostalgia here, but instead a colossal escapism wrapped in traces of the fifties religious revival. These films tended to get somewhat more absurd as the decade wore on, and no one batted an eyelash when King Vidor cast George Sanders as a Hebrew prince in **Solomon and Sheba.** Audiences kept right on coming, and if not for visions of the **Cleopatra** fiasco dancing in their heads, what's left of Hollywood would probably still be grinding out lust-in-the-dust, or "Tits and Sand" epics, as they were affectionately referred to in the industry.

But perhaps the most indicative change was that which befell the biographical film. Starting in the thirties, these stories had glorified the lives of great scientists, artists, and even bankers. But by the fifties the public could no longer accept the joyous accession to fame of a **Yankee Doodle Dandy.** Biopix now focused on "giants" who were revealed as emotional cripples: Jeanne

James Dean's brief career spanned only three films, but their impact was enormous. Some stars like Wayne or Crawford have built up their reputations over decades, but Dean's career lasted for just a few months in 1955-1956. That he could make so strong an impression in his own time is understandable, though his hold today on the public's enthusiasm is largely the result of the high-quality films he did appear in. George Stevens's **Giant,** with Elizabeth Taylor, was the last.

51-37

Above: The final outpost of the "film noir"—Orson Welles, Janet Leigh, and Akim Tamiroff in **Touch of Evil** (1958). Welles directed this brilliant work almost by accident, thanks to the timely intervention of its star, Charlton Heston, but he was unable to promote another directing job for himself in Hollywood. Working successfully within the studio framework was difficult, but it was accomplished by directors like Minnelli. **Lust for Life** (r) was among his best films, with Kirk Douglas in the role of Van Gogh (1956).

Eagels with dope, Helen Morgan with alcohol. In **Love Me or Leave Me,** Doris Day played her finest role as Ruth Etting, mired in a self-destructive relationship with husband/manager James Cagney, "the Gimp." As written by Isobel Lennart, the film was a dry run for her later **Funny Girl,** but its most interesting aspect was a view of marriage as a manipulative association akin to a crooked business partnership, a protofeminist slant which would seem more at home in the seventies. Even in such unremarkable works as **The Buster Keaton Story** or **The Eddie Duchin Story,** the concentration seemed to be on traumas of the great lives. **Lust for Life,** Minnelli's fine film on Van Gogh, implied most strongly of all that trauma and art were inextricably bound. A few old-fashioned biographies were still made, like Anthony Mann's **The Glenn Miller Story,** but public acceptance was chancy and some, like **The Spirit of St. Louis,** were shot down by audiences. By the sixties the reliable old biopic, like practically everything else on the American screen, had mutated into almost unrecognizable form.

As film audiences dwindled, many large old theaters were forced to close, selling their valuable downtown property. Occasionally an old theater resurfaced as a supermarket or an appliance store. As financial returns to the producers fell off, the number of features made by Hollywood plummeted, starving those exhibitors still struggling to remain in the business. Statistics over the decade show that U.S.-produced features dropped from 391 in 1951 to 131 in 1961. Frantically searching for a supply of film for their theaters, exhibitors turned on a large scale to foreign producers. Imported features rose from 263 to 331 over the same period. Foreign films grew from forty percent of the market to an astounding seventy percent. Early in the fifties it was the Italian films in the late neo-realist vein that attracted the most attention: Fellini's **La Strada** and De Sica's **Umberto D.** and **Miracle in Milan.** But, again, what came across the Atlantic was heavily filtered. The early Michelangelo Antonioni was practically unknown, as were Robert Bresson and Roberto Rossellini after the Ingrid Bergman hysteria. The Japanese made a few films to crash the Western market and hoarded the rest. Teinosuke Kinugasa's **Gate of Hell,** with its delicate Eastmancolor, won prizes from the New York Film Critics and at the Cannes Festival, and even a Hollywood Oscar. Akira Kurosawa was known for **Rashomon,** but much of his work was unseen until later. And the finest Japanese directors, Yasujiro Ozu and Kenji Mizoguchi, were almost unheard-of in the West until the late sixties. Often when a truly great film was imported, it met an icy critical reception—which was more than enough to discourage other thoughtful distributors. This is what happened to Carl Dreyer's **Ordet** in 1957 (and to his **Day of Wrath,** made in 1943 but not released in America until 1948, and to **Gertrud,** made in 1965—all recognized much later as films of timeless value, but panned by many of the New York critics). Instead, the critical establishment promoted Satyajit Ray and his Apu Trilogy. Sometimes a **Nights of Cabiria** would brighten the screens of small metropolitan theaters, but by the decade's end the foreign imports seemed as morose as the term "art film" might suggest. Ingmar Bergman became a fit subject for discussion in theological circles (though not Catholic ones, where the Legion of Decency had condemned most of his work), and pop sociology wallowed in a new consciousness of alienation and existentialism. It was the French "new wave" that blew life back into the movies.

The "new wave" was made possible by changes in the French government's attitude toward film subsidies, a financial quirk which permitted dozens of young filmmakers to make their first features at the close of the fifties. Although most of this work was uninteresting, 1958-59 saw the first features of Jean-Luc Godard **(Breathless),** François Truffaut **(The 400 Blows),** Claude Chabrol **(Le Beau Serge** and **The Cousins),** Alain Resnais **(Hiroshima, Mon Amour)** and Eric Rohmer **(The Sign of Leo).** This incredibly vital and multifaceted burst of creative energy quickly transformed the rest of European, British, and American film. Its creators were mostly film critics affiliated with "Cahiers du Cinéma," a magazine which had promoted the concept of the "caméra stylo"—the idea that the tools of the moving picture could and should be employed as personally as the writer uses his pen. This concern with personal creativity was linked closely with a study of the filmmakers themselves, and "Cahiers" was noted for an

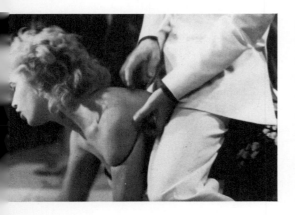

artist-centered form of film criticism known as the "politique des auteurs." They elevated the director to star status and found even in the work of those formerly regarded as studio journeymen (for example, Robert Aldrich and Raoul Walsh) strong underlying themes and stylistic devices. Indeed, the discovery of a director's "personality" in a work became far more important than the presence of any self-conscious "content." In their own films, they reacted strongly to the ossified quality of much of the fifties French cinema—all very literate, smoothed out, and respectable. Instead, they let the rough edges of their work show, emphasizing to audiences the peculiar nature of the movie experience. Actors stopped and talked to the camera/director/audience; the introductory slates to individual shots might not be removed; jump cuts and self-conscious references to other movies and moviemaking abounded.

The low budgets of many of their early features provided an echo of the early days of one of their favorite movements, Italian neo-realism, with its extensive—and artful—urban location shooting by nimble, hand-held cameras. Through American directors they developed an appreciation of cinematic action, and in their first films, at least, tried to keep things moving at all times. They projected Jean-Paul Belmondo as the new Bogart, but such starmaking almost seems an afterthought, for it has been the director who has ruled as superstar from the days of the new wave on.

This Parisian outburst paralleled the flowering of the "angry young man" school across the Channel, where the work of writers like John Osborne and Alan Sillitoe provided the nucleus for a revival of creative cinema in Britain. Although their French comrades might have accused them of concentrating too heavily on "big themes," the new English cinema began a grim study of postwar social and economic problems. Tony Richardson's **A Taste of Honey** and **The Loneliness of the Long-Distance Runner,** Karel Reisz's **Saturday Night**

The decedence of Roman society which Fellini pictured in his explosive **La Dolce Vita** (opposite, top) shocked viewers in 1961, but the film's deep moral lesson was implicit. Left: **Lolita** was filmed by Stanley Kubrick in 1962 and considerably underrated by critics and audiences alike. Not the least of its accomplishments was re-creating American highway and motel life on English locations. With James Mason, Sue Lyon, and Shelley Winters. Above: Laurence Harvey and Angela Lansbury in John Frankenheimer's **The Manchurian Candidate** (1962), one of a spate of political thrillers.

and Sunday Morning, John Schlesinger's **A Kind of Loving,** and Lindsay Anderson's **This Sporting Life** created a new vision of working-class England, cast in the image of Tom Courtenay, Albert Finney, and Richard Harris. Although somewhat depressing even to art-house audiences in America, these films seemed to have a franker approach to social and sexual problems than was possible in Hollywood, and their exaggerated realism appeared hopelessly ahead of standard Hollywood fare. Even more startling in this regard was the sudden turn in the Italian cinema. In Antonioni's **L'Avventura, La Notte,** and **L'Eclisse,** the old neo-realist strain had changed into a moody and introspective examination of the failure of modern man and modern society. What Pauline Kael referred to as the "come-dressed-as-the-sick-soul-of-Europe party" captured screens across the continent. A wealthy crowd composed of jet-setters, old nobility, and effete intellectuals wandered around the endless corridors of baroque hotels, spas, mansions, or maybe just the streets of Rome. There were many and varied comments on the meaninglessness of it all, the failure of personal relationships, and the general loss of innocence. "Oh, Marcello, I'm so bored . . ." went the dialogue. If Resnais's **Last Year at Marienbad** was the formal peak of this movement, then Fellini's **La Dolce Vita** marked its grandest expression. Halfway between his neo-realist period and his three-ring-circus phase, Fellini presented his version of our fall from grace as a modern Apocalypse covered by a Roman gossip columnist. From the moment the helicopter-borne statue of Christ sails over the bikini-clad sunbathers, we know that we are in for some real social criticism, early sixties style. Fellini manages to convey with rare skill his own love-hate relationship with "la dolce vita," and just as skillfully he walks De Mille's tightrope between sex and morality. Even with Nadia Gray's famous striptease, the stern moral lesson behind **La Dolce Vita** won it an "unobjectionable for adults, with reservations" rating from the Legion of Decency, an organization which condemned outright the "amorality" of **Breathless, Jules and Jim, Knife in the Water, L'Avventura,** and many others. It is no exaggeration to say that frank sexual content was in large part responsible for the success of foreign films in America in the early sixties. In 1961 the Legion condemned less than one percent of American productions, but fully twenty percent of foreign releases. The boom in art-house attendance in this period was largely related to the more open sexuality evident in European films. When American films in the late sixties were free to deal with the same subjects, the bottom fell out of the American market for European producers.

But in the early years of the decade, American films reacted hardly at all to any of the challenges from abroad. Indeed, it seems that the fifties did not end until the middle of 1963. Hitchcock and Ford still dominated this period with ease—**Psycho** and **The Birds** capping Hitchcock's fabulous output, while Ford's **The Man Who Shot Liberty Valance** sums up many of his ideas on myth and reality that had been developing since the thirties. Spectacles still soaked up much of Hollywood's time and money, and a few, like **Exodus,**

Cinema in the early sixties ran off
in several divergent directions.
Left: A massive moment from Anthony
Mann's **The Fall of the Roman
Empire** (1964), one of the better
costume spectacles. Above: Slim
Pickens in Kubrick's black comedy,
**Dr. Strangelove, Or: How I
Learned to Stop Worrying and Love
the Bomb** (1964). Below: Marcello
Mastroianni in Fellini's **8½**
(1963), one of the most popular imports
then breaking into the market.

Spartacus, and **Lawrence of Arabia** really seemed worth the effort. But films were coming more and more to require a special reason for being, and these years marked the final appearance of the well-crafted Hollywood property of the old school. Established directors like George Cukor **(Heller in Pink Tights),** Vincente Minnelli **(Two Weeks in Another Town),** Elia Kazan **(Splendor in the Grass),** and Fred Zinnemann **(The Sundowners)** gave us the last offerings of a Hollywood about to suffer permanent stylistic schizophrenia. Younger directors like TV's John Frankenheimer, in **The Bird Man of Alcatraz** and **The Manchurian Candidate,** cautiously began to explore the potential of the new media, but only in the context of the older tradition. Only Stanley Kubrick explodes to life in this period, with the still underrated **Lolita,** and the even more startling **Dr. Strangelove,** a film whose freewheeling, macabre manipulation of Cold War conventions seemed to single-handedly bring the introverted fifties to an end and inaugurate the freer, much less inhibited style of the high sixties.

This mid-decade style was very much related to the phenomenon of "swinging London" as analyzed (and largely constructed) in the pages of "Time" magazine. British taste, which had long seemed the epitome of staid conservatism, suddenly and totally came to dominate the pop cultural world of fashion, music, and film. Led by Twiggy, the Beatles, and James Bond, the new "mod" life-style quickly found its clearest expression in the movies.

The Bond films themselves had started as recognizable entries in the secret-agent genre, but after **From Russia with Love** they became more concerned with projecting the specific Bond image of supercool sex and violence spiked with a fetish for mechanics and technology in its most advanced forms. In creating this paramount image of wish-fulfillment (really a picturization of the "Playboy" philosophy), the Bond films rapidly became the most popular series ever made, each new release somehow out-grossing the one before. They created their own genre of mod international spy film, which instantly went through an entire life cycle and produced such clever archetypal inversions as **The Spy Who Came in from the Cold,** with Richard Burton not Sean Connery, **Casino Royale,** and **Modesty Blaise** (starring Monica Vitti as a female secret agent loose in a psychedelic Pop Art wonderworld). These films, especially Sidney J. Furie's **The Ipcress File,** were stylistically hyped up with second-hand devices borrowed from the new wave. The king of this rip-off style was Richard Lester, director of **A Hard Day's Night, The Knack,** and **Help!,** and it is strange today to read the praise heaped on the first of these films, praise which soon turned to ashes when the emptiness of the style became apparent in the repetitious sequels. The masters of the "angry young man" school also adopted this mannerism, but to somewhat better effect. Tony Richardson's **Tom Jones** seemed truly fresh and imaginative at the time, and John Schlesinger's **Darling** combined the earlier social concern with the new techniques, finding in Julie Christie a quintessential image of swinging London. Karel Reisz directed what in retrospect seems the best example of this school, **Morgan!,** a wacky

Above: British filmmakers introduced a number of "big themes" that had been ignored in earlier days of stricter censorship. Here are Dirk Bogarde and Julie Christie in John Schlesinger's **Darling** (1965), at the time one of the most highly regarded films, but already somewhat dated. Right: The Americans followed up as soon as they were able. Mike Nichols filmed Edward Albee's **Who's Afraid of Virginia Woolf?** with Richard Burton, Elizabeth Taylor, George Segal, and Sandy Dennis (1966), a landmark in on-the-screen use of dirty words.

psychopathic farce brilliantly played by David Warner and Vanessa Redgrave. By 1967 the mod movement began collapsing into auto-critique: Peter Watkins' **Privilege** attacked the power of rock music and the media, and actually compared the potential of the current scene to Nazi Germany! Soon the new politically conscious cinema would sweep all this frivolity before it, but for a time England seemed the place to be, and everyone went there to make films. Truffaut's lyrical science-fiction film **Fahrenheit 451** misfired, but Roman Polanski's **Repulsion** still remains a chilling combination of surrealism and horror. The transportation of the Italian cinema to England created a true masterpiece in Antonioni's **Blow-Up,** a search for truth set in a swinging London not so far removed from the decadent Roman scene of a few years earlier.

The Italian cinema itself had undergone changes very much like the British cinema. From moody black-and-white seriousness at the decade's start, it exploded after Fellini's **8½** (1963) into a riot of color and expressionism. Antonioni in **Red Desert** (1964) produced a landmark color film which carefully investigated the relationship between a disintegrating personality and her disintegrated environment. **8½** itself seemed very close to the new wave's concern for the special nature of filmmaking, but unlike the later **Day for Night,** this film approaches Joycean dimension in its view of the artist and society. **Juliet of the Spirits** marks the farthest limit of Italian neo-expressionism and the height of sixties chic, but Fellini already seems uncertain in repeating without sufficient variation themes which were to obsess him for the next few years.

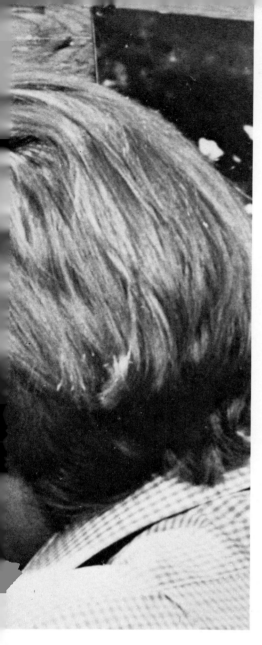

A number of European directors achieved worldwide prominence in the sixties, moving from one country to another and creating a new, international style of filmmaking. Above: David Hemmings as the curious photographer in Michelangelo Antonioni's **Blow-Up** (1966). Mod London was now heir to the decadent Roman scene of a few years earlier. Jean-Luc Godard and François Truffaut were the two most important talents to emerge from the "new wave." But soon they split along political lines. Far left: Juliette Berto and Michel Semianko in Godard's **La Chinoise** (1967). Left: Claude Jade and Jean-Pierre Léaud in Truffaut's **Bed and Board** (1971).

The rest of the European cinema seemed split between the best of Bergman and Godard, and the occasional interesting flash from other directors, skilled and not so skilled. Popular style was instantly captured by Claude Lelouch's **A Man and a Woman** and Bo Widerberg's **Elvira Madigan,** dreamy and romantic films whose soft-focus photography and lyrical camera movements seemed a conscious return to high-thirties style. Striking at the time, this style quickly degenerated into a mindless cliché in student films and television commercials. More lasting was the effect of Buñuel's **Belle de Jour,** the perversely erotic triumph of the old master of surrealism. Buñuel, ironically, seemed the popularizer of investigations launched much more obliquely by Bergman in **The Silence** and **Persona,** studies in the deeper sexuality of modern woman. But in 1967, sex was about to be replaced by politics as the main theme of modern cinema, largely thanks to the work of Jean-Luc Godard. Of all the early members of the new wave, Godard was the only one to swing radically to the left and infuse his work with Marxian politics. Truffaut became a poet of personal relationships, Chabrol a director of Hitchcock-style thrillers, and Rohmer a philosopher, but Godard's cinema leaned toward Bertolt Brecht and agit-prop theater. His investigation of the position of women in society **(My Life to Live** and **Two or Three Things I Know About Her)** turned gradually to a discussion of that society itself, in **Masculin Féminin, Made in U.S.A.,** and **La Chinoise.** To allow the audience to objectively study these "children of Marx and Coca-Cola," Godard built barriers between audience and film, becoming highly conscious of the mechanical elements of this dispassionate form which he once had hoped dispensed truth twenty-four times a second. By 1968 he was the idolized master of the new cinema, the dominant creator of its new style and the chief exponent of its new politics.

By contrast, film in America had reached a distinct low point in the mid-sixties, aping European models in nearly all creative respects. Large-scale costume and period films were generally more thoughtful than previously, but Zinnemann's **A Man for All Seasons** seemed very remote from contemporary dilemmas, while David Lean and MGM turned **Dr. Zhivago** into a veritable remake of **Gone With the Wind. The Sound of Music** set the tone for a series of gargantuan musical adaptations, but the majority of these failed badly, and studios were often left with dead investments of ten or even twenty million dollars tied up in unsalable musical spectaculars like **Paint Your Wagon.** This trend still continues, the success of a **Funny Girl** or a **Cabaret** giving rise to flops such as **On a Clear Day, Lost Horizon,** and **Man of La Mancha.** The established directors of a few years earlier began to produce films which failed at the box office and confused critics. Ford's **Seven Women,** Hitchcock's **Torn Curtain,** and Wilder's **Kiss Me, Stupid** seemed flawed and insignificant beside their brilliant European counterparts, and American directors seemed to lack not only the answers to the day's problems but even a passing understanding of what the questions should be. A few films, like Wilder's **The Fortune Cookie** (despite its

Opposite, top: Omar Sharif and Julie Christie
in David Lean's **Doctor Zhivago** (1965).
Dustin Hoffman and Jon Voight in John
Schlesinger's **Midnight Cowboy** (1969). Above:
Antonioni's American film, **Zabriskie Point** (1970).
Whatever happened to Daria Halprin and Mark Frechette?

unfortunate ending), Howard Hawks's **El Dorado,** and John Huston's **Reflections in a Golden Eye,** seemed to show some life remaining in the Hollywood tradition, but their like was few and far between. Orson Welles sent back **Falstaff** from Europe and critics shook their heads in confusion. Only the most glib directors in Hollywood seemed up to form. Stanley Donen produced the slight but stylish **Charade** and **Arabesque,** and the rather more interesting **Two for the Road,** an examination of a failed marriage which seemed heavily influenced by the nonlinear style of Resnais. This lull did give us the early work of some directors who would later become important for having worked with themes and structures that would blossom more creatively in the future.

Two films by new directors set the tone for the great changes that followed at the close of the sixties: Mike Nichols's **The Graduate** and Arthur Penn's **Bonnie and Clyde.** Nichols had not shown any particular brilliance in **Who's Afraid of Virginia Woolf?,** but **The Graduate** won him great critical admiration and an immense following, its bouncy Simon and Garfunkel score setting the tone for dozens of "youth films" to follow. **The Graduate** was actually preceded by Francis Ford Coppola's **You're a Big Boy Now,** in many ways a superior film, but one whose quirkiness kept it from being the smashing success **The Graduate** quickly became. **Bonnie and Clyde** (originally intended by authors Robert Benton and David Newman for Jean-Luc Godard) ignited the debate on screen violence which grew to overwhelming proportions with Sam Peckinpah's later work, its slow-motion massacre establishing another stylistic innovation that quickly became a cliché. Also of interest were Penn's **The Chase,** Boorman's **Point Blank,** and even Roger Corman's **The Wild Angels,** wherein it became clear that Hollywood's obsession was violence, not sex.

The year 1968 made one of the stronger demonstrations that art really does follow life and that film is the art which follows it most closely. Student riots not only in Paris but throughout Europe and even in the United States suddenly burst into the headlines. The Democratic National Convention in Chicago, the Czech invasion, the marches on Washington to protest the Vietnam War and poverty, the assassinations of Martin Luther King and Robert Kennedy, Weathermen blowing up buildings, political repression, rioting in the streets—in Yeats's terms the center did not seem to be holding very well, and mere anarchy had been loosed. "Relevance" was the order of the day and the Woodstock nation seemed to be giving the orders. In France, Godard's cinema became politicized after **Weekend,** a final dalliance with the old narrative film format and another knock at the apparently doddering capitalist system. Later, in films like **Le Gai Savoir, Wind from the East,** and **Vladimir and Rosa,** Godard buried himself in political work, vanishing from screens around the world while promoting his Dziga Vertov film collective, named after the Soviet documentary pioneer. His return to the story film with Jane Fonda and Yves Montand in **Tout Va Bien** caused barely a ripple of excitement or even notice.

More successful with political material was Henri Costa-Gavras,

When it finally came, the censorship breakthrough was almost laughably abrupt, as if the pent-up forces of decades of repression had all shot to the surface at the same moment. Top: **The Damned** (1970) was an examination of the more perverse roots of Nazism, an international co-production with Luchino Visconti at the helm. Bottom: Master of bad taste, Britain's Ken Russell flourished briefly in this period with films like **The Devils** (1971), a near-surrealistic tale of convents, exorcism, sexual repression and torture, all handled in Russell's most florid style.

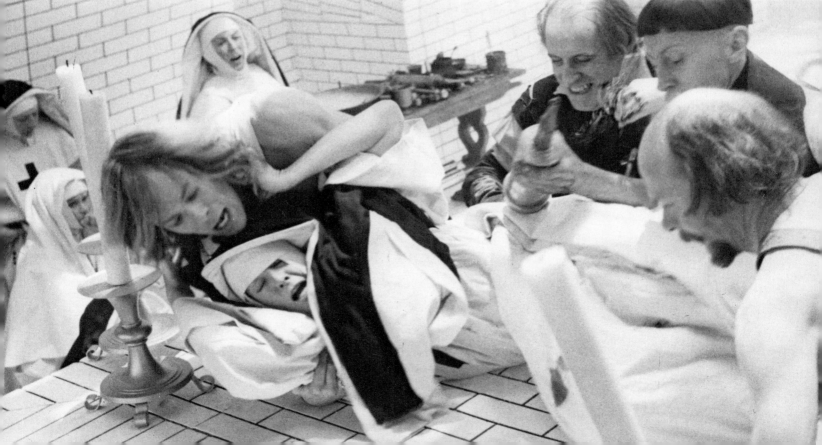

Popular tastes rocked back and forth in the early seventies, first following trends, then reacting against them. Far left: The sentimentality of **Love Story** (1970), with Ali MacGraw and Ryan O'Neal ("What can you say about a 25-year-old girl who died?") was a welcome retreat to the past. But Jane Fonda's role in **Klute** (l) was something else entirely (1971). The most important trend was fashioned in 1969 by **Easy Rider** (below), which ignited the youth-film market. With Dennis Hopper (who also directed), Jack Nicholson, and Peter Fonda.

who found ways of using commercial screens to transmit political messages in **Z** and **State of Siege.** Gillo Pontecorvo's revolutionary-political films were not so widely shown but probably were more effective. **The Battle of Algiers** detailed the struggle of the Algerian FLN and **Burn!** actually emerged as a Hollywood-sponsored textbook for revolution.

In America new social and political themes merged with the growing wave of youth films. Haskell Wexler's **Medium Cool** was set against the backdrop of the riots at the Democratic National Convention in Chicago in 1968, tying up the personal story of the plot with the public struggle of the real events. In **Easy Rider,** Dennis Hopper had his two motorcycle heroes travel the landscape of a grotesque America, meeting a violent end at the hands of shotgun-wielding rednecks. The phenomenal success of this film made producers willing to back almost any director under thirty in any sort of youth-oriented project. Because of this, screens were swamped with films like **The Strawberry Statement, Two Lane Blacktop, Panic in Needle Park, Vanishing Point, Drive, He Said, A Safe Place,** and **The Last Movie,** each more self-indulgent than the next. Some of the new directors showed the benefits of this temporary freedom, like Noel Black with **Pretty Poison** and Bob Raphelson with **Five Easy Pieces,** but the general level of these films was so poor that soon the entire movement dissolved. Yet before the excitement cooled, America became once again the place to come to capture the spark of the moment.

Instead of going to London, European filmmakers came to the United States. John Schlesinger made **Midnight Cowboy,** and Claude Lelouch, Jacques Demy, and Michelangelo Antonioni also undertook to capture the American experience. **Zabriskie Point** emerged as the disappointing final word on the whole youth-political-international "angst" period of the late sixties. Later works, like Jan Troell's **The Emigrants** and **The New Land,** took a somewhat more sober look at the country. From this group two young directors emerged, linked mainly by their connection to the king of the B Pictures, Roger Corman. Francis Ford Coppola was Corman's soundman and assistant when given the go-ahead to film **Dementia 13,** his first film and still one of his most interesting. Coming from the ranks of student filmmaking, Coppola had a hard time establishing himself even in those days, alternating studio jobs like **Finian's Rainbow** with personal projects like **The Rain People** and **The Conversation.** But the prodigious success of **The Godfather** assured his future.

Peter Bogdanovich had been an auteur-school film critic before working on Corman's **The Wild Angels,** then convinced Corman to finance his first film, **Targets.** The huge critical and commercial success of **The Last Picture Show** established his reputation and set the tone for the rest of his work, a single-handed attempt to revive classic Hollywood. With **What's Up, Doc?** and **Paper Moon** he re-created the thirties spirit, and in Daisy Miller he evoked the glamourized Hollywood adaptations of the Henry King days.

But classic Hollywood itself still twitched on occasion. Norman

91

Among the more interesting directors to achieve prominence are Bernardo Bertolucci and John Boorman. Bertolucci's greatest success has come from **Last Tango in Paris,** although **The Conformist** (1970) is more interesting. With Jean-Louis Trintignant and Stefania Sandrelli (above). In Boorman's early films like **Point Blank** he showed his talent for stylish pacing and movement, but his best film is probably **Deliverance,** opposite, with Ned Beatty, Herbert Coward, Burt Reynolds, and Jon Voight (1972).

Jewison's **The Thomas Crown Affair** dressed up the caper film with incredibly stylish multi-image pyrotechnics, a grab bag of cinematic tricks held together by Hollywood flash and star personalities (Faye Dunaway and Steve McQueen, emblems of the late sixties). Franklin Schaffner's **Patton,** illuminated by George C. Scott's bravura performance, was both high-style biography and high-style war movie (or was it antiwar?). As an intelligent spectacle it was only surpassed by Stanley Kubrick's **2001: A Space Odyssey,** which Kubrick had filmed in utmost secrecy for several years. On its appearance in 1968, this most expensive of underground movies startled everyone, but overcame weak reviews and opening business to develop a solid following which grew steadily over the years. Today this tremendously ambitious panorama of man's spiritual odyssey seems one of the key works of the age. More typical of MGM, though, was **Ryan's Daughter,** a failed attempt to repeat the success of **Dr. Zhivago,** right

down to the advertising. One reason for this disaster was the film's constant undercutting of its romantic story—a bad mistake in a movie advertised as a grand romance in an era addicted to the syrupy romanticism of **Love Story.**

While most of Hollywood's time and attention went into such updated soap opera, or the production of still more giant musicals like **Funny Girl, Hello, Dolly!,** and **Mame,** a few filmmakers managed to combine the old Hollywood craftsmanship with the creativity of the youth explosion. Robert Altman's **M*A*S*H** captured the public imagination in a way that **Brewster McCloud** did not, but his **McCabe and Mrs. Miller** and **The Long Goodbye** emerged as highly personal, and relatively successful, reexaminations of the western and private-eye genres. In Europe, classicism seemed to return by the end of the sixties. Truffaut's Antoine Doinel films and **The Wild Child** and **Day for Night** seemed oblivious to earlier "political" necessities. Richardson's **The**

Charge of the Light Brigade and Reisz's **The Loves of Isadora** brought back the period film and the biography with a dash of sixties style. And nothing but sixties style were the films of Ken Russell, especially **The Music Lovers, The Devils,** and **Savage Messiah,** fascinating exercises in bad taste on both technical and aesthetic grounds. **The Boy Friend** showed that Russell's vaunted surrealism couldn't stand comparison with Busby Berkeley's. Although his subjects seemed very stylish and advanced, Luchino Visconti's late-sixties work perhaps more than anyone else's set the stage for the neo-classic revival. The expressionism of **The Damned** harked back to the style of the German films of 1930, and was largely responsible for the sudden wave of nostalgia that crested in the early seventies. See Bernardo Bertolucci's **The Conformist,** or De Sica's **The Garden of the Finzi-Continis,** or even Bob Fosse's **Cabaret,** for further examples of this obsession with the thirties, art deco, and the "déjà-vu" sensation of dancing on the brink of the volcano. Fellini, of course, remained unaffected by all this. **Satyricon** and **Roma** (actually **Fellini Satyricon** and **Fellini's Roma**) were caricatures of his earlier visions, although **The Clowns** was certainly worthy of his best work.

In the past few years trendiness has come to dominate the international cinema, and the success or failure of any film seems connected with its ability to fit into, or initiate, some all-pervasive trend. In 1971-72 the cult of exaggerated violence monopolized critical discussion. Peckinpah's **Straw Dogs** (and his earlier **The Wild Bunch**), Kubrick's **A Clockwork Orange,** Hitchcock's **Frenzy,** and Boorman's **Deliverance** raised argument and counterargument over the effect of their concentrated dosage of ultraviolence. Gangsterism, this time seen with an economic or a political slant, attracted wide attention in **The Godfather** and **The French Connection,** and always there were a dozen little films to follow in the wake of each big success—**Prime Cut** or **The Friends of Eddie Coyle,** for example.

By 1972 the experimentation with form and structure so typical of the sixties had vanished. Neo-classicism was the prevailing style, in films as disparate as **Travels With My Aunt, The Last Picture Show,** and **Last Tango in Paris.** These films may have explored new areas of content, but stylistically they snuggled back to the early fifties. The difference between the convoluted Bertolucci style of **The Conformist** or **The Spider's Strategem** and the linearity of **Last Tango** is striking and worthy of attention. It is a style necessarily linked to nostalgia and an evocation of the past. The sixties were not interested in this. Life and art were exploding in all directions and we were offered abstract formal puzzles in even the standard Hollywood fare. Now with films like **American Graffiti, The Way We Were, The Great Gatsby,** and **Daisy Miller,** filmgoing has become much less troublesome. We are offered a respite from the stylistic strains of the sixties. Nostalgia is big business and high art as well, and will continue to be so until we can bring ourselves to stop looking backward and turn our faces ahead.

With all the changes that the film world has gone through, producers still return to the tried-and-true methods when the market is unsettled. For the major Paramount release, seen at left, David Merrick took a pre-sold property **(The Great Gatsby),** hooked into a current fad (nostalgia), cast some big stars (Mia Farrow and Robert Redford), and spent big money for production and exploitation. Of course, even the best of the old methods don't work all the time.

SUPERSTARS

Preceding pages:
KATHARINE HEPBURN and
SPENCER TRACY
The rare exceptions: two
stars who were able to work
together on screen in a
completely effortless yet
wholly satisfying manner.

MAE MARSH
The innocent little "Dear
One" of D. W. Griffith's
films, this sentimental
heroine of 1917 inspired
the poet Vachel Lindsay.

By some vague, collective whim, the movie audience selects from the galaxy of film players a handful of people for that unique, impressive, and often uncomfortable role—stardom. The selection is the public's doing entirely. It was so in the beginning and is so today.

The early producers wanted their performers to remain nameless. They knew well the lesson of the theater, where "name" performers commanded enormous salaries—and worse, control of their own productions as well. But the early moviegoing public began to recognize the nameless performers they saw on the screen each week, and they gave these actors and actresses sobriquets in a conscious effort to personalize them. The magic of the screen compelled them to identify with these performers. Those who caught audiences' imaginations first had distinctive looks or mannerisms—golden curls, dimples, big dark eyes—which were reflected in the early nicknames and came to be an important element of star quality.

The public demanded stars. Borderline independents like Universal and Fox gambled that they could crack the power of the film trust by manipulating this insistent clamor. Previously known only as "the Biograph Girl," Florence Lawrence was hired away by Universal's Carl Laemmle and given a name of her own. The star system had officially begun.

When other producers finally recognized this "fait accompli," they spent fortunes on promoting as screen stars the already established stars of stage and grand opera, legendary performers like James O'Neill and Mary Garden. But the public would have none of this; it wanted its own stars, new stars for a new medium.

As the studio system grew, producers became more adept at presenting the public with likely material. But to say that producers "made" stars is a complete misreading of film history. Likely performers were thrown onto the screen by the fistful, and the public chose for itself. No one ever foisted an unwanted star on the public, at least not for long. Not Griffith with Carol Dempster, not Goldwyn with Anna Sten, not even Hitchcock with Tippi Hedren.

Some of the stars who did make it are included here. Mostly they are the larger-than-life stars of the golden period of the movies, the ones Gloria Swanson keeps talking about in **Sunset Boulevard.** The ones with faces. Now that films have been cut down to size, there is no need for the luminous constructions of earlier days. Today Dustin Hoffman, Al Pacino, and Gene Hackman offer exactly what's called for in seventies cinema: superb acting without recourse to the frills and backlighting of the classic Hollywood style.

. . . But back in the good old days, they did have faces.

NORMA TALMADGE
The great romantic heroine of the silent screen, an aristocratic beauty whose fabulous career vanished with the coming of sound.

MARY PICKFORD
Not just America's sweetheart, but a Hollywood princess who married Douglas Fairbanks and reigned over the movie colony during its golden age.

LOUISE BROOKS
An actress of rare intelligence and beauty whose talents were fearfully misused by Hollywood, but whose glow still illuminates a handful of silent masterpieces.

RUDOLPH VALENTINO
Perhaps the first male star
whose success was based on
direct exploitation of sex
appeal, shown here in his greatest
role in **Blood and Sand,** 1922.

JOHN GILBERT
Popular in both straight
dramatic and romantic leads,
he was the screen's great
lover in the days before
talkies brought an
end to his career.

LON CHANEY
An early portrait of "the
man of a thousand faces,"
years before he thrilled
millions as Quasimodo
and "the Phantom."

DOUGLAS FAIRBANKS
This all-American hero is
best remembered today for
his romantic swashbucklers—
The Thief of Bagdad, 1924,
being the most imaginative.

THEDA BARA
With a few straggling exceptions, she construc an entire career by portraying "the Vamp," in this **Salome** of 1918.

LILLIAN GISH
Her best performances glow with an inner vitality that keeps them fresh and exciting to this day, like her Mimi in **La Boheme,** 1926.

GLORIA SWANSON
Best known for romantic dramas of considerable opulence, her finest performances were always underlined with a touch of the comic.

MAE MURRAY
The superheated qualities
of her impassioned romances
seem laughable today, but
twenties audiences adored
her "bee-stung" lips.

CLARA BOW
A surprisingly reflective
moment for Clara, otherwise
the most aggressive of the
jazz-age flappers.

GRETA GARBO
A young Garbo, hardly a
star, not yet a legend,
but already possessed of that
classic presence in
this revealing early portrait.

RONALD COLMAN
Hollywood's image of the
sophisticated man of the world,
his impressive silent career
was greatly enhanced by the
arrival of talking pictures.

RICHARD BARTHELMESS
A silent star whose successes
ranged from pastorals to
costume romances, he was
unable to find a suitable
image in the thirties.

FREDRIC MARCH
The matinee-idol beginnings
of a wide-ranging career
that spanned four decades
on stage and screen.

MARLENE DIETRICH
The most exotic of
Hollywood's creations,
a screen goddess of the
thirties whose image
remains eternally haunting.

TALLULAH BANKHEAD
Did the movies ever make
full use of Tallulah's
wildly erratic talents?
Probably not, preferring
to waste her in trash
like **My Sin,** 1931.

EDWARD G. ROBINSON
On screen often a dangerous
hood or hard-bitten hero,
the real-life Robinson was
a connoisseur who built up
one of Hollywood's finest
art collections.

LIONEL and JOHN BARRYMORE
Members of a distinguished
theatrical family, they
carried on the best
of its traditions both before
and after sound, as here in
Grand Hotel, 1932.

JOHN WAYNE
The longest reigning of
Hollywood's big box-office
stars, seen here at the
beginning of his
career with Fox in 1930.

NORMA SHEARER
MGM's symbol of refinement
and style, Mrs. Irving G.
Thalberg poses gracefully
in an art deco mood.

BARBARA STANWYCK
A sweet pose from a girl
whose career was highlighted
by some of the toughest
performances in screen history.

JEAN HARLOW
One of the brightest stars
in the Metro galaxy, an
earthy blonde whose talents
as a comedienne helped create
a new definition of sex appeal.

111

SHIRLEY TEMPLE
At the age of nine, not only the ultimate child star, but the savior of the Fox studio as well.

CHARLES LAUGHTON
Master of the character role, seen here as Captain Bligh in the 1935 **Mutiny on the Bounty.**

CLAUDETTE COLBERT
A warm and well-loved heroine of the thirties and forties, equally at home in screwball comedies or costume epics.

BORIS KARLOFF
Hollywood's master menace, here having a little villainous fun in **The Secret Life of Walter Mitty,** 1947.

JUDY GARLAND
A very early (1937) portrait of the future star of **The Wizard of Oz** and **A Star Is Born.**

GARY COOPER
Strong, thoughtful, and dependable—equally comfortable in buckskins or a three-piece suit.

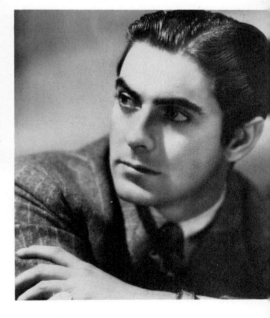

CAROLE LOMBARD
Paramount's lovely
purveyor of romantic comedy,
here at the peak of her
career in 1937.

ROBERT TAYLOR
The charming, if lightweight,
star of so many MGM
romances, at the start
of his career in 1935.

[BE]TTY GRABLE
[W]orld War II's most popular
[pi]n-up queen, and the most
[sp]arkling of the famous
[Fo]x blondes.

[C]HARLES BOYER
[Th]e epitome of continental
[so]phistication, and France's
[mo]st successful gift to
[th]e Hollywood Casbah.

JEAN ARTHUR
The down-to-earth working
girl, secretary, reporter, or
congresswoman—she gave them
all an indisputable star presence.

TYRONE POWER
Not only the most handsome
of Fox's leading men but also
an actor who often rose well
above the level of his material.

113

CARY GRANT
One of Paramount's
handsome, young romantic
leads, in a photograph
taken in 1934 for
the fan magazines.

BETTE DAVIS
As an ingenue in 1933,
well before the ever-present
cigarette, the classic mannerisms,
and the brilliant performances.

JOAN CRAWFORD
A star whose film
career spanned some forty years,
shown here as Miss Flaemm in
the all-star **Grand Hotel.**

ERROL FLYNN
Dashing and heroic,
Warners' incomparable
romantic hero poses
unflinchingly for the
studio photographer.

MAE WEST
A typically grand gesture,
but thrown away on one of
her lesser films, **Every
Day's a Holiday,** 1938.

JOHN GARFIELD
A likeable hero who wore
the stamp of
the tough New York streets
he grew up on.

HENRY FONDA
A true professional who
brought a particular conviction
to many of the screen's
finest social dramas.

JAMES STEWART
Unforgettably warm and
believable, creator of the
performances at the heart
of so many screen classics.

117

LANA TURNER
At eighteen, not far from
the drugstore counter, but
not yet the femme fatale of
The Postman Always Rings Twice.

RITA HAYWORTH
The love goddess of Columbia
Pictures, the haunting
vision of **Gilda** and **The
Lady from Shanghai.**

OLIVIA De HAVILLAND
Not just one of Hollywood's
loveliest stars, but an actress
with a well-deserved pair of
Oscars to her credit.

GENE TIERNEY
Cool, bewitching, and
unattainable—the far-off
beauty of **Laura** and
Leave Her to Heaven.

JAMES CAGNEY
An incredibly talented
performer who could play
any role, from song writing hoofer
to psychopathic killer,
with complete grace and
utter believability.

INGRID BERGMAN
One of the most thoughtful
and radiant of Hollywood's
heroines, always retaining
a hint of the foreign and exotic.

CLARK GABLE
"The King," the ultimate
rugged-romantic movie hero,
as he looked when he returned
from the war in 1945.

ELIZABETH TAYLOR
Always appealing—as a
precocious child star, as
a patrician beauty, and finally
as an actress of talent.

AVA GARDNER
The queen of postwar
Hollywood sensuality, the
heroine of **The Killers**
and **The Barefoot Contessa**.

MARILYN MONROE
A strange and wonderful
mixture of the innocent and the
erotic, a brilliant comedienne
whose target was often her
own fifties sexpot image.

PAUL NEWMAN
Brooding and rugged, one of the few fifties romantic stars with an even greater reputation today.

JAMES DEAN
A turbulent, meteoric star who embodied all the fears, desires, obsessions, and frustrations of youth.

HUMPHREY BOGART
Years after his death, still the very image of the sensitive loner surrounded by a flint-hard wall of psychic protection.

ROBERT REDFORD
A modern romantic hero in the classic tradition, tall and blond, and quite definitely a star.

 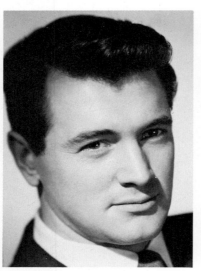  

GREGORY PECK
Seen here in the 1947 **Gentlemen's Agreement,** one of his many social message pictures.

ROCK HUDSON
Still the ruggedly handsome hero he created in so many of the classic melodramas of the fifties.

BURT LANCASTER
An actor of often uncredited range and power, and the hero of some of the strongest postwar dramas.

MARLON BRANDO
The most dynamic actor of his generation, whose career is periodically renewed by performances of magnetic power.

SOPHIA LOR
A beauty whose star shir
brightly on both sides
the Atlantic, and
Oscar-winning actress
rare intensi

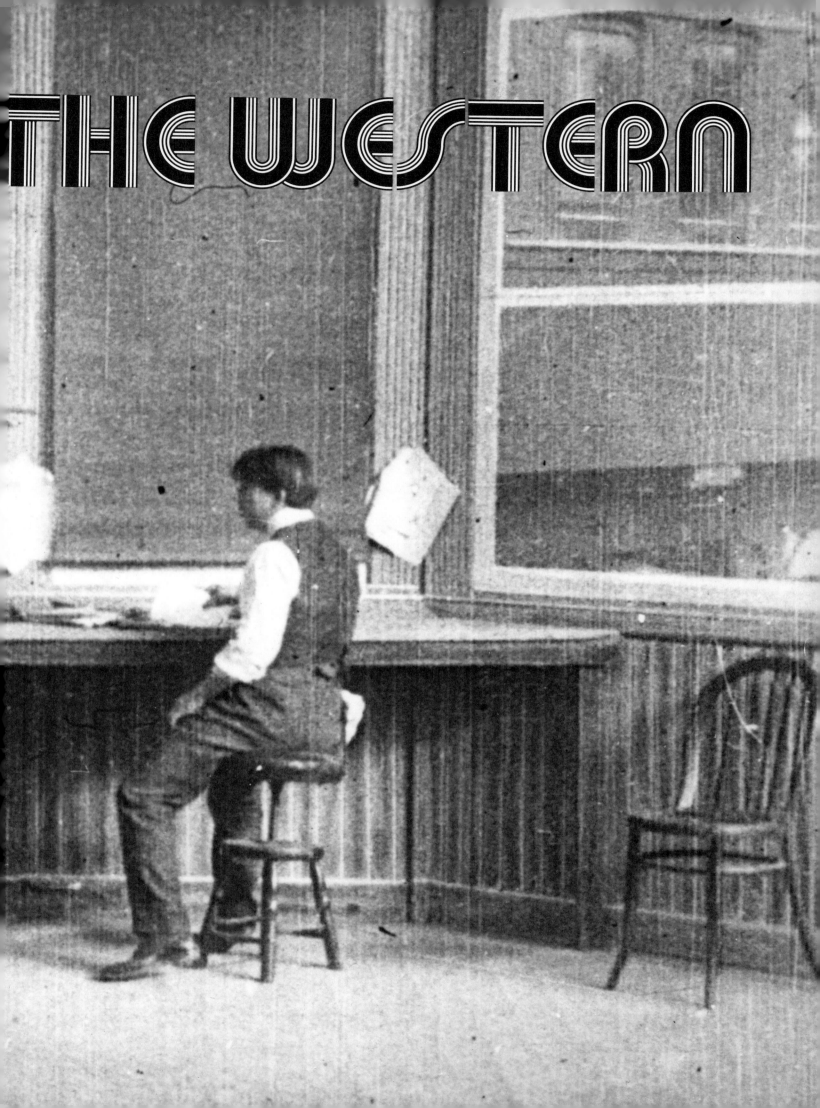

THE WESTERN

The pulp western novel was enjoying its heyday at the turn of the century, and early filmmakers immediately sensed the terrific screen potential of this material. Westerns presented the opportunity of leaving the studio and taking the camera into the great outdoors, showing theater audiences for the first time the reality of wind and rain, of stampeding cattle and broad, rolling landscapes.

It so happened that the early ones were mostly photographed in and around East Orange or Fort Lee, New Jersey, but audiences didn't seem to mind. The simple chases and romances of those lively one-reelers were constant crowd pleasers. The fact that most of the action could be taken on location, thus saving the cost of sets and freeing valuable studio space for other productions, was one major economic factor in the rise of early western production. Edison copyrighted **Cripple Creek Barroom** in 1898 and by 1903 had produced **The Great Train Robbery,** a landmark not only in the history of the western but in any survey of the American narrative film. In one of those strange filmland coincidences, the picture introduced G. M. Anderson to the screen in a tiny bit role (he's been identified as the passenger shot by the train robbers). Realizing the tremendous potential of the western, Anderson began to investigate film work more fully and soon co-founded the Essanay Film Manufacturing Company in Chicago. Here, in a series of some five hundred short films produced during the mid-teens, he established not only the first movie western series but also the first movie western character, the rather overdressed good-badman, Broncho Billy. Anderson's work, what little of it survives, still stands up well today and many historians now credit him with having spelled out the whole formula of the genre in these pioneer films.

But raising the western film to an art form was not the doing of Anderson, an Eastern dude who knew the West only through dime novels. In 1914 William S. Hart joined Thomas Ince and began the creation of a new type of western character, one based not on pulp fiction but on firsthand knowledge of the real West. Hart was an actor of considerable ability, having played Messala in the original stage production of **Ben Hur,** and he constantly underplayed his screen western roles. The realism which this relatively modern style of acting contributed to his films was enhanced by careful attention to the details of western life and lore. This was startling and fresh to audiences, who flocked to see this new-style hero in films like **Hell's Hinges, The Narrow Trail,** and **The Toll Gate.** Hart had complete control over his films and carefully developed the screen character of a loner, an outsider, often a badman, redeemed by the true love of the heroine. Hart's popularity peaked around 1920, and he is today remembered best for his last major film, **Tumbleweeds,** an epic of the Oklahoma land rush, released in 1925. But by this time he had begun to lose his following. Audiences of the twenties, preferring color and excitement to Hart's gritty realism and increasing sermonizing, had replaced him in their affections with Tom Mix.

Mix had actually entered films before Hart but did not hit his

Preceding pages:
An important step in early film history, Edwin S. Porter's **The Great Train Robbery** (1903). Porter cut boldly between cardboard interiors like this and the real outdoors, opening up the stage-bound film to the "western" landscapes of New Jersey. Less than a decade later, Broncho Billy Anderson created the screen's first western hero. Note the fanciful Indian warpaint in this scene from **Cowboy Trails**.

126

The first to bring the authentic
flavor of the West to the screen was
William S. Hart, above, who scorned
the pulp-novel version of the
West pictured by Broncho Billy and others.
The spiritual redemption of
the hero was also a hallmark typical of
Hart, shown here in **The Gun Fighter**
(1917), one of his Thomas Ince films.

stride until his series for Fox after 1920. Shying away from the good-badman role, Mix might often appear as a ranger or government agent, and his films featured incredible stunt riding, breathtaking location work, and fast-moving action. One of the most popular stars of the silent screen, Mix dazzled his audiences in films like **Just Tony** (dedicated to his famous horse) and **Sky High,** in which the villains are smuggling aliens into the country. His **The Great K & A Train Robbery** is one of the most delightful of western action films, full of fancy riding and good humor, and magnificently photographed by Dan Clark. Mix gradually withdrew from films as westerns declined in popularity in the thirties, but he left behind a definite contribution to the genre—a touch of the comic that was later developed by such stars as Ken Maynard and Gene Autry.

Although westerns had always been successful in their B-picture markets, the major studios shied away from including them as featured portions of their annual schedules until Paramount released **The Covered Wagon** in 1923. Though it looks rather tired and overblown today, the film appealed to critics and audiences as well, and serious commentators began to notice the potential for epic drama in this previously scorned genre. It created a vogue for films about America's past that included **The Pony Express, The Vanishing American,** and John Ford's **The Iron Horse** and **Three Bad Men.** Ford had been making westerns since 1917, many of them at Universal with Harry Carey. This experience came in quite handy when the western epic arrived in the late twenties. **Three Bad Men** is perhaps the finest of this tradition, the story of a Dakota land rush that carries with it the theme of westward migration as well.

When sound arrived, westerns achieved a brief moment of prominence, as Raoul Walsh's **In Old Arizona** and Wesley Ruggles's **Cimarron** swept many of the important Oscars in 1929 and 1930. **In Old Arizona** was promoted as the first outdoor talking picture, with microphones ingeniously hidden in bushes and sagebrush. But Warner Baxter's performance as the Cisco Kid gave it a spark of life, more than could be found in the dull **Cimarron,** which conned audiences on the strength of its size and the popularity of Edna Ferber's novel. Films like **The Virginian,** with Gary Cooper, really hold up much better today than this overrated classic.

The early talking western was also a key item in the attempt to introduce 65- and 70-mm film. King Vidor's **Billy the Kid,** with Johnny Mack Brown as Billy and Wallace Beery as Pat Garrrett, was MGM's experiment in the new wide-film process, but its senseless killings and brutality—an attempt to link the western outlaw to the modern gangster—did not sit well with audiences. More successful was Fox's widescreen "Grandeur" production **The Big Trail** (1930), a covered-wagon trek directed by Raoul Walsh in his usual gutsy style. John Wayne had his first major role in this film, but he languished for a decade, as did westerns in general, until John Ford made **Stagecoach** in 1939.

Depression audiences were more attuned to glossy and ur-

banized stories than to western action, so the genre largely went underground during the thirties. Although some of these films (like Edward Cahn's **Law and Order**) were exceptionally well made, critics of the time took no notice until the arrival of **Stagecoach.** Not the greatest of western films, it took several of the key motifs, particularly the Indians versus the Cavalry and the good-badman, and presented them in an elaborate and well-produced package. The script by Dudley Nichols was sprinkled with enough liberal clichés to please most critics, while Ford's direction provided more than enough action for the mass audience, which had been starved for such material for almost a decade.

Ford's career as a western director was astonishing. More than anyone else he was able to use the genre to project his feelings about the family, society, and the American way of life. Ford saw the frontier as a land to be subdued by a special class of settlers and lawmen whose great sacrifices make the land safe for those who come after. These early westerners were giants who deserved the legendary status they earned, and the civilized townsfolk who followed must always hold them in awe. Ford's westerns often employ flashbacks that emphasize the historicity of this approach. In **Wagonmaster,** for example, folk songs on the sound track tell us of the hardships of the pioneers of a century ago, and Ford shows them to us in almost documentary fashion. In one sequence the train is camped in a circle and the settlers decide to hold a square dance. To fashion a dance floor they have to lay boards over the desert sand, and with this ritual celebration Ford shows the defeat of the wilderness through the metaphor of boarding over the land.

Just as he reveres the heroes of a century ago, so within his films the heroes are usually older and more accomplished men who have helped conquer the West in much the way they might break some wild stallion. Like John Wayne in **She Wore a Yellow Ribbon,** they are now turning over the easier work to come to younger, and lesser, replacements. In **The Searchers,** his greatest film, Ford tells us that the body and blood of the pioneers must be buried in the ground to fertilize it, to prepare it to bear fruit for the generations to come. This idea is given its fullest expression in **The Man Who Shot Liberty Valance,** in which James Stewart, now a Senator of a new Western state, thinks back to the time he first arrived in the wild, unsettled territory. Liberty Valance, an unchecked outlaw presence, had been terrorizing the region until he was shot by John Wayne, a man of action who, for Ford, represents the pioneer spirit of the West. But the young lawyer (Stewart) had been credited with the killing and gained fame so wide that he was able to help make the territory a state. The man of action has to clear the path for the civilized man of the law who inevitably follows. Yet when Stewart confesses the truth to a newspaper editor at the funeral of the now-forgotten Wayne, the editor dismisses his confession with a typical Fordian response, "When the legend becomes fact, print the legend."

Although not comparable to the finest Ford films, the post-**Stagecoach** western boom did produce many interesting works. There was

After years of wallowing in
B-picture budgets, the western
suddenly was overtaken by the
epic tradition of the mid-twenties.
James Cruze's **The Covered Wagon,**
above, was the first of these.
When sound arrived, location
shooting proved no problem,
as was demonstrated in Raoul
Walsh's **In Old Arizona** (1929).
Warner Baxter (r) as the
Cisco Kid won the year's acting
Oscar. John Ford's **The Iron Horse**
(1924), opposite, gave a human
dimension to the building of the
transcontinental railroad. George
O'Brien and Madge Bellamy starred.

a revisionist cycle which made heroes of badmen, notably the James Brothers in **Jesse James** and **The Return of Frank James,** and Billy the Kid in **The Outlaw.** Tyrone Power and Henry Fonda as Jesse and Frank James were pictured as popular heroes who courageously fought the encroachment of the railroads. Well directed by Henry King and Fritz Lang, these splashy Technicolor films raised a considerable amount of protest because of their historical distortion, but Hollywood went right ahead with a further series of whitewashes. The strangest of these was undoubtedly Howard Hughes's **The Outlaw,** a western that based most of its appeal on the proportions of Jane Russell's bust. Held up by the censors for years, **The Outlaw** seems today a film of considerable humor, though of an outlandishly sexist variety. Jack Beutel and Walter Huston swap Jane back and forth like a pack horse, but without the usual aura of importance given to horse trading. Hughes designed a new bra for Miss Russell based on the principle of the cantilever span, and cameraman Lucien Ballard worked out a special system of cross-lighting that threw her cleavage into deep relief. But nobody bothered very much with the "western" elements of the story; everyone did pretty much what he wanted. Gregg Toland, who shot most of the film,

Although shot in Fox's wide-screen "Grandeur" process, Raoul Walsh's **The Big Trail** (1930, opposite top) was not a big success, and westerns languished during the decade. But 1939 saw a revival in the form of Henry King's **Jesse James** (r), with Tyrone Power and Henry Fonda, and John Ford's **Stagecoach**. The director's brother Francis is the one on the right wearing the Civil War hat.

135

Another element that helped
revive the western in 1939 was
comedy, as in George Marshall's
Destry Rides Again (above),
with James Stewart and Marlene
Dietrich. Right: Madeline Kahn
and Cleavon Little spoofed
this spoof in Mel Brooks's
Blazing Saddles (1974), a film
which rode roughshod over the
whole western genre. Far right:
Randolph Scott in Fritz Lang's
Western Union (1941). Ironically,
the German émigré became one of
Hollywood's top western directors.

worked out camera angles twice as outrageous as any he had used in **Citizen Kane** the year before.

A much finer "adult western" was King Vidor's **Duel in the Sun,** in which Jennifer Jones appeared as Pearl Chavez, the half-breed temptress who destroys everyone she comes near—especially lover Gregory Peck in the final, outlandish showdown. The psychological elements which were introduced in crude fashion in films like **Duel in the Sun** were developed to a much greater degree in Howard Hawks's **Red River,** perhaps the most thoughtful of western epics. John Wayne as the cattle baron prodding his men and his herds beyond endurance on a classic western trail drive turned in one of his finest performances, while the young Montgomery Clift made his first great impression as the youngster who rebels against Wayne's twisted sense of power.

The fifties developed this theme so strongly that it soon came to be regarded as the decade of the psychological western. Henry King's **The Gunfighter** returned to the William S. Hart style of realism in showing the lonely fate of the West's fastest gun, played by Gregory Peck in a droopy handlebar moustache.

The postwar period produced many of the most enduring western classics. Opposite: Montgomery Clift backs up John Wayne as he guns down "quitters" in Howard Hawks's **Red River** (1948). Top: Gregory Peck, Lillian Gish, and Jennifer Jones in David O. Selznick's **Duel in the Sun** (1946), largely directed by King Vidor. Left: An aged John Wayne in John Ford's **She Wore a Yellow Ribbon** (1949), the second film of his cavalry trilogy. Below: The beautiful and nostalgic **Wagonmaster** (1950), Ford's tribute to the courage of the pioneers.

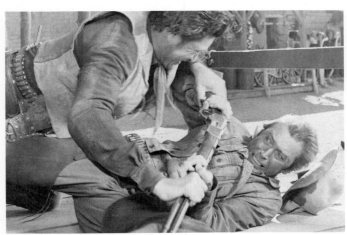

The fifties marked the richest period of the western's long career, exploring every facet of the genre from the classic conflict to the then-stylish "psychological approach." Above: Gary Cooper and Grace Kelly in Fred Zinnemann's **High Noon** (1952). Opposite: Randolph Scott in Budd Boetticher's **Ride Lonesome** (1959, top l); Natalie Wood, John Wayne, and Jeffrey Hunter in John Ford's **The Searchers** (1956, top r); Anthony Perkins in Anthony Mann's **The Tin Star** (1957, center l); James Stewart in Mann's **Winchester 73** (1950, bottom l); and Ricky Nelson and John Wayne in Howard Hawks's **Rio Bravo** (1959).

Other attempts at reworking the classic western themes were much more successful at the box office, but today seem patently arty and self-conscious to no good purpose. George Stevens's **Shane** glorified the standard homesteaders-versus-cattlemen plot (a staple as far back as Ford's first feature, the 1917 **Straight Shooting**), and benefited from the superb Technicolor photography of Loyal Griggs. **High Noon** was a textbook film, the story of a marshal who looks for help from his townspeople when an outlaw gang comes to town to get him, then finds he really didn't need it anyway. This plot so incensed Howard Hawks that he filmed **Rio Bravo** as a reaction to it, with John Wayne as the marshal who thinks he is a superman and needs no help, but is constantly bailed out by a woman, a boy, an old man, and a drunk.

The most self-consciously artistic western of the sixties, and possibly of all time, was Marlon Brando's **One-Eyed Jacks,** which he both directed and starred in. Overlong, and with a script jammed full of "meaningful" clichés—as many as could be heard through Brando's mumbling—the film was made bearable only by Charles Lang's VistaVision photography of the Big Sur

142

country. Indeed, it might be noted that whatever else fails, westerns have always been able to fall back on their photography.

In retrospect some of the best westerns of the time were those directed by Anthony Mann and Budd Boetticher, straightforward and unpretentious, but each with an interesting approach to the requirements of the genre. With the films of Hawks and Ford, these westerns were among the most important influences on Godard, Truffaut, and the other members of the French new wave. Mann's were the more prestigious, usually featuring James Stewart, who, with John Wayne, was the fifties' biggest box-office draw. In films like **Bend of the River, The Far Country,** and **The Man from Laramie,** Stewart's little-used dramatic capabilities gave life to the complex moral and psychological forces that drive Mann's heroes. Boetticher, on the other hand, operated within a much narrower framework. His series of Randolph Scott westerns, including **Seven Men from Now, The Tall T,** and **Ride Lonesome,** featured a strangely Hart-like character on an elaborate revenge mission, played out amid the perils of a menacing landscape.

As Boetticher and Mann withdrew from the field in the sixties, Sam Peckinpah came to the fore. Peckinpah chronicles the changes that have affected the West. His films are often set at the end of the "Wild West" period, late enough for the hero of **The Ballad of Cable Hogue** to die in an automobile accident. In **The Deadly Companions** and **Ride the High Country,** Peckinpah seems to be drawing close to Ford in his use of the West as a concentrated image of American life. But Ford could never have directed **The Wild Bunch,** Peckinpah's famous and bloody tale of an outdated gang of desperadoes. Peckinpah seems to alternate between the explosiveness of films like this, or the near-western **Straw Dogs,** and the calm introspection of **Cable Hogue** and **Junior Bonner.** The public prefers the explosiveness.

Like several other film genres, the western must now depend on violence and bloodshed for its following, and the relatively calm investigation of moral truths that marked the fifties has been forgotten. Howard Hawks still continues in his **Rio Bravo** mold with **El Dorado** and **Rio Lobo,** films that seem anachronistically classical beside such bizarre if interesting recent work as Robert Altman's **McCabe and Mrs. Miller.** Given all the conflicting pressures the modern western must come to terms with, the only director to master them all has been Sergio Leone. Making a box-office reputation with the witty Clint Eastwood series, including **A Fistful of Dollars** and **The Good, the Bad and the Ugly,** Leone showed in convincing fashion that he could handle sex, blood, and a very dark brand of humor. He wangled a Hollywood contract and created that most extraordinary of western films, **Once Upon a Time in the West,** a lyric tribute owing more to Murnau and Hitchcock than to William S. Hart and John Ford. In retrospect, **Once Upon a Time** is the fairy-tale ending to the saga of the American western, an Italian confection too rich for Times Square audiences, but right at home in the Museum of Modern Art.

In recent years the western has become increasingly self-conscious, feeding on its own history and conventions, and often twisting them into strange new forms. The only thing that remains a certainty is violence, in ever-increasing doses. Top left: The railroad comes through in Sergio Leone's **Once Upon a Time in the West** (1969). Top right: Bloody end for Sam Peckinpah's **The Wild Bunch** (1969). Center right: Dustin Hoffman in Arthur Penn's **Little Big Man** (1970). Bottom left: Julie Christie and Warren Beatty in Robert Altman's **McCabe and Mrs. Miller** (1971). Bottom right: Robert Redford and Paul Newman in George Roy Hill's **Butch Cassidy and the Sundance Kid** (1969).

FANTASY

Ever since Georges Méliès discovered the tricks by which the camera could seem to do the impossible, fantasy has found its true home in the world of the cinema. The first trick films were full of mysterious disappearances, diabolical actions, and spectral apparitions—Méliès's gift to the filmmakers of England, France, and the United States. But when the novelty wore off, the fantasy theme was dropped abruptly, and only in Germany did the macabre film flourish in the silent period.

Hollywood limited itself to a few versions of **Dr. Jekyll and Mr. Hyde,** the most interesting of which starred John Barrymore (1920), and an occasional experiment like **The Lost World,** in which papier-mâché models menaced Bessie Love and Wallace Beery. Even Lon Chaney's grotesque films were far from fantasies. All had rational explanations behind them, and whatever horror they contained was the work of warped minds and bodies. In **The Hunchback of Notre Dame** it was a poor cripple and in **The Phantom of the Opera** it was just a mad, misshapen musician.

German audiences, however, found a steady diet of the supernatural and the inexplicable. The German silent classics were well based in the romantic tradition of E.T.A. Hoffmann's stories and in the growing wave of expressionism in architecture and the graphic arts. The expressionist artists externalized the interior passions of their subjects by distorting the shapes and colors of the universe they moved in. The combination of the romantics' interest in madness and the supernatural gave rise to the most important of all cycles of film fantasy. **The Cabinet of Dr. Caligari** (1919) showed the world of madness as warped, twisted out of harmony with its inhabitants. Its reception prompted further expressionist experimentation, including some of the first films of the supernatural, Paul Wegener's cabalistic **The Golem** and F. W. Murnau's classic vampire film, **Nosferatu. Destiny, Warning Shadows,** and **The Hands of Orlac** further developed the haunted, fatalistic themes of romantic expressionism. Fritz Lang's **Metropolis** mixed occult elements with an early form of science fiction, and Murnau's **Faust** was perhaps the most hauntingly beautiful of them all. While the films were not great successes in America, Hollywood respected the talents of the filmmakers and asked them to continue their work here. Paul Leni, who had directed the eerie **Waxworks,** filmed **The Cat and the Canary** and **The Last Warning** for Universal, while Benjamin Christensen, the Danish creator of **Witchcraft Through the Ages,** was brought over to do **Seven Footprints to Satan** and **The House of Horror.** All these American films were "dark house" thrillers in which the "supernatural" goings-on are exposed as the actions of criminals. Audiences here would not accept supernatural explanations, it was believed. Even in Tod Browning's **London After Midnight,** one of his most famous Lon Chaney films, the "vampire" is exposed at the end as a fraud.

Browning's **Dracula** was the first film to break with this tradition, presenting a supernatural vampire who was not debunked in the last reel. This new twist, combined with Bela Lugosi's sinister performance and the real

Preceding pages:
Distorted planes and shadows of German expressionism first startled moviegoers in **The Cabinet of Dr. Caligari** (1919). Werner Krauss as the doctor was modeled on an analyst the writer had known in World War I. The Edison studio (1910) produced the screen's first version of **Frankenstein** (l). Monster was shown as a reflection of baser side of creator's soul. Charles Ogle of the Edison Stock Company starred.

A few rare examples of silent film fantasy. Top left: Arctic apparition from **Conquest of the Pole** (1912), one of Georges Méliès' last films. Right: Cadaverous **Nosferatu** from F. W. Murnau's 1922 vampire film. Compare with suave Lugosi version on p. 153. Bottom: Bessie Love menaced by a brontosaur in **The Lost World** (1925), in which Willis O'Brien developed animation techniques he later perfected in **King Kong.** Below: Frank Tuttle's now-lost 1923 chiller, **Puritan Passions.**

P-17-135P

149

beauty of the film's opening sequences, created a whole new horror genre which Universal immediately came to dominate. **Frankenstein** (produced right after **Dracula**) established Boris Karloff as a star after years of playing in bit roles. It was filmed by James Whale, Universal's top director, who quickly followed it with **The Old Dark House, The Invisible Man,** and **The Bride of Frankenstein.** The style and elegance of Whale's horror films have seldom been surpassed, although they have long been eclipsed in the blood-and-gore field. Karloff in **The Mummy** and Lon Chaney, Jr. in **The Wolf Man** played the last of the great Universal monster heroes. Larry Talbot's plaintive cry, "I couldn't **help** myself," humanized this werewolf in a way never quite attempted with the earlier monsters, but by the time he appeared both Universal and the monster cycle had fallen on bad times.

Universal also attempted other, nonmonster horror films in the thirties, among them **Murders in the Rue Morgue,** shot almost as a remake of **Caligari** by Karl Freund, the great German cameraman (**Metropolis,** among others), and Edgar G. Ulmer's **The Black Cat,** the most bizarre of the whole series, with Karloff and Lugosi conducting satanic rites in an art-deco mansion in modern Transylvania. When the hero of this strange film complains that Lugosi's explanations sound like a lot of supernatural baloney, Bela answers in his characteristic tones, "Supernatural, perhaps. Ba-lo-ney, perhaps not!"

Other studios were busy as well, for Depression-era audiences piled into any horror film they could find. The greatest of horror epics came from RKO: the story of a giant gorilla and his one true love. Since **King Kong** crashed one hundred and two stories into the middle of Thirty-fourth Street his reputation has grown and grown until now he exists as a genuine twentieth-century folk hero. Forty years later "King Kong died for our sins" was a well-established piece of graffiti, and in 1974 the film played a one-day return engagement at the Radio City Music Hall.

Warner Brothers, that most realistic of studios, contributed **Svengali, Dr. X,** and **The Mystery of the Wax Museum,** all of which were staunchly nonsupernatural. Harder to believe was Paramount's **Island of Lost Souls,** in which Charles Laughton turned animals into semihumans. And Rouben Mamoulian's **Dr. Jekyll and Mr. Hyde** was another odd entry from Paramount, notable for some technical fireworks and Fredric March's stylized, Oscar-winning performance.

Moving back to Metro after a brief stay at Universal, Tod Browning shocked even horror fanciers with **Freaks.** Returning to his major theme, the lives of circus and sideshow performers, Browning assembled the world's most famous freaks at the MGM studios (something which caused consternation in the commissary at lunchtime). The ultimate in "realistic" horror, the film was peopled by truly deformed humans who were more disturbing than anything that ever emerged from Karloff's makeup kit. A magnificent film, though a terrible box-office failure, Browning followed it up with **The Mark of the Vampire**

Two of Lon Chaney's thousand faces he created for silent screen. Opposite: In costume as "The Red Death," Erik the Phantom crashes opera's masked ball in **The Phantom of the Opera** (1925). This sequence, shot in early Technicolor process, showed up cape in bright crimson. Above: Chaney as phony vampire in **London After Midnight** (1927), one of many films he made for director Tod Browning.

Left: One of numerous scenes
cut from English and American
prints of Fritz Lang's
Metropolis (1926), a heavily
allegorical tale of the
future. Hollywood's answer
was **Just Imagine** (above),
a 1930 science-fiction
musical. Maureen O'Sullivan
and Frank Albertson
were lovers in 1980 New York.
Dracula (r) and **Frankenstein**
(below) began new horror
cycle in 1931. Karloff got
role of monster after
Lugosi, who disliked dialogue
grunts and makeup, rejected it.

(a remake of **London After Midnight**) and **The Devil Doll,** in which Lionel Barrymore shrank people to the size of puppets. Although these were two of his best films, Browning vanished from the screen for three years, emerging only to direct the minor **Miracles for Sale** in 1939, then retiring into obscurity.

The forties brought a continuation of Universal's stock company of monsters, often appearing in teams, as in **Frankenstein Meets the Wolf Man,** or en masse, as in **House of Dracula.** Yet, somehow arising out of this genre of decay came a new type of horror film, subdued and underplayed, and largely the work of RKO producer Val Lewton. Lewton's production unit, which included the young directors Robert Wise, Jacques Tourneur, and Mark Robson, specialized in B-budget horror films with a very shadowy touch (shadows are very effective in masking cheap sets). The Lewton films emphasized psychological horror instead of mere shock, and played out much of their action in contemporary settings. A Greenwich Village witch cult was the subject of **The Seventh Victim,** and Manhattan offices and apartments were the locale for **The Cat People.** Lewton used a small New Mexican border town for **The Leopard Man** and set **The Curse of the Cat People** in Tarrytown, New York, far from the Transylvanian locales of most of the early horror films—a useful device for bringing the weird occurrences closer to the audience. **I Walked with a Zombie** remains one of the most literate of horror films, **Isle of the Dead** one of the most claustrophobically terrifying. Lewton's extremely popular series of shadowy horrors influenced other, higher-budgeted films as well, and his touch can be felt in such films as **The Uninvited** and the British **Dead of Night.**

Like the twenties, the fifties rejected the supernatural monster out of hand and established a genre of its own—science fiction—in which rational explanations could always support the most incredible happenings. There are a handful of earlier examples of screen science fiction, such as Lang's **Metropolis** and **Woman in the Moon,** or the British **Things to Come** and **Transatlantic Tunnel** (or even our own Flash Gordon and Buck Rogers), but the genre really got its start in 1950 with **Destination Moon.** This near-documentary was followed by **The Conquest of Space** and a score of films on planetary exploration, most of them considerably less serious. **Fire Maidens of Outer Space,** perhaps the most esoteric of these titles, can be recognized by the stock shot of the German V-2 that passes for the spaceship. Space people visiting us (usually with evil intent) was the focus of **The Thing, Earth vs. the Flying Saucers, It Came from Outer Space,** and **The War of the Worlds,** although **The Day the Earth Stood Still** featured Klaatu (Michael Rennie) as a Christ-like visitor trying to bring us the gift of peace. Related to these extraterrestrial invasion stories was Don Siegel's **Invasion of the Body Snatchers,** the most terrifying of science-fiction films, and one quite closely related to the vampire genre (with mysterious forces waiting to take over our souls).

The third major trend in fifties sci-fi was the "kill it before it multiplies" school, in which the earth is threatened by a sudden infestation of

Some highlights of golden age of film fantasy, the 1930's. Top left: Behind the scenes on **Freaks** (1932) with director Tod Browning. Right: Bela Lugosi drains blood of Arlene Francis in **Murders in the Rue Morgue** (1932). Center left: Fredric March in Oscar-winning role as Dr. Jekyll/Mr. Hyde (1932). Right: Most famous fantasy-film scene, King Kong atop Empire State Building (1933). Bottom left: Claude Rains's first screen "appearance" in **The Invisible Man** (1933). Right: Preparing for trip to the moon in H. G. Wells's **Things to Come,** a 1936 British film. Depression-era audiences never seemed to tire of such fantastic escapism.

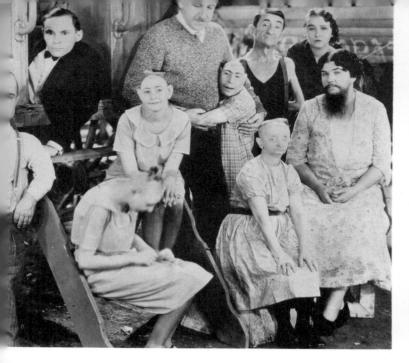

By the 1940's, classic themes of horror and science fiction had begun to degenerate, but for a few notable exceptions. Left: **Dr. Cyclops** revived shrunken-people gimmick of **The Devil Doll,** a 1936 success, on more elaborate scale. **The Wolf Man** (top), a worthy entry in Universal's monster cycle, established Lon Chaney, Jr. as a minor star. After the war, sci-fi began to dominate the genre, even influencing the serial. Note Commando Cody above, in **Zombies of the Stratosphere.**

157

Throughout the 1950's, science
fiction drove old-fashioned
horror films into hiding
with elaborate special-effects
exercises like **The War of the
Worlds** (1953, top) and
This Island Earth (1955, r).
But new decade saw
return to earlier tastes, as
in Roger Corman's Poe series.
Above: Vincent Price in
The Pit and the Pendulum (1961).

giant insects (or other suitably nasty critters). The ants of **Them!** were quickly joined by **Tarantula, The Deadly Mantis, The Black Scorpion,** and **The Spider,** but soon this, too, descended into self-parody with **The Giant Gila Monster, The Killer Shrews,** and **The Giant Claw,** with its mangy, oversized buzzard from outer space. Atomic testing and fallout were usually the unnatural acts which triggered these mutations, an idea encountered again in Jack Arnold's **The Incredible Shrinking Man,** perhaps the best remembered of fifties science-fiction films. If national A-bomb paranoia seems indicated in these films, it emerges as the key element of Japanese science fiction. In **Rodan** atomic testing cracks open dormant dinosaur eggs, and the newly hatched beasts make straight for Japan, leveling a few cities when they get there. The same pattern was followed in a whole series of Godzilla pictures, Japan's cities being flattened in each and every sequel.

By the late fifties, horror was once again making a comeback, although often mixed with various amounts of fantasy and science fiction. In England, Hammer Films revived the old Universal monster series, and Peter Cushing and Christopher Lee turned up in such well-produced films as **The Horror of Dracula** and **The Curse of Frankenstein.** Later sequels, as usual, were disappointing. Italy's Mario Bava produced a group of florid chillers, including the notable **Black Sunday** with Barbara Steele, and the underrated classic **Black Sabbath,** in which Karloff made his last great horror appearance. America's William Castle banked on theatrical gimmicks for his success. He sent an inflatable skeleton flying over the audience in **The House on Haunted Hill** and wired theater seats for a "shock" effect in **The Tingler,** a tongue-in-cheek tale of a mad coroner and the proprietor of a silent-movie revival theater ("the tingler" gets loose during a showing of **Tol'able David**). But the most memorable American entries in the early sixties were Roger Corman's Edgar Allan Poe series, most of them starring Vincent Price, and all produced on a shoestring budget for American-International Pictures. Relying on such talent behind the camera as Floyd Crosby (photographer of Murnau's **Tabu**) and screenwriters Richard Matheson, Charles Beaumont, and Ray Russell, Corman pleased critics by bringing out the psychosexual slant in Poe's stories, while he delighted Times Square audiences with grotesque makeups and loud noises. Starting with the rather primitive **The House of Usher,** the series quickly improved until by the time of **The Premature Burial, The Masque of the Red Death,** and **The Tomb of Ligeia,** Corman was the most respected of horror filmmakers. He had been well served by his fifties apprenticeship, when he directed such minor classics as **Attack of the Crab Monsters** and **A Bucket of Blood.** But he soon tired of directing, and now functions solely as a producer and distributor. (Among the films handled by his New World Pictures are **Stacey and Her Gang Busters, Night of the Cobra Woman,** and Ingmar Bergman's **Cries and Whispers.**)

While Corman was conquering the B-picture field, both horror

Original 1967 version of
Planet of the Apes, with Kim
Hunter, Charlton Heston,
and Roddy McDowall, above, was
the best of what soon became
an increasingly puerile series.
More stylish, although more
cheaply produced, were Christopher
Lee films of England's Hammer
Studios. The best of these,
like **Dracula Has Risen from the
Grave** (r), were directed
tongue-in-cheek by Freddie Francis.
Opposite: Stretching the scope
of sci-fi, Stanley Kubrick's
2001: A Space Odyssey won
long-deserved recognition for
this once-despised genre.

and science fiction were being picked up by major studios and directors. Alfred Hitchcock's **Psycho** began a whole trend toward films about murderous maniacs (**Berserk, Homicidal,** etc.). Interestingly enough **The Birds**—a more demanding and in some ways a better film, especially the unforgettable attack of the birds—puzzled critics and audiences alike when it first appeared. Roman Polanski followed Hitchcock's lead with great success in **Repulsion,** though his **Fearless Vampire Killers** pleased no one. Roger Vadim had more luck with vampires in **Blood and Roses,** introducing an element of lesbianism that had been dormant since Carl Dreyer's **Vampyr** in 1932. And science fiction made a very strong comeback in the mid-sixties, Stanley Kubrick's **2001: A Space Odyssey** emerging as the masterpiece of the genre, but with respectable showings by films like **The Andromeda Strain, Silent Running,** and **THX-1138,** films that worked present-day social and ecological concerns into classic science-fiction plots. On a more popular level were the Planet of the Apes series and **Night of the Living Dead,** a fifties-style horror film punched up with violence and blood. In the early seventies science took a back seat to the occult, and mediums and satanists made strong appearances. The first and best of these subjects probably was Polanski's **Rosemary's Baby** (a William Castle production), but the 1973 entry, **Legend of Hell House,** was also quite good, notably in its documentary-style approach to the whole business of hauntings and séances. William Friedkin's **The Exorcist** is on its way to becoming one of the most popular films of all time. One might argue about including the recent occult films in a discussion of horror and science fiction at all, because they simply don't present themselves as fantasy. They seem to believe implicitly in what they are talking about. And what is even stranger in this Aquarian age we live in is that most of the audience believes in it too.

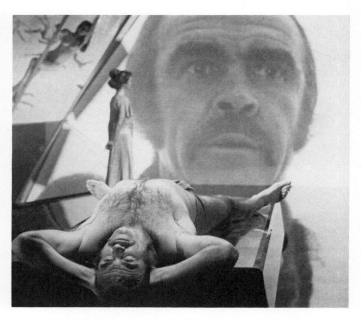

Do recent trends indicate a
swing away from science fiction,
back toward the supernatural?
Old-style chillers like
grade-B **Night of the Living Dead**
(top l), have proven bonanzas,
while elaborate futuristic films
like **Zardoz** (top r), have
disappointed at the box office.
The religious element, successfully
exploited in Roman Polanski's
Rosemary's Baby (r),
has been sensationally developed
in William Peter Blatty's
The Exorcist (l), directed by
William Friedkin. Expect
to hear more about witches and
demons in the near future.

COMEDY

Right from the start comedy was a major part of the motion-picture experience. **The Sneeze** was probably thought of as a comic subject, but most film historians consider **L'arroseur Arrosé** the first true film comedy. It was a part of the first Lumière showing in Paris, London, and New York in 1895 and 1896. Sometimes known as **A Practical Joke on the Gardener,** the film consists of a single shot showing a gardener getting soaked by his own hose and the mischievous prankster responsible for the trick being chased off screen. Film historian Kemp Niver writes that most early film comedies consisted of someone emptying a bucket onto someone else's head. In slightly more ambitious films this was followed by a chase, and **L'arroseur Arrosé** contains both these elements in primal form. For the first dozen years of film, slapstick and the chase provided the nucleus of screen comedy, although more sophisticated touches were added by the screen's first magician, Georges Méliès. His charming, "artificially arranged scenes" today seem like fin-de-siècle postcards come to life, and for them Méliès devised the first camera tricks to startle his audiences. Nearly every trick of double exposure and stop motion was invented by him and used in such wonderful films as **The Inn Where No Man Rests, A Trip to the Moon,** and **An Impossible Voyage.** His films were so popular that they were blatantly stolen and duplicated by Edison and other American distributors, while our filmmakers copied all of his technical innovations for their own work. Edwin S. Porter's **Dream of a Rarebit Fiend** (1906) is almost pure Méliès, while J. Stuart Blackton's astonishing **Princess Nicotine, or The Smoke Fairy** even outdoes the master. But by the time it appeared in 1909 the originator of all this magic was practically out of business, a victim of the cutthroat practices of the film's earliest days.

It is doubtful, though, that Méliès could have adapted to the audience's changing demands. Simple slapstick, chase, and trick films were quickly swept away as the narrative advances of the dramatic film began to be absorbed by film comedy. The Vitagraph Company of Flatbush was among the first to produce sophisticated story-comedies, and created the first comedy stars, John Bunny and Flora Finch, whose humor depended on material personally tailored to their specific screen images: the rotund, Pickwickian Bunny, and the tall, crane-like Flora Finch. An important step forward in comedy construction was taken by Vitagraph in its series of Mr. and Mrs. Sidney Drew comedies beginning in the mid-teens. They played a well-to-do couple who got tangled up in recognizable comic situations involving embarrassing relatives, household dilemmas, and troublesome servants. Since they were not grotesque or funny in looks or costume, their comedy grew completely out of believable situations, thus setting an early standard for all the Lucy-Desi-style family sitcoms of the television years. This sophisticated tradition was carried to its height in the early Douglas Fairbanks films, mostly the work of Anita Loos, who used the Fairbanks character of an energetic New York playboy as a peg on which to develop satires of spy thrillers, Wild West romances, or such popular fads as Couéism, inspired by Émile Coué and in vogue during the late teens and

Preceding pages:
Two of the greatest comics of the talking screen, Mae West and W. C. Fields, worked together in only one film, **My Little Chickadee** (1940). George Moran played Fields's faithful Indian companion, Clarence. These two are still sure laugh-getters, mainly because their verbal humor supplemented, but did not extinguish, the visually comic elements of their style— as this demonstrates.

Above: Some typical Keystone slapstick. Ford Sterling, Fred Mace, and Mabel Normand in **Mabel's Adventures** (1912), a Sennett film. Right: Douglas Fairbanks added a touch of sophistication to early comedies. This is a gag shot, taken around 1920, for one of his breezy, fast-moving satires. Far right: Fatty Arbuckle in one of his last films, **Gasoline Gus** (1921). The tranquil mood is not very typical of Fatty, whose comedies seldom were caught napping.

early 1920's ("Every day in every way, I am getting better and better!").

But sophisticated comedy was not the dominant mode of the day. This was still slapstick, a little refined, perhaps, but slapstick nonetheless, and perfected largely at the Mack Sennett studio.

Sennett originally was a boilermaker who drifted into films with D. W. Griffith at Biograph, and gradually came to direct most of the Biograph comedy releases. But his comedy tastes and Griffith's did not coincide and there was friction. Sennett wanted to make films poking fun at policemen, but Griffith found this idea quite disrespectful. Sennett had go to out on his own to make the Keystone Comedies, and Sennett's work dominated the comic side of film as Griffith's dominated the dramatic side. Sennett's comedies were consciously patterned on deflation of authority, with pie-throwing and other assorted violence indulged in as a harmless, though messy, manifestation of infantile disrespect. In an article written in 1918, Sennett wrote in all seriousness, "Nearly every one of us lives in the secret hope that some day before he dies he will be able to swat a policeman's hat down around his ears." Sennett's films allowed his audiences to experience this delicious pleasure vicariously, thumbing their noses at the world while in the comfortable anonymity of a movie house.

But while Sennett knowingly employed this undercurrent of disrespect, he was seemingly unconscious of the stream of pure anarchy which ran through his work, and which delighted the French surrealists of the twenties. Without bothering to think about it, he demonstrated Henri Bergson's theories of comic automatism, in which men are reduced to machines, and then proceeded with the zeal of a true anarchist to destroy the machine world of consumer America. Cars, planes, trains, food, and clothing were all sacrificed over the cliff in what might have been an early version of **Zabriskie Point.** The main difference is that Sennett used fast motion instead of slow motion, opting for an extra gag instead of pseudo-poetry.

Sennett's studio was known as "the fun factory," and it certainly is true that his humor was of the assembly-line variety. The mass production required for his heavy release schedule prevented him from spending time in developing comic personalities for his stars, and he preferred to work with comedians like Ford Sterling, Ben Turpin, and Chester Conklin, funnymen with interchangeable styles, who could dish out a pie or take it—whatever the situation demanded. When a comedian rebelled, hoping to get away from the assembly-line conception and more deeply into a comic character, Sennett dropped him, an unfortunate response which caused him to lose Fatty Arbuckle, Harry Langdon, and most importantly Charlie Chaplin.

In 1913 Chaplin was touring America as the star of Fred Karno's "A Night in an English Music Hall." Sennett caught the show at the Empress Theatre in Los Angeles and was impressed. He arranged to have a contract offered to "Charlie Chapman," who was playing the part of a gentleman drunk. It has been suggested that Sennett was not only confused by the name but never

Acclaimed by many Chaplin critics as his first masterpiece, **A Dog's Life** (1918) was a three-reel short featuring Charlie and a mongrel named Scraps. The teaming prefigured the Jackie Coogan feature, **The Kid.** Here, Charlie and Scraps visit Edna Purviance, the perennial leading lady of Chaplin's early films. Later successors like Georgia Hale and Paulette Goddard never matched her quiet charm.

even saw Chaplin at all, that the man playing the lead that night was not Chaplin but his understudy—Stan Laurel.

All ironic eventualities aside, it was Chaplin whose films started appearing for Keystone early in 1914, where he quickly learned the rudiments of filmmaking and soon began to write and direct all of his own comedies. His spell began to work on audiences at once, even in such primitive Keystones as **Caught in a Cabaret** or **Dough and Dynamite,** and he was quickly offered a fabulous contract by the Essanay Company. Here he was allowed to play down the slapstick and begin to develop the pathos which marked his later style. **The Tramp** (1915) is perhaps the first indication of the hand of the genius. All that was needed for a theater to attract an audience was a life-size poster of Charlie out front bearing the caption, "I Am Here Today." The success of Chaplin grew so monumental that an even more fabulous contract was offered by Mutual. For them he created the finest of his early comedies, including **The Vagabond, Easy Street,** and **The Immigrant,** films which began to introduce Chaplin's classic social concerns and brought out the Everyman qualities of the little tramp. It was here that Chaplin really surpassed the work of Max Linder, the French comic whose genteel mannerisms were closely related to the tramp's, and whose early success was almost as great as Chaplin's. Chaplin's mature work began with his First National period in 1918, and technically and thematically he never really progressed very far beyond **Shoulder Arms, The Kid,** or **The Pilgrim,** in which all of his characteristic mannerisms reached their fullest development.

By the time he came to direct his United Artists features, Chaplin was being hailed as the greatest artist of modern times, and men like Bernard Shaw and Sergei Eisenstein came to pay tribute to him. This pressure began to tell and he slowed down his comedy output. His first UA film was a drama, **A Woman of Paris,** in which he only appeared in a walk-on, and he did not release **The Gold Rush** until 1925. This film was one of the most thoughtfully crafted comedies ever made. Each bit of business was honed and polished, and shot over and over again until it reached perfection. Chaplin intended **The Gold Rush** to be a masterpiece, and he succeeded. The tramp as a prospector in the Far North looks for gold and winds up not only with the treasure but with the girl as well, an untypically happy ending for Chaplin, but an extremely satisfying one for audiences. The film is a catalogue of Chaplin's most familiar scenes —the dance of the breakfast rolls, Charlie turning into a chicken, the house at the edge of the cliff—and all of this welded into what is, for Chaplin, a very strongly developed story line. Much looser in construction was **The Circus,** largely because its production was constantly interrupted by one of Chaplin's messier legal problems. Indeed, the film occupied so little of Chaplin's attention that he fails to discuss it in his autobiography. Yet it is refreshing, light, and unpretentious, a nearly biographical sketch of a tramp who becomes a great star by making people laugh. The whole film captures the easy, open feeling of his Mutual films, and closes with one of the finest of Chaplin's triste endings, the

Chaplin's foremost competitors during comedy's golden age. Top: Buster Keaton was a creative and innovative filmmaker with somewhat surrealist tastes. Here he hunts decoy ducks in **The Balloonatic** (1923). Bottom: Harold Lloyd's comic style featured an aggressive young man who often found himself in embarrassing or dangerous situations like this one, high above Los Angeles in **Never Weaken** (1921).

Silent comedy ranged over a wide field, from knockabout slapstick to sophisticated bedroom farce. Opposite, top: Charlie Chaplin, Tom Murray, and Mack Swain in Charlie's most famous silent film, **The Gold Rush** (1925). Below, left to right: Raymond Griffith, a sophisticated favorite of the mid-twenties, in Paul Bern's **Open All Night** (1924); Marie Prevost as a sophisticated flapper in Lubitsch's **Three Women** (1924); and Bea Lillie with Harry Myers in **Exit Smiling,** one of her all too rare screen appearances (1926). This page, top left: Harry Langdon in a moment of Mack Sennett foolishness in **His First Flame** (1926). Top right: Hal Roach's original Our Gang serenades fellow travelers in **A Pleasant Journey** (1923). Above: W. C. Fields in his best silent comedy, **So's Your Old Man** (1926), with Frank Montgomery. Gregory La Cava directed.

173

tramp being left behind by the departing circus wagons.

Chaplin's major competitor, artistically and commercially, was Buster Keaton, although critics who took Charlie's films "seriously" refused to do the same for Buster. Chaplin's films had easily recognizable Everyman themes, but Buster's just seemed funny. Today it is clear that Keaton was much the finer director, that as a filmmaker his command of editing and camera placement was somewhere between Griffith and King Vidor, and that for sheer cinematic imagination he was surpassed only by Abel Gance and the Russians, notably Eisenstein. The movie-house episode of **Sherlock, Jr.,** in which Keaton wanders completely into another film and battles the spatial discontinuities of that other film's montage (one instant he is in a garden, the next on a rock in mid-ocean, etc.) is without parallel in the silent American cinema. Yet audiences never warmed to Keaton and he failed to capture their imagination the way Chaplin did. His films were too cold, his character too distant, and sometimes his main gags were so technically complex that they were more puzzling than funny. One very expensive gag designed for **The Navigator** is an example of this. Keaton had dozens of large rubber fish constructed as props for an underwater sequence, and a complicated mechanical system was designed to move the fish through the water on cue. On the sea floor in a diving suit, Buster plays traffic cop by holding up the stream of rubber fish with a stop sign, allowing one little fish to scurry across the traffic flow. Preview audiences were so stunned by the mechanics of the sight gag that they forgot to laugh, and Keaton regrettably cut the whole routine from the final version.

Keaton came from the vaudeville stage and began his film work as one of Fatty Arbuckle's company in 1917. Arbuckle had left Sennett and estab-

By the late silent period the best of the comics had gained complete mastery over their medium and their own extremely personal styles. Above: Laurel and Hardy put Blue Boy above the piano in **Wrong Again** (1929), a film which is said to have influenced Buñuel. Right: Buster Keaton's **The Navigator** (1924), one of the best of his man-versus-machine comedies. Holding the helmet is Kathryn McGuire, a typical Keaton heroine.

lished his own unit, quickly demonstrating his considerable talents as a director and enhancing his great popular following. He had an understandable weakness for fat-boy jokes and a habit of playing in drag, but as a comic director he was probably unmatched at the time. Keaton learned much from appearing in such Arbuckle-directed gems as **Out West** and **The Garage.** Fatty's own career came to an abrupt end in 1921 after he was charged with manslaughter in the death of Virginia Rappe, a young starlet who was along for a Labor Day orgy he hosted in San Francisco. The tabloids accused him of rape, however, and when the scandal broke, his films were banned by local citizens' committees. In at least one case, enraged self-appointed censors actually tore down the screen in a theater where an Arbuckle film was playing. Paramount refused to release his last film. The fact that he was acquitted after a third trial did him no good, and Arbuckle practically vanished from the screen.

Keaton, fortunately, turned down an invitation to that party and continued his popular series of shorts. He never seems to have gone through the trial-and-error period that Chaplin underwent, and his earliest shorts, like **One Week,** in which he constructs a do-it-yourself house, seem as polished as such later masterworks as **The Boat** or **Cops.** When Keaton began making features in 1923, his real talent as a filmmaker became apparent. The elaborate narratives of his films made Chaplin's plotting seem flimsy by comparison, and his sure handling of dramatic material marked him as one of the finest silent directors. **Our Hospitality** and **The General,** for example, are among the most sophisticated of silent-film stories and are superb comedies as well. Keaton very often set himself against a machine—an ocean liner in **The Navigator** or a train in **The General** (films that are actually named after the machines), and explored the comic possibilities of the man-and-machine encounter to the point where he and his stone face sometimes became an extension of the machine. One of the machines he was most interested in was the motion-picture machine, and his films are filled with elaborate tricks designed for the camera's eye, feats of engineering that Keaton recalled with pride decades later. His career ended rather abruptly at the close of the twenties, after he gave up his own company and moved to MGM. Louis B. Mayer never gave Keaton much of a chance in talkies, undercutting his pantomimic strengths by teaming him with the fast-talking Jimmy Durante, then filling the screen with wise-cracking dialogue. Keaton's career was mismanaged out of existence, some say sabotaged by Mayer merely out of spite.

While Keaton's career may have been sabotaged at MGM, Harry Langdon's demise was entirely his own doing. Discovered by Sennett in 1923, he appeared in a large number of two-reelers in which his own brand of guileless innocence and delicate pantomime vied uneasily with the stock antics of the Sennett "fun factory." **Boobs in the Woods** and **Feet of Mud** were two of the best of these, but Langdon was unhappy and took his gag writer Frank Capra, and his director Harry Edwards, and started his own production company.

Their very first film brought a revolutionary new form of comedy to the screen: the rapid-fire wisecrack. Zeppo, Chico, Groucho, and Harpo Marx in **The Cocoanuts** (1929, top), with Mary Eaton and Margaret Dumont. Yet Chaplin kept his silence in **City Lights** (1931, far l) with Virginia Cherrill. George Hill was one of Metro's best directors of the period, and his **Min and Bill** (1930, l) made a popular comedy team of Wallace Beery and Marie Dressler.

Tramp, Tramp, Tramp (directed by Edwards) established Langdon's reputation as a major comedian, one which grew quickly to rival Chaplin's with **The Strong Man** and **Long Pants,** both directed by Capra. Langdon then began to believe his own publicity, fired his old collaborators, and took over complete control himself. The result was a fiasco. **Three's a Crowd,** an attempt at Chaplinesque comedy, was all pathos and no humor. **The Chaser** was filled with admirable mime, but rather stingy with laughs. It contains perhaps the best example of Langdon's peculiar sense of black comedy, unrelieved by the touch of Sennett or Capra: Harry wants to commit suicide and swallows the contents of a bottle he mistakenly believes is poison. He lies down on the floor to die, and the camera grinds away for long moments. Nothing happens. This kind of gag was not appreciated by audiences of the twenties, and even today it elicits more astonishment than laughter. Left to his own devices, Langdon engineered the collapse of his career so rapidly and so completely that by 1930 he was supporting Slim Summerville in a pathetic little comedy called **See America Thirst.**

If many of the great comedians rebelled at the inflexible construction of Sennett's comedy, there was another studio tradition to turn to—that of Hal Roach. Roach carefully developed screen personalities for his stars, beginning with Harold Lloyd in 1915. Together they tried two very different personality types (at least one of which was a direct steal from Chaplin's tramp) before settling on the famous "glasses character" with which Lloyd achieved his great fame.

Roach was most responsible for developing the situation comedy format which had been pioneered at Vitagraph. The plots, gags, and characterizations were worked out in the finest detail, and an aura of reality surrounded even the zaniest of his comedies. Lloyd, for example, was always given background motivation and infused with the work ethic, the desire to climb to the top. Somehow it never seemed unreasonable that he should find himself dangling from the ledge of a skyscraper. Roach's films always made a funny kind of sense. In a series of fast-moving short comedies, Roach quickly established Lloyd as the epitome of the go-getting young man of the twenties, yet he was successfully able to go against type in films like **Grandma's Boy,** set largely in Civil War days, by utilizing the same basic character traits of innocence and earnestness.

Lloyd today is remembered mainly for his "human fly" films like **Never Weaken** and **Safety Last,** but these were only a small part of his standard gag construction. Lloyd's feature films were put together by specialists, tried out on audiences, analyzed, and put together again. They have built into them a sense of audience reaction which is perfectly timed and tuned, and the gags are spaced around tested audience responses. For this reason, a good Lloyd comedy will always get more laughs from an audience than a comparably good Chaplin or Keaton—whose films were often concerned with more than just laughter. This is not to demean Lloyd, whose grasp of the capabilities of film was

Top left: Cary Grant made his first big impression with Mae West in **I'm No Angel** (1933). Her pre-Code comedies did a lot to raise the temperature of censorship groups all over the country. More fuel was supplied by Jean Harlow who, like Carole Lombard and Marilyn Monroe, was an accomplished comedienne. Top right: Lee Tracy and Hattie McDaniel with Jean in Victor Fleming's **Bombshell** (1933). Right: Two comics from silent days who found sound not a bit of a problem—Stan and Ollie in **Beau Hunks** (1931).

179

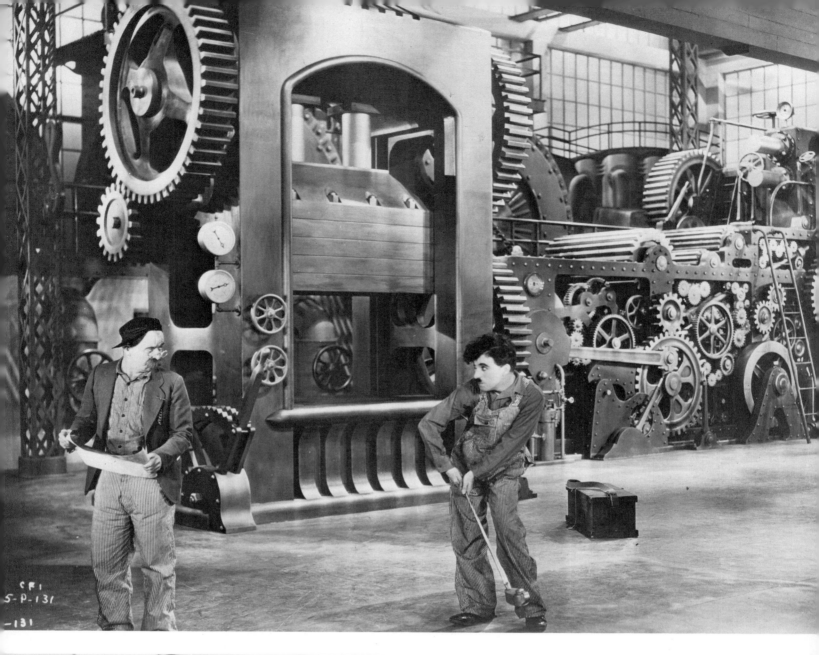

The comedy style of the thirties encompassed the typical antics of some of the screen's great clowns and a sophisticated, romantic format all its own. Top: W. C. Fields (l) closes down his store in **It's a Gift** (1934), and a slightly daffy Charlie Chaplin (r) puzzles Chester Conklin in **Modern Times** (1936). Bottom: Gary Cooper, Fredric March, and Miriam Hopkins form an unusual "ménage à trois" in Lubitsch's **Design for Living** (1933, l); March and Walter Connolly silence Carole Lombard in William Wellman's **Nothing Sacred** (1937, c); and Katharine Hepburn and Cary Grant pamper Baby in Hawks's **Bringing Up Baby** (1938, r).

The screwball comedy begins to take itself a bit more seriously. In **Holiday** (1938), with Jean Dixon, Katharine Hepburn, Lew Ayres, and Edward Everett Horton, George Cukor elicited fine performances from the entire cast, especially from the usually underrated Lew Ayres, playing the family's alcoholic brother.

nearly the equal of Keaton's. His late silent features contain excellent examples of this: the wild bus ride in **For Heaven's Sake,** or the brilliant use of camera movement as he climbs higher and higher up the tree in **The Kid Brother.** But most of the Lloyd features have been withheld from public view for so long that his reputation has inevitably suffered.

Lloyd was Roach's most important star, but certainly not the only one to demonstrate his strategies of story and character construction. Will Rogers was carefully presented as a free spirit, a homespun-philosopher type, though gag writers on the Roach lot concocted most of his material. His hayseed comedies are still funny, though a bit too dependent on titles. But what has held up very well are two short but brilliant satires on the movies, **Uncensored Movies** (1923) and **Big Moments from Little Pictures** (1924).

In a parallel vein, the original "Our Gang" comedies were introduced by Roach in 1922 and demonstrated how careful writing and direction of material prepared for specific personalities (each of the gang had his own carefully established identity) could successfully carry a whole situation-comedy series. "Our Gang" starred not only noncomedians but children who were nonactors as well (at least in the beginning). Roach carried this concept to its logical conclusion with a successful series of animal comedies later on.

Of all the great Roach comics, Charlie Chase is the least remembered today, but in his late silent comedies Chase developed the archetypal role of the harassed, middle-class husband to hilarious perfection. Although he never had enough of a following to go into feature pictures (thus sealing the historical oblivion which has befallen him), his work is today being recognized, and his talents as a highly stylish director and performer are now clear, at least to silent-film buffs. His tradition is carried on in the work of Dick Van Dyke, whose material bears more than a slight resemblance to Chases's familiar domestic situations. In fact, Van Dyke starred in a film called **The Comic,** a tribute to the early comedians of the Roach and Sennett days, and in it one could find a good deal of the personality of one of Van Dyke's major influences, another Roach protégé, Stan Laurel. As mentioned earlier, Stan Laurel had been Chaplin's understudy in the Karno company, and he quickly followed Charlie into the movies. Stan's early career as a performer in the late teens was somewhat stunted because the old orthochromatic film stock could not register the blue of his eyes, leaving his face with a permanent Orphan Annie expression, a fate which befell many early film actors. But by the mid-twenties he was well established as a comedy writer and director, and had a successful series of shorts to his credit, films like **Oranges and Lemons** and **Kill or Cure.** In these early solo appearances he played a fast-talking, pushy sort of character, more like Bob Hope in the forties than the dummkopf role of the Stan-and-Ollie series.

Then, in 1927, Roach called on him to appear in a series of slapstick comedy shorts, where he ran into Oliver Hardy, and the magic between the two was immediately obvious. In a series of brilliant silent comedies Laurel

and Hardy laid the groundwork for their even wider success in talking films. Although the direction of their comedies is credited to a wide variety of talented filmmakers, including Clyde Bruckman, Leo McCarey, and James Parrott, it was Stan Laurel who provided the creative energy for their films (just as Keaton and Lloyd did on films officially credited to others). Their finest silent films, like **Two Tars, That's My Wife,** and **Big Business** established Laurel and Hardy's comedy as the comedy of social relationship. Comic problems arise whenever the boys try to deal with one another (the classic battles of graduated destruction), when they try to relate to another human being (selling Christmas trees to Jimmy Finlayson), or when they face the world at large (the orgy of automobile destruction in **Two Tars**). Laurel and Hardy's films seem to tell us that personal relationships on any but the most childish level are invariably self-destructive, but impossible to avoid. Because their voices matched their screen images so well, and because they had an instinctive understanding of when not to use dialogue in their talking films (**Busy Bodies** [1933] is practically a silent movie), they easily moved to even greater success after the coming of sound.

The great comedians (Chaplin, Keaton, Langdon, and Lloyd) and the great comedy producers (Sennett and Roach) may dominate any discussion of silent comedy, but the studios produced a steady output of comedies on their own, often using Broadway material and stars imported from the legitimate stage, vaudeville, or the follies. Today one cannot accept the critical opinions of the time about these films. They have aged in various ways, and while some seem to have ripened over the years others have gone completely sour.

Mal St. Clair's **The Show-Off** is unwatchable today, although he succeeded much better with **Are Parents People?** or **A Woman of the World.** William Seiter made a charming film of **Skinner's Dress Suit** for Universal, starring Reginald Denny and Laura La Plante, while Howard Hawks showed early evidence of his comic talents in **Paid to Love,** a spoof of Erich von Stroheim and Elinor Glynn. King Vidor proved Marion Davies to be among the screen's great comediennes in **Show People** and **The Patsy,** two delightful comedies of 1928 which can stand comparison with the best work of the great comedians. So can Bea Lillie's hilarious **Exit Smiling** or Eddie Cantor in the silent **Kid Boots.** But few critics know these films today. They have only recently been made available for reevaluation after years of mouldering in the vaults, and what reputation they once had slowly disappeared over the decades. Who today talks of Lewis Milestone's **Two Arabian Knights,** a film which defeated Chaplin and Lloyd for the 1928 comedy Oscar and which had a cast including Billie Dove, William Boyd, and Louis Wolheim? Who can discuss James Cruze's early expressionist comedies, **Hollywood** and **Beggar on Horseback**? The scarcity of material has even obscured the early work of so important a figure as W. C. Fields. Fields had made a short called **Pool Sharks** in 1915 which, seen today, seems the equal of anything Chaplin or Arbuckle was doing at the time, and of course years ahead of Keaton and Lloyd—yet Fields abandoned films for

After 1938 these high-style comedies of the idle rich began to suffer noticeably at the box office, owing to public apathy toward such irrelevant goings-on. The right move was into the supernatural, and the Topper series filled the bill. Above: Roland Young and Constance Bennett in **Topper Takes a Trip.**

nearly a decade. In the mid-twenties he played supporting roles in a pair of mediocre Griffith films, and then starred in seven additional features for Paramount. These films, especially **So's Your Old Man,** show all the Fields situations and bits of business in incipient form. The family, the drinking, the juggling, the braggadoccio—everything is here just waiting for sound to come, to capture the asides which drip silently from Fields's lips even in these films.

The only part of the studio comic tradition of the twenties which remains relatively well known today is the work of Ernst Lubitsch. Imported from Germany on the strength of his direction of spectacles, Lubitsch quickly changed his concentration to witty and somewhat risqué comedies of manners and bedroom farces. Usually set in Paris or Vienna or Old Heidelberg, these films injected the flair of continental romance into American comedy, a strain which was to bloom fully in the thirties. In films like **The Marriage Circle** (1924) and **So This Is Paris** (1926), Lubitsch introduced the comedy of objects. Under his peculiar handling, place cards, checkbooks, and especially doors took on immense comic significance. And no one ever mastered as well the sly look or the surreptitious glance. Lubitsch and his Adolphe Menjou school of comedy served as a model for a whole flock of Hollywood-continental directors, most notably Harry D'Arrast. It was sometimes hard to tell a film like D'Arrast's **A Gentleman of Paris** or Mal St. Clair's **The Grand Duchess and the Waiter** from the work of Lubitsch himself, and occasionally the imitators even surpassed the original. But this sophisticated, Europeanized tradition had to wait for the coming of the thirties, sound, and screwballism to hit its real stride.

Lubitsch's twenties comedies were made for Warners, a studio never noted for the elegance of its production values. But when sound arrived he found his true niche at Paramount, where art director Hans Dreier and cinematographers like Victor Milner and Charles Lang could fashion a rarefied, glistening setting for the elegant, romantic liaisons that dotted the Lubitsch landscape. His early sound musicals are discussed elsewhere, but in **Trouble in Paradise** (1932), Lubitsch set the high-water mark in sophisticated Hollywood comedy. Herbert Marshall and Miriam Hopkins are jewel thieves in art-deco Europe, stealing hearts as well as diamonds while they work their way across the Continent. But an encounter with Kay Francis, the worldly head of Colette Cosmetics ("It doesn't matter what you say, it doesn't matter how you look—it's how you smell!") disrupts their happy partnership. Lubitsch juggles all of this with the grace of the Restoration stage—and just a dash of Noël Coward thrown in for spice. In fact, Lubitsch next turned to Coward's **Design for Living,** a Jules-and-Jim sort of triangle which he successfully produced from a Ben Hecht screenplay that proudly avoided all of Coward's dialogue.

The stylish **Desire, Angel,** and **Bluebeard's Eighth Wife** followed in the late thirties, and Lubitsch closed out the decade with his most famous film, the culmination of his comedies of continental seduction, **Ninotchka.** "Garbo laughs " was the advertising line, and the Lubitsch touch certainly humanized

Preceding pages:
Among the revelers in
Capra's **You Can't Take It With You** (1938): Jean Arthur, James Stewart, Lionel Barrymore, Dub Taylor, Spring Byington, Edward Arnold, Ann Miller, Mischa Auer, Donald Meek, Eddie Anderson, Samuel Hinds, Halliwell Hobbes. Opposite, top: Stewart, Cary Grant, and Katharine Hepburn in Cukor's **The Philadelphia Story** (1940). Far left: Greta Garbo and Melvyn Douglas in Lubitsch's **Ninotchka** (1939). Center: Mickey Rooney and Lewis Stone in **Andy Hardy Gets Spring Fever** (1939), directed by W. S. Van Dyke. Bottom: Stewart again, here with Margaret Sullavan in Lubitsch's **The Shop Around the Corner** (1940).

Right: Cary Grant implicates Alma Kruger in Howard Hawks's **His Girl Friday** (1940). Rosalind Russell starred in this remake of **The Front Page.** Far right: Jean Arthur, Charles Coburn, and Joel McCrea share the bathroom in **The More the Merrier** (1943), directed by George Stevens. Below: Napaloni is entertained by Hynkel and Garbitsch. Jack Oakie, Charlie Chaplin, and Henry Daniell in Chaplin's **The Great Dictator** (1940), his most political comedy.

this goddess and brought her down to earth. Whether this was all for the good is unclear. Certainly Garbo's last film in this vein, **Two-Faced Woman,** was a complete failure and hastened her retirement from the screen, while for Lubitsch **Ninotchka** seems at times a tired recapitulation of material he handled with more verve in earlier films. But the magic of Melvyn Douglas melting the unsmiling commissar appealed to audiences, and both Lubitsch and Garbo are today best remembered for this one film together.

Lubitsch was not the only director turning out stylish cream puffs, of course. Coward's **Private Lives** was brilliantly put on the screen by MGM's Sidney Franklin, a director noted for his responsible treatment of film adaptations. His version of **The Guardsman** brought the Lunts to the screen in their great stage success (their first and only film, alas), while his handling of more serious material in **Reunion in Vienna** and **The Barretts of Wimpole Street** demonstrated the broadest scale of his tasteful sensibilities.

MGM under Irving Thalberg was a company that could shift from the elegance of **The Guardsman** to the not-so-elegant **Min and Bill,** and do justice to both. The latter, an earthy comedy directed by the long-neglected George Hill, reestablished the faded star of Marie Dressler and permitted Wallace Beery to add, "Aw, Min" to his gallery of great dialogue.

Metro had discovered the considerable comic talents of Jean Harlow in **Red-Headed Woman** (1932) and **Bombshell,** and teamed her with Beery, Dressler, and the rest of the stars on the lot in George Cukor's **Dinner at Eight,** the apex of MGM style. **Dinner at Eight** (1933) was based on the 1932 Broadway hit comedy written by George S. Kaufman and Edna Ferber, and its star-studded cast included Marie Dressler, John and Lionel Barrymore, Wallace Beery, Jean Harlow, Lee Tracy, Billie Burke, Madge Evans, Karen Morley, Edmund Lowe, and Jean Hersholt.

The clothes-horse opulence with which Adrian and Cedric Gibbons bedecked the high-thirties Metro releases just missed the lightness of Paramount's style, the grace of Van Nest Polglase's RKO designs, the streamlined chic of Danny Hall's interiors at Universal. Each thirties studio had its own definite look, and MGM's overheated decoration seemed completely opposed to the airiness needed for the production of that most typical of thirties comedies, the screwball.

In the early part of the decade there were a number of zany, fast-talking, fast-moving comedies that laid the groundwork for the screwball comedies to come. **The Front Page** set the tone for a cycle of breathless newspaper comedy-dramas, such as James Cagney's delightful **Picture Snatcher** (1933). While the speed of dialogue delivery was here, the action was still too dramatic and the characters too close to reality. **The Half-Naked Truth** by Gregory La Cava came close to the screwball ideal, but Lee Tracy as the con man who swindles New York by passing off a kootch dancer as a princess was still too real a character; he carries the authenticity of the newsroom around with

The top two comedy teams of the forties, exponents of a style of humor intimately bound up with wartime and postwar attitudes. Above: Paramount's entry, Bing Crosby and Bob Hope in **The Road to Zanzibar** (1941). These two would travel the world battling over Dorothy Lamour. Opposite: Bud Abbott and Lou Costello in **Africa Screams** (1949), made after their best Universal comedies. Slapstick, but in verbal form.

him wherever he goes. Frank Capra's **Platinum Blonde** introduced the super-rich into the screwball equation, but lacked the sheer craziness of the latest films.

Perhaps James Whale's **Remember Last Night?** (1935) first brings together all of the elements of the classic screwball comedy—beautiful people with money to burn involved in some distinctly exotic activity, totally unaware of the realities of the outside world, living life at the fastest possible speed and lost in the dreamlike exhilaration of movement, laughter, and romance. The opening of **Remember Last Night?** sets the standard for this: a dizzying sequence of Long Island socialites on an all-night binge, a wild night of booze and partying which ends up with everyone in the wrong bed the next morning. Really a mystery-comedy, the mystery portion may be inferior to **The Thin Man,** but the pace and movement are pure screwball. Howard Hawks's **20th Century** (1934) was also early screwball, with John Barrymore and Carole Lombard creating the first great performances of the genre, a style later monopolized by Cary Grant. In **The Awful Truth, Topper,** and **Holiday,** Grant developed the perfect screwball hero—quick-witted and debonair, projecting an easy elegance that enabled him to glide with a straight face through the zany twists and turns of the fast-moving screenplays. Of course, he was ably matched here by Irene Dunne, Constance Bennett, and Katharine Hepburn, each in her own way an incarnation of thirties chic and femininity. But in the finest of the screwball comedies, **Bringing Up Baby,** Grant reversed the type, playing an introverted hunter of dinosaur bones who falls prey to Katharine Hepburn and her pet leopard. A truly magical film, **Bringing Up Baby** (1938) flies high without losing touch with its own crazy logic, the chief glory of the best screwball comedies. Peter Bogdanovich's unofficial remake, **What's Up, Doc?** (1972), wisely refrained from trying to capture this very special feeling, and settled, with much less luck or wit, for the easy zaniness of a Looney Tunes cartoon, instead.

But Grant's was not the only screwball image. William Powell playing the servant to a whole wacky family in **My Man Godfrey,** Jean Arthur accepting the mink coat that drifts down from heaven in **Easy Living,** or Claudette Colbert smiling her way through **Midnight,** one of the last of the genre, immediately come to mind as high points of screwballism. On the other hand, **Nothing Sacred,** often cited as one of the great screwball comedies, is really too serious-minded and Capraesque to fit this tight category. The exploitation of a supposed death by radium poisoning is really too grim to sit well in the same category as **Topper** and **The Awful Truth,** and this startling Ben Hecht satire really belongs more to the muckraking **The Half-Naked Truth** school—with one foot settled firmly on the ground.

The thirties may not have been as dominated by great comedians as the silent period, but at least some of the great comics of the talkies could out-screwball anything and anyone else on the screen. The Marx Brothers came to films in direct reproductions of their stage hits **The Cocoanuts** and **Animal**

Crackers, but soon were developing new screen material with the aid of George S. Kaufman and S. J. Perelman. The talking film was an absolute necessity for the Marxes who, unlike Fields, would have floundered aimlessly in the silent cinema. Their comedy was based on communication, and each brother presented a different aspect of its confusions. Groucho with his nonstop delivery snowed opponents under an avalanche of words, not all of which made very much sense to anyone but him. Chico's impossible puns twisted the language into knots, but the most fiendish twisting was his New York-Jewish accent inexplicably trying to pass itself off as New York Italian. In **Animal Crackers** he asks Abie the Fish Peddler from Czechoslovakia how he happens to be masquerading as the wealthy Mr. Chandler. "Say, how did you come to be an Italian?" retorts Abie. Harpo's silence speaks for itself, an untainted retreat from the confusion of words to a mute eloquence that finds its outlet in elaborate pantomime. Groucho and Chico have all sorts of problems with the speakeasy password in **Horse Feathers,** but Harpo gets across "swordfish" without a wasted breath. Zeppo might have been needed to provide a stable reference for all this in vaudeville, but the wider scope of their films only emphasized his irrelevance. The Marxes closed out their Paramount period with **Duck Soup** (1933), directed by Leo McCarey and probably their masterpiece, an insane and unrelentless attack on nationalism, patriotism, and international diplomacy. Its box-office failure severed their relations with Paramount. They moved to MGM where Irving Thalberg forced them to endure the strains of Allan Jones. But while **A Night at the Opera** and **A Day at the Races** were the Marxes' top-grossing films, they lacked the inspired madness of the earlier features.

Unlike **Monkey Business** or **Duck Soup,** their MGM films are clearly divided into the Marxian scenes and the non-Marxian, and their fans found plenty of time to go out for popcorn while they were off the screen. This "saving" of comic business by padding the films with subplots may have made box-office sense, but certainly watered down the comedy.

W. C. Fields suffered the same problem in many of his films, and his finest thirties comedies are definitely not those in which he hangs around the fringes of the plot, like **Six of a Kind** and **Mississippi.** It is only in the unadulterated Fields vehicles, comedies and shorts, that his comic imagination worked overtime. **It's a Gift** is certainly one of these, especially notable for the episode in which the blind man destroys Fields's general store, or **The Man on the Flying Trapeze,** with its horrendous picture of marriage and its "burglars singing in the cellar." It is interesting to note that after having been a star of elaborate silent features, Fields, at the introduction of sound, was reduced to supporting roles and cheap, short comedies. But with everything else pruned away, Fields easily turned these two-reelers into perhaps his most completely successful films.

The Dentist contains one of Fields's most hilarious sequences, extracting a tooth from lanky Elise Cavanna, an episode so suggestive that it

Film comedy apparently lost its direction during the war, the old styles and comics falling behind or producing very peculiar work. Above: Jack Benny disguised as a Nazi in Ernst Lubitsch's black comedy, **To Be or Not to Be** (1942). Opposite, top: Harold Lloyd returned to the screen in Preston Sturges's **Mad Wednesday** (1947), a reexamination of the values promoted by Lloyd's earlier films. Bottom: A new version of the battle of the sexes. Spencer Tracy, George Kezas, and Katharine Hepburn in George Stevens's **Woman of the Year** (1942).

was heavily censored when the film was reissued to post-Code audiences. Even more astonishing is **The Fatal Glass of Beer,** a bizarre film whose pacing seems closer to Samuel Beckett than to Fields, Sennett, or anyone else on the screen. With the laconic mumbling of, "And it ain't a fit night out for man nor beast " Fields receives a bucketful of prop snow everytime he opens the door to his North Woods cabin. He mocks the phoniness of the snow, the sets, and the inept back-projection of a rampaging herd of "elks," while telling the story of his son Chester who was seduced by the wiles of the city. "The city ain't no place for women, gal, but pretty men go thar," we are told.

In films like these Fields managed to come across without the inevitable handicaps of studio padding, but Mae West never really went beyond her one-liners. And after the Hays Office cleaned these up, Mae had to struggle along as only she knew how. "Some men are all right in their place—if they only knew the right places," was one that she managed to slip past the censors, although it lacks the outrageous quality of "Are you packin' a rod, or are you just glad to see me?"

Coming to terms with the structure of the feature picture was a trick that few comedians managed with complete success, and Laurel and Hardy in the thirties were no exceptions. Although they made their first feature **(Pardon Us)** in 1931, they alternated short and full-length productions until 1935. This allowed them to appear in all-star comedy revues and Hal Roach operettas like **Fra Diavolo** and **Babes in Toyland,** while simultaneously developing the best elements of their comic style in shorts like **Scram** and **Their First Mistake.** And when suitable feature material arose they could turn a story like **Sons of the Desert** into one of their finest and most typical works. Their late thirties features seem less assured. Their basic assortment of gags and the whole comic structure are somewhat attenuated. Even so, **Way Out West** is happily one of their best films, and even **A Chump at Oxford** contains much great material. In general, the late thirties was not so good a time for the great comedians of the old school, like Fields, the Marxes, or Laurel and Hardy. Attention was shifting more and more to the handsome and expensive screwball comedies or to the romantic farces of the Lubitsch school. And a whole new genre was developing, which its chief exponent himself referred to as "Capracorn."

Frank Capra had moved from his association with Harry Langdon to a top position at Columbia, where he directed adventure films **(Dirigible, Flight),** topical melodramas **(The Miracle Woman, American Madness),** and standard comedies like **Platinum Blonde** and **Lady for a Day,** where his famous populist streak first became strongly evident. **It Happened One Night** is nearly a screwball comedy, with madcap heiress Claudette Colbert leading a frivolous, irrelevant existence in a world of unlikely autogyros and European nobility. But she is straightened out by man-of-the-people Clark Gable (a reporter, of course) who pulls her out of the screwball world and down into what passes for the real one. Gable projected a sense of realism that was strong enough to deflate any

Spencer Tracy and Joan Bennett in Vincente Minnelli's **Father of the Bride** (1950), a fine example of the situation comedies which began to dominate the field in the years right after the war. Opposite: Broderick Crawford and Judy Holiday in George Cukor's **Born Yesterday,** from the play by Garson Kanin (1950). Judy brightened some of the best high comedies of the fifties.

screwball screenplay, an effect completely the opposite of casting Cary Grant in a role. Capra was involved with the proletariat for most of his career, and he would only use an actor like Grant for so frivolous a farce as **Arsenic and Old Lace.** For the populist manifestos that were closest to his heart Capra preferred to employ Gary Cooper or Jimmy Stewart, "Aw, shucks" boys from down home who could stand in for the little people in a way that city slicker Grant never could. In **Mr. Deeds Goes to Town** and **Mr. Smith Goes to Washington** Capra grew so concerned with social commitment that the term "comedy" hardly applies, while **Meet John Doe** has fewer laughs than **Lost Horizon.** In the Deeds-Smith-Doe trilogy Capra was expressing his ideas through original material, but even in adapting a solid property from outside, like George S. Kaufman and Moss Hart's **You Can't Take It With You,** he transformed all into his own image. The farcical problems of the eccentric family here were transformed into a classic battle of the individualist against giant corporate forces (Edward Arnold), a classic Capra confrontation. Frank Capra may have been

the dominating factor in the socially conscious comedy of the thirties, but his works certainly didn't stand alone. Leo McCarey's **Ruggles of Red Gap** must sneak onto any such list, if only for Charles Laughton's impassioned recitation of the Gettysburg Address. Indeed, McCarey is certainly the best all-around comedy director of the thirties, having left Laurel and Hardy to direct the best Marx Brothers film **(Duck Soup),** one of the finest screwball comedies **(The Awful Truth),** and **Ruggles**—this warm, folksy, and intensely personal masterpiece in the Capra tradition.

The Depression, of course, gave Charlie Chaplin ample opportunity to develop the socially conscious elements in his little tramp character. But this element is sacrificed to Chaplinesque pathos in **City Lights,** as the tramp falls in love with a blind flower girl, played by Virginia Cherrill, and manages to pay for an operation to cure her blindness. Her image of her friend and benefactor has been that of a rich tycoon, so when she sees the tramp for the first time at the film's conclusion, Chaplin pulls out all the stops. Innocent of the facts, she

Right: The fifties' most sensational comedy team, Jerry Lewis and Dean Martin, in **Money From Home** (1954), one of their most typical. Far right: British comedies introduced a touch of dark humor to American screens as a sophisticated contrast to the slapstick of Martin and Lewis. Here Stanley Holloway and Alec Guinness in **The Lavender Hill Mob** (1951) pack solid-gold models of the Eiffel Tower. Below: Guinness and Dennis Price in **Kind Hearts and Coronets** (1949). Below right: Comedy in CinemaScope. Betty Grable, Rory Calhoun, Lauren Bacall, Cameron Mitchell, Marilyn Monroe, and David Wayne in **How to Marry a Millionaire** (1953), directed by Jean Negulesco.

wants to be kind to the funny little man who stares at her like a new "admirer," and presses a flower into his hand. With this touch she suddenly recognizes her old friend. "You!" says the silent title card, as Chaplin the director cuts to an unbearably poignant close-up of Chaplin the star, and the jolt of this realization reverberates through the audience.

City Lights contains many brilliant bits and comic scenes but is knitted together quite poorly, like a group of shorts strung together to make a program feature. Much finer is **Modern Times,** an extraordinary and unique work which somehow seems today the classical masterpiece of thirties comedy. Dominated completely by social motifs springing from the Depression, the problems of workers and the unemployed, **Modern Times** is a comedy of class struggle. Stealing a loaf of bread is enough to bring on police-state brutality, like an updated **Les Miserables,** but Chaplin never lets the film descend to mere agit-prop. The tramp in his last real appearance battles the newly arrived machine age, and confronts the social realities of a terrifying new world which is quick to beat him over the head with a nightstick and throw him in the clink. But **Modern Times** is a hopeful statement by an artist who didn't always have much hope for his hero or for his society. When it's time to walk back down the road of life at the end of **Modern Times,** the dirt road may have become a superhighway, but at least he doesn't have to walk down it alone.

In the same way as thirties comedy functioned under the cloud of the Depression, forties humor had to deal with the realities of World War II. Films about madcap heiresses began to get scarce, but no cohesive genre of forties comedy rose to take their place. Instead, comedy became very diffuse, and as different forms and styles proliferated the well-developed traditions and styles of the thirties gradually weakened. Even Chaplin radically changed his approach. Not only did he talk for the first time in **The Great Dictator,** but he played two new roles, Adenoid Hynkel, dictator of Tomania, and a look-alike Jewish barber who was one of his unwilling subjects. His most serious film to date, **The Great Dictator** was lightened mainly by some of Chaplin's most elegant pantomime—Hynkel's mad ballet with the globe of the world, for example. A strong dose of physical comedy was also included, but somehow the sight of storm troopers slamming Charlie off the cobblestones was a bit too unsettling. By the time **The Great Dictator** appeared, the war in Europe had already begun, and no one was laughing much at the antics of dictators anymore. War-related comedy themes centered more on home-front activities. Billy Wilder's first film, **The Major and the Minor,** dealt with a military academy and Ginger Rogers's effort to disguise herself as a twelve-year-old, while in **The More the Merrier** Jean Arthur had apartment troubles in housing-short Washington, both typical examples of standard thirties situations dressed up in battle gear. Preston Sturges mocked the adulation of the military with Eddie Bracken in **Hail the Conquering Hero,** a tricky enough feat in wartime America, but Sturges sur-

Top: Tom Ewell and Marilyn Monroe as the two halves of the fifties comedy couple, harried husband and blonde bombshell, in Billy Wilder's **The Seven-Year Itch** (1955). Bottom left: Paul Newman caught with his pants down by Joan Collins in Leo McCarey's **Rally Round the Flag Boys!** (1958). Right: Jayne Mansfield and Tony Randall in **Will Success Spoil Rock Hunter?** (1957). Directed by ex-cartoon maker Frank Tashlin, this film got most of its laughs in thoroughly raucous, comic-book fashion.

By the end of the fifties a new
form of light romantic comedy
had evolved, as shown by these hits
from 1959. Above: Cary Grant
and Arthur O'Connell in Blake
Edwards's **Operation Petticoat.**
Right: The original caption on this
still from **Pillow Talk** reads:
"Doris Day, already in bed, is
thrilled to get a call from Rock
Hudson after their first date."
Opposite: Tony Curtis does
his Cary Grant imitation for the
benefit of Marilyn Monroe and a
thinly disguised Jack Lemmon in
Billy Wilder's **Some Like It Hot.**

passed himself with **The Miracle of Morgan's Creek.** While the Hays Office was sleeping, Betty Hutton attends an all-night "kiss the boys good-by" party and the next day can't remember whom she "married" the night before. After much panic and slapstick carrying-on, Bracken is corralled into being "the father," but disaster is averted on Christmas Eve when Betty gives birth to sextuplets and the couple become national heroes.

If **The Miracle of Morgan's Creek** seemed strange to wartime audiences, they were completely befuddled by **To Be or Not to Be.** Perhaps the first black comedy of the screen, this astonishing work came from Ernst Lubitsch, of all people, and dealt with a troupe of Shakespearean actors in Warsaw at the time of the Nazi invasion. Like Chaplin's **The Great Dictator,** the film ran hot and cold as high-comedy sequences were interspersed with stark tragedy, and it was attacked in some quarters for milking laughs from a decidedly unfunny situation. Still, no one who sees the film can forget the delicious absurdity of Nazi commandant Sig Rumann rolling his tongue over lines like, "So they call me 'Concentration Camp' Erhart . . .?" The rest of Lubitsch's late work is similarly distinct from his flip, jazzy romances of the early thirties. **The Shop Around the Corner** is a warm, completely uncynical love story with James Stewart and Margaret Sullavan (later musicalized as **She Loves Me**), while **That Uncertain Feeling** only showed that Lubitsch himself was uncertain about returning to the style of an earlier decade. Lubitsch's last two films are testimonial works, comparable to the last films of John Ford or Jean Renoir, as the great artist wraps up the concerns of a lifetime in their final, fully matured form. For Lubitsch this was **Heaven Can Wait,** the life story of a wicked Lothario whose "wickedness" is laughed at by the devil himself. Being a rat with women doesn't count for much on the world's scale of evil, and the suave seducer of an earlier day seems mildly comic by 1943. With this mellow film, Lubitsch made his last wry comments on a genre that he had once commanded, and he allowed his romantic hero a very private demise behind a closed door, the most melancholy of Lubitsch touches. In his next film, **Cluny Brown** (1946), Lubitsch contented himself with much lighter material, and demonstrated how completely he had abandoned the cynicism of his younger days. Here intentions are honorable and motives are pure, and Jennifer Jones and Charles Boyer glow with a warmth more human than anything he managed in his days at Paramount.

But this nostalgic reverie was far from the main interests of wartime audiences, which leaned much more to the verbal slapstick of Abbott and Costello. Bud and Lou made a smash hit with **Buck Privates** (1941), where they immediately established themselves as the characteristic funnymen of the forties. How or why this relatively uninteresting and derivative team so captured the country's imagination has never been fully explained, but audiences flocked to **Hold That Ghost, Pardon My Sarong,** and anything else that Universal put the pair into. When their popularity began to wane at the decade's end, they were teamed up with the Frankenstein monster, Dracula, and the Wolf

New wave of comedic sophistication in the early sixties was firmly established by the great success of **Breakfast at Tiffany's** (1961), skillfully directed by Blake Edwards. With Audrey Hepburn as Holly Golightly, Henry Mancini's "Moon River" on the sound track, and an ultra-chic visual style, the film was a perfect embodiment of the wildly popular Jackie Kennedy image.

Man in one of their more ambitious productions, but Bela Lugosi and Lon Chaney, Jr. stole the show.

In the same tradition of Brooklynesque comedy was Danny Kaye, whose style and personality created a sensation with the zany patter songs of **Up in Arms.** Further success followed in **The Kid from Brooklyn,** and Kaye's abilities as a dancer and mimic seemed to open up a whole new chapter in American screen comedy. But his madcap qualities were subverted by Sam Goldwyn as early as **The Secret Life of Walter Mitty,** and by the fifties Kaye had lost his manic Borscht Belt energies.

Red Skelton was another clown whose wartime comedies **(Whistling in Dixie)** found a wide audience, but after **The Fuller Brush Man** he did his best work in television.

Less chaotic, but equally based on a pleasing personal style were the "Road" comedies of Bob Hope, Bing Crosby, and Dorothy Lamour. Sprinkled with inside jokes about the series, the Paramount studio, and moviemaking in general, these films traveled from Morocco to Singapore to Utopia in a free and easygoing style, a distinct change from the double-talk of most wartime comedy. Hope and Crosby were reunited in **The Road to Hong Kong** in 1962, and some of the old nonchalance was still there, a bit puffier around the edges, perhaps. But none of these wartime progeny could be called great comedians or be said to have produced great comedy. While the best of the prewar comedies still seems fresh, these films have invariably dated, their extreme topicality limiting their appeal for modern audiences to occasionally amusing bits and pieces.

Of the great comedians of the thirties who continued into the war years only W. C. Fields maintained his old touch. While his teaming with Mae West in **My Little Chickadee** did not result in the comedy classic the studio claimed it to be, **The Bank Dick** and **Never Give a Sucker an Even Break** were, however, true Fields spectaculars. The latter film especially, produced from an incoherent scenario by Otis Cribblecoblis, remains the high point of the Fields style, with complete contempt expressed for the niceties of Hollywood story construction. Unhampered by subplots or romantic interest, Fields reads a scenario to Franklin Pangborn, head of Esoteric Studios, and we jump to these unconnected scenes being played out. In the course of this, Fields gets off cracks at everyone from waitresses to Margaret Dumont, while keeping ingenue Gloria Jean carefully in line. The formal discontinuities of **Sucker** are so striking that we have to turn to Ole Olsen and Chic Johnson's **Hellzapoppin** to find anything to compare them with. Here the humor comes almost completely from manipulating the filmic image and spoofing the illusionism of the movies. The film within a film within a film within a film narrative is impossibly complex and at times seems a parody of films made twenty years later (**Citizen Kane** is already one of its targets). It was unfortunate that this self-conscious and imaginative work was a mere fluke, and that this kind of surrealist madness was

Some of the older directors continued to make their comedies in the same old way. Above: John Ford put Lee Marvin and John Wayne in the South Seas with instructions to horse around in **Donovan's Reef** (1963). Following in the Lubitsch tradition, but a little more cynically, was **Irma la Douce** (1963). Jack Lemmon and Shirley MacLaine were both out walking the beat in Billy Wilder's Paris (r).

allowed to wither. But even the Marx Brothers couldn't come to terms with the forties. **Go West** (1941) was their last really satisfying film, and only sporadically amusing episodes dot **The Big Store, A Night in Casablanca,** and **Love Happy.** While age was beginning to tell on Harpo and Chico, limiting their effectiveness as clowns, some effort might have been made to arm Groucho with suitable Marxian dialogue, but either he or his writers didn't feel up to it at the time. His renaissance had to wait for fifties television and "You Bet Your Life."

The Marxes were refugees from the thirties making an uncomfortable adjustment to the world of the forties, but they were certainly not alone. Katharine Hepburn in the delightful **The Philadelphia Story** carried the screwball tradition to a premature conclusion, then turned to films like **Woman of the Year,** her first with Spencer Tracy, and one of the growing cycle of wartime films focusing on women in a more active and aggressive societal role. In the comedy field the finest of these was Howard Hawks's **His Girl Friday,** a rewrite of **The Front Page** with a female Hildy Johnson and Rosalind Russell's finest performance. A few years later, Hawks directed with thirtyish finesse a typically fortyish story of masculine insecurity, **I Was a Male War Bride,** which starred Ann Sheridan and, of course, Cary Grant. Grant was also along on **The Philadelphia Story** and **His Girl Friday**—an eternally charming thirties presence in the often uncertain world of forties comedy. These films marked an updating of the screwball tradition, and their toughness made them quite acceptable to no-nonsense forties audiences.

But that other staple of thirties screens, the homespun message humor of Frank Capra, had entirely different problems. After completing his wartime Signal Corps work, Capra poured all of his energies into **It's a Wonderful Life** (1946), the story of a good man who suddenly feels that his life has been valueless. The film is not only the most "corny" of Capra's works, but his greatest achievement as well. Like Lubitsch with **Heaven Can Wait,** Capra succeeded in producing one ultimate statement of his ideals and obsessions, here a charming and ageless fable of optimism triumphant. Using Jimmy Stewart as his hero once again, Capra created a vulnerable, defenseless film which wore its heart on its sleeve. The hard-nosed audiences of the forties sensed this and tore it to pieces. They seemed to resent the fact that it lacked the wise-guy, hard-shell attitude of the forties, and that it dared to flaunt its openness and sincerity. They made sure that that mistake would not be repeated for a long time.

One could never have accused Preston Sturges of wearing his heart on his sleeve. The writer/director of **Hail the Conquering Hero** and **The Miracle of Morgan's Creek** always seemed to give the least emphasis to that particular portion of the anatomy. Noted as the first Hollywood screenwriter to make the step up to major director, Sturges's comedies were odd mixtures of elegantly crafted dialogue in the Lubitsch tradition, and expansive slapstick à la Mack Sennett. His romantic farces, **The Lady Eve** and **The Palm Beach Story,** were the equal of anything done in the thirties, and he even turned the trick

Opposite, top: An attempt to recapture the spirit of the great comedies of the past, **The Great Race** (1965) worked much too hard for the few laughs it produced. Here Tony Curtis stands aloof from the world's messiest pie fight.
Bottom right: Jerry Lewis in perhaps his zaniest comedy, **The Nutty Professor** (1963). He invents a potion which turns him into a singing idol amazingly similar to Dean Martin!
Far right: Jean-Pierre Léaud as a detective in François Truffaut's **Stolen Kisses** (1969), one of the delightful Antoine Doinel films.

206

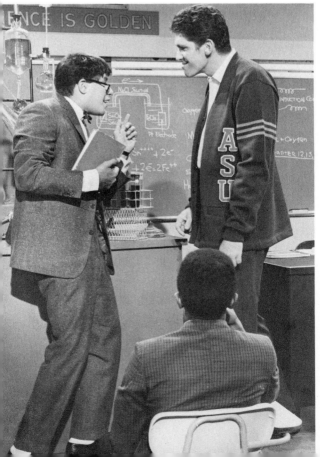

without Cary Grant. But more exotic subjects offered Sturges more room to be outlandish. In **The Great Moment** he created the most offbeat biopic of the forties, turning the story of the discoverer of ether into a slapstick comedy with plenty of dentist gags. His **Sullivan's Travels** (1941) is the best comedy about Hollywood, the saga of the director of **Ants in Your Pants of 1939** who longs to direct a message picture called **Oh Brother, Where Art Thou?** Disguised as a tramp, he tours a United States still very much in the grip of the Depression and in one nightmarish sequence gets railroaded into a chain gang. Often referred to as the comic **8½,** the film really turns a much neater trick in that Sturges succeeds in giving his audience both **Oh Brother** and **Ants in Your Pants** wrapped up in the same film, thus satisfying everyone, most especially the fans of Veronica Lake, who lights up the film while serving as romantic interest.

The strangest film of Sturges's career was probably **Mad Wednesday,** a follow-up of Harold Lloyd's 1925 **The Freshman,** for which Lloyd himself returned to the screen. Sturges cynically explodes the naïve, go-getting idealism of the Lloyd character and shows him decades later as a self-made failure, still mouthing the pious work-ethic platitudes of the twenties. A wildly uneven work, **Mad Wednesday** (1951), does succeed in revealing the disillusionment which was at the heart of the forties veneer of wise-guy cynicism. By the end of the war, America had long since stopped believing in the ideals of those far-off years, and had substituted a philosophy completely stripped of idealistic aspirations. Preston Sturges was probably the only director who found this funny.

Team comics Dean Martin and Jerry Lewis emerged from the nightclub circuit at the close of the forties and quickly filled the vacuum left by the demise of Abbott and Costello. Their relationship was much the same, that of an innocent naïf and his smoother, straighter pal, while the gags were also similarly structured, the dunce trying to win the approval of the buddy who is constantly ripping him off. The comic situation of being shot down while striving for affection is emphasized more strongly in the Martin and Lewis team, and reflects a very topical postwar insecurity, later developed by many of the stand-up comics of the early sixties. The emotional vulnerability of one of the partners was definitely not a factor in such prewar teams as the Marx Brothers or Laurel and Hardy, and Martin and Lewis are important for adding emotional pain to the nearly depleted slapstick arsenal of physical pain. In **My Friend Irma, At War With the Army,** and **Scared Stiff,** their first wildly successful comedies for Paramount, Martin and Lewis developed their own particular brand of "misfit comedy," with Dino always close at hand to provide a standard of social grace and physical attractiveness. It was not until the team joined talents with Frank Tashlin, however, that the real emotional underpinnings of their comedy became clear. Tashlin had been trained in the Looney Tunes unit at Warner Brothers, where he specialized in surrealist physical gags of the Daffy Duck sort, but he was also

Above: British comedies reached a peak with the bizarre **Morgan!** (1966), with David Warner. Karel Reisz directed this black comedy about a psychotic Marxist who envisions himself as King Kong. Right: Charlie Chaplin bid farewell to the screen with **A Countess from Hong Kong** (1967), starring Sophia Loren and Marlon Brando. Panned on release by those happier with mid-sixties madness, the film today reveals considerable warmth and romantic charm.

interested in satirizing the more vulgar elements of pop culture. He carried over this cartoon style to his own live-action films, and it is particularly successful in **The Girl Can't Help It,** full of wild stabs at consumerism, rock-and-rolling teen-agers, and fiftyish sexual hangups. (This is the film in which Jayne Mansfield appears clutching a pair of milk bottles to her breasts.) Tashlin took over the team in **Artists and Models,** where he had some fun with the horror-comics craze, and **Hollywood or Bust,** with Anita Ekberg standing in for Miss Mansfield. After the famous breakup he continued with Lewis alone, and in films like **Cinderfella** brought out the uncomfortable strain of sexual infantilism in Lewis's character. By this time Lewis was ready to direct his own comedies, and **The Bellboy** and **The Ladies' Man** are very much in the Tashlin mold. Tashlin's famed vulgar streak first brought out the humor of bumbling sexuality in the Jerry character, and the Woody Allen image of the seventies owes much to the Tashlin and Lewis films of the fifties.

The leering gags of such Tashlin comedies as **Will Success Spoil Rock Hunter?** were present as well, though in a more refined form, in the fifties comedies of Billy Wilder, **The Seven-Year Itch** and **Some Like It Hot.** The first was the more Tashlinesque, with Wilder using Tom Ewell in a role which recalled his appearance in **The Girl Can't Help It,** here paired not with the brash Jayne Mansfield but the somewhat more demure Marilyn Monroe. The quite considerable differences between these archetypal blonde sexpots of the fifties marked the distinction between the comic styles of Tashlin and Wilder as well, Tashlin's flat-out vulgarity being superseded by the more restrained, Lubitsch-influenced touch of Billy Wilder (one of **Ninotchka's** screenwriters). **The Seven-Year Itch** is sheer fifties high comedy, with kids, television, and the strains of family life proving the butt of much of the humor. Wilder's debt to Lubitsch shows clearly in the sparkle of the performances, the underrated Tom Ewell and Marilyn Monroe in her first great comic role enlivening a situation which might have descended to the banal in lesser hands.

Some Like It Hot is a very different kind of film, with Monroe's comic potential now fully established, and co-stars Jack Lemmon and Tony Curtis cavorting in the best screwball tradition. Indeed, Curtis even gets to do his Cary Grant imitation. The riotously funny **Some Like It Hot** is, in many ways, the beginning of the sixties tradition in comedy, as Tashlinesque bad taste recedes to be replaced by cool sophistication in the stylish tradition of the thirties. Sex is no longer the object of lecherous guffaws, but raises wry smiles in an almost Lubitsch fashion. The ground-breaking work in supplanting this overheated approach to sexual humor was done by Otto Preminger—another Lubitsch protégé—who managed to release **The Moon Is Blue** in 1953. (Indeed, Preminger served as co-director with Lubitsch on a 1948 release, **That Lady in Ermine,** but did not receive screen credit for his work.) This was quite a feat, as the film had been denied a Code seal and was condemned by the Legion of Decency—all due to the appearance of the words "virgin," "mistress," and

One of the oddest comedies of the sixties, Clive
Donner's **What's New Pussycat?** is one of the best examples of the
free-wheeling farces of the period. Woody Allen made his debut
here in a small part, but the big stars of the 1965 film were Peter Sellers
and Peter O'Toole. Sellers must certainly be the most durable comedy
star of the postwar period, successfully moving back and forth from England to
Hollywood for over two decades and creating a gallery
of grotesque comic caricatures.

"seduction" on the sound track. That this innocuous little comedy could have raised such an uproar seems incomprehensible, not just in the light of seventies cinema, but in the context of the leering sexpot comedy of the time.

By the time the fifties stopped ogling Jayne Mansfield's milk bottles, a more self-consciously sophisticated style of comedy had arisen. One can see glimmers of it as early as **How to Marry a Millionaire,** a film whose sophistication is only skin deep and which all too often falls back on the physical attributes of Lauren Bacall, Betty Grable, and Marilyn Monroe. **Bus Stop** at least gets most of its comedy from the interplay of the two stars, underplaying Marilyn Monroe's sex appeal, while Leo McCarey in **Rally Round the Flag Boys!** hedges his bets throughout. This failed comedy, which wraps up all the fifties preoccupations with suburbia, television, kids and sex, is nearly redeemed by Joan Collins and her superb fifties bombshell routine, but scampering about in suburban bedrooms is an element McCarey did not feel comfortable with. Not until Ross Hunter's **Pillow Talk** did this frothy sub-genre of romantic comedy come into its own, and the teaming of Rock Hudson and Doris Day began a cycle that lasted well into the sixties. By that time mere titillation was not enough for movie entertainment. By their very nature the Hudson-Day type of comedy had to deliver a lot less than it promised. Driven from the big screen, they found a natural home in the innumerable TV sitcoms of the sixties.

One of the few rewarding offshoots of the otherwise obnoxious school of fifties "dumb broad" comedies was the work of Judy Holliday. Her great success in **Born Yesterday** unfortunately typed her in the role of the not-so-dumb blonde, freshly presented in this George Cukor adaptation of the Garson Kanin-Ruth Gordon comedy, but a type which she began to lose interest in as the fifties wore on. **It Should Happen to You** (1954) continued her association with Cukor and Kanin. In this film she is Gladys Glover, an average New York girl who has her name put up on a giant billboard. Being another of the satires on fifties advertising, the film soon finds her an overnight celebrity, a girl with that all-important something: a name. Jack Lemmon made an impressive screen debut in this amusing and often overlooked minor comedy. Judy's career was next taken over by Richard Quine, one of the fifties' best comedy directors, who had made the zany 1955 version of **My Sister Eileen. The Solid Gold Cadillac** was very much a return to her earlier films with Cukor and Kanin, but in **Full of Life** she borrowed a page from Lucille Ball's "I Love Lucy" antics and played a comedy about an expectant mother. Her last film was Vincente Minnelli's delightful **Bells Are Ringing,** in which "The Party's Over" ironically served as her rather poignant screen swan song before she died of cancer. Quine's career lasted through the sixties, but he never recaptured the flavor of his best fifties comedies.

Kim Novak as the modern Manhattan witch in **Bell, Book and Candle** and Doris Day and Jack Lemmon selling lobsters in **It Happened to Jane** are typically light and breezy examples of the best late fifties style. Quine also

211

directed **Operation Mad Ball,** a pre-**M*A*S*H**-style service comedy about a wacky troupe of medics in postwar Europe, for which he got his usual fine performances from Jack Lemmon and Ernie Kovacs. The service comedy had always existed around the fringes of the war genre, but it reached a particularly well-developed point amid the quirky comedies of the fifties, probably because of the success of the comic relief episodes in Billy Wilder's **Stalag 17.** The best of these, John Ford and Mervyn LeRoy's **Mister Roberts,** provided James Cagney with a delightful comic-psychotic role, and emerged almost as a comedy version of **The Caine Mutiny.** Jack Lemmon turned in another winning performance and the film suffered only from a change of directors in mid-production. Blake Edwards (one of the writers on **Operation Mad Ball**) gave us Cary Grant and Tony Curtis aboard a submarine in **Operation Petticoat,** but his best work came in the sixties. Perhaps the most incredible of these service comedies was Josef von Sternberg's **Jet Pilot** (largely reshot by Howard Hughes), in which Janet Leigh plays a Soviet fighter pilot who lands her MiG in Alaska in an attempt to seduce John Wayne and get him to defect to the Russians!

While Tashlin, Quine, and Edwards emerged as the new comic directors in the fifties, such old reliables as Cukor, Minnelli, Hawks, and even Chaplin all produced just as many laughs. Mentioned earlier were Cukor's Judy Holliday films, but perhaps his best work in these years were his films with Katharine Hepburn and Spencer Tracy, **Adam's Rib** and **Pat and Mike.** Cukor had directed Hepburn several times previously, notably in **Holiday** and **The Philadelphia Story,** but teaming her with Tracy in these two Kanin-Gordon vehicles brought out entirely new aspects of her personality. **Adam's Rib** saw them as a husband and wife team of lawyers on opposite sides of the same case, a worthy successor to their first teaming in **Woman of the Year** back in 1942, and a film notable as well for introducing fifties stalwarts Tom Ewell and Judy Holliday to the screen in supporting roles. A follow-up in **Pat and Mike** was just as successful, with Hepburn as an athlete and Tracy as her manager, but their special relationship needed the warmth that Cukor, Kanin, and Gordon provided so well, and a later film like Walter Lang's **Desk Set** (1957) seemed much more a formula job. But Hepburn and Tracy turned in brilliant performances in their other fifties films as well, she opposite Bogart in Huston's **The African Queen** and he as Elizabeth Taylor's dad in Minnelli's **Father of the Bride.**

A return not to the forties but to the thirties world of **Bringing Up Baby** was provided by Howard Hawks in his zany **Monkey Business.** Once again featuring Cary Grant in his absent-minded professor routine, the problem here is that of a rejuvenation drug, B-4, which gets out of hand when a laboratory chimp pours it into the water supply. Hawks has a lot of fun as Grant and co-star Ginger Rogers revert to infantilism, but he also uses the drug to strip away their social inhibitions, giving us a brief but terrifying glimpse of a world without the restraints of adult responsibility, sort of a comic parallel to **Bigger Than Life.**

In box-office terms, the biggest comedy hit of all time has been Mike Nichols's **The Graduate** (far r). The 1967 release noticeably affected the nation's college generation; it made a star of Dustin Hoffman and a household expression of "Mrs. Robinson," played by Anne Bancroft. Neil Simon's **The Odd Couple** (1968, r), one of the many successful film versions of Simon's Broadway hits, starred Jack Lemmon and Walter Matthau.

And not belonging very clearly to the thirties, forties, or fifties was Charles Chaplin's 1957 feature **A King in New York,** not released in the United States until 1973. The story of a small-time European monarch who comes to New York and recoups his fortunes by renting himself out for TV commercials, the film marked Chaplin's last screen role, and one quite removed from that of the little tramp. Like many fifties comedies, **A King in New York** attacks such elements of pop culture as advertising, television, rock 'n' roll, and wide-screen movies, but does so with a strange bitterness, as if Chaplin felt personally affronted by these external manifestations of fifties society. He saves his real bitterness for McCarthyite witch hunts and the House Un-American Activities Committee, insane aberrations on the American scene, but, at the core, suggests Chaplin, manifestations of the same temporary madness that afflicts us with CinemaScope and rock 'n' roll. Charlie tells us it all will pass, and he will be glad to come back when it does. Put together with such a lack of cinematic dexterity that Chaplin seems to dare us to disregard the form and concentrate on the content, **A King in New York** is dotted with fascinating, though isolated, Chaplinesque bits—the most insane of which shows him soaking the Committee with a fire hose, then being cited as a friendly witness.

Had Chaplin's film been shown when it was made, it would have suffered the fate of other fifties black comedies. Audiences of the time wanted their humor straight, with no undercurrents of politics, serious social criticism, or just plain perversity. Huston's **Beat the Devil,** for which Truman Capote wrote the screenplay, was a send-up of the classic intrigue film of **The Third Man** variety, with stalwarts Humphrey Bogart and Peter Lorre along to make it look real. The shaggy-dog ending was decidedly unsatisfying to audiences of the time, but the film slowly began to develop a cult by the sixties. Hitchcock miscalculated just as thoroughly in **The Trouble With Harry,** the story of a meandering corpse in a New England village, and a film whose touch was close to that of the popular Charles Addams cartoons of the time.

American audiences preferred to follow such macabre high jinks on Hitchcock's weekly television series, but English producers were very successful with black comedy, so long as Alec Guinness played in it. The postwar comedies of the Ealing Studio often featured rather bizarre stories of murder and mayhem presented with the most finely drawn English reserve, and usually played out by Guinness, Alastair Sim, and the whole Ealing stock company. In Robert Hamer's **Kind Hearts and Coronets,** Dennis Price plays a disgruntled member of a noble family who decided to dispose of all the relatives between him and the title he wants to inherit. He finds imaginative ways to get rid of each of them, but most of the humor comes from watching Guinness play the whole family—he appears in nine different roles. In **The Lavender Hill Mob** he is a mild bank clerk planning a sensational robbery, while in Alexander Mackendrick's **The Ladykillers,** he and his whole mob fall victim to an innocent Katie Johnson. (Guinness starred as well in a nonmurderous capacity in **The Man in the White**

Walter Matthau seems perfectly cut out for the long string of light comedies in which he has been cast so successfully in the past decade—films like **Cactus Flower, The Odd Couple,** and **Plaza Suite** (1971, above). In this last, his performance was a triple-faceted tour de force. Here he lures his daughter out of the bathroom in the wedding episode.

Suit; he played the inventor of an indestructible fabric who suddenly must consider the full impact of his discovery.) Bodies piled up with complete sangfroid in these films, but many of the best Ealing comedies present an entirely different picture, a tranquil England on which the sun never sets, and where the only concerns are preposterously antiquated. In **Passport to Pimlico,** Margaret Rutherford and her friends managed to establish their own sovereign state in the middle of London, thanks to an old land grant, while Mackendrick's **Tight Little Island** centered on the residents of an isolated Scottish island and their problems with a shipload of liquor. The hero of **Genevieve** was an ancient motor car, while an old-time cinema was the focal point of **The Smallest Show on Earth.** The great difference between the British and American comedies of the fifties lies in Hollywood's incessant investigation of the vulgarities of postwar America and Ealing's nostalgic idealization of a simpler and sunnier England. By the end of the fifties the British realized that Hollywood was right.

Fifties style and fifties filmmakers continued to dominate the new decade for the first few years in both comedy and drama. In the early sixties the major comedies were all the work of men like Cukor, Ford, Hawks, Minnelli, and Lewis, and carried on pretty much in the standard fifties vein. Cukor's **Heller in Pink Tights** featured Anthony Quinn and Sophia Loren as the leaders of a troupe of traveling actors in the Old West, and was one of his most delightful excursions into the world of the theater. Unjustly neglected, the film has considerable visual charm as well, particularly in its lush Technicolor photography. John Ford relaxed from the somber introspection of his late films and directed **Donovan's Reef,** a freewheeling comedy of two old Navy men (John Wayne and Lee Marvin) who retire to a South Seas island and engage in lots of typical Fordian hell-raising.

Man's Favorite Sport was another of Howard Hawks's variations on the theme of the insecure male and the predatory female—here Rock Hudson is a famous authority on fishing who has never actually gone out to catch a fish. The usual sexual innuendo Hawks allows was perhaps laid on a bit less securely here, however.

Vincente Minnelli's **Goodbye, Charlie** was an even more embarrassing finish to the Debbie Reynolds-Tony Curtis-style comedy of the fifties, with reincarnation the dubious theme. George Axelrod, on whose flop stage play this was based, had also written the originals of **The Seven-Year Itch** and **Will Success Spoil Rock Hunter?** but is more important to sixties cinema for writing, producing, and directing that ground-breaking bad-taste film, **Lord Love a Duck,** one of the first of the dirty-minded comedies of the mid-decade.

And Jerry Lewis continued at the same old stand, only watering down his zaniness with stronger and stronger doses of sentimentality. Although Tashlin continued to direct some of his films **(It's Only Money, The Disorderly Orderly),** Lewis's most interesting films were those he directed himself, including the amazing **The Nutty Professor** (1963). One of the key works behind the

French Jerry Lewis cult, this film shows Jerry as a mousy little scientist who invents a Jekyll-and-Hyde potion that turns him into Buddy Love, a thinly disguised version of Dean Martin. It carries to its logical conclusion the early Martin and Lewis humor, where Jerry was always wishing he could be more like his suave buddy, all innocent of the less attractive parts of Dino's personality. But while Lewis's popularity soared among audiences that didn't understand English, most American critics found his work a failed mixture of Tashlin's vulgarity and Chaplin's sentimentality.

Blake Edwards was the first of the fifties group to come to terms with the new decade. His **Breakfast at Tiffany's** captured the glossy, high-style New York image of the swinging sixties, thanks largely to Audrey Hepburn's Holly Golightly and Henry Mancini's "Moon River," a melody that was hard to avoid in the early sixties. Mancini's contribution may have been greater than realized at the time. His lightly orchestrated pop sound tracks for this film, **The Pink Panther,** and **Days of Wine and Roses** had much to do with demolishing the heavily scored tradition of Max Steiner and Erich Wolfgang Korngold, thus transforming Hollywood movies from overorchestrated to underorchestrated in a few short years.

The Pink Panther and **A Shot in the Dark** teamed Edwards and Mancini with Peter Sellers, who by the early sixties had become the new Alec Guinness. In these two Inspector Clouseau films Sellers could indulge his tastes for disguise and Ealing-style silly-ass comedy, but it was Edwards's slick pacing that held the films together. By the time of **The Great Race,** Edwards began to lose his grip, however, and this well-intentioned tribute to the slapstick days collapsed of its own weight. The theory that if one pie in the face was amusing a hundred would be uproarious was once more laid to rest in the film's unfortunate conclusion.

Of course, the greatest example of overproduced comedy in the early sixties, possibly of all time, was Stanley Kramer's **It's a Mad, Mad, Mad, Mad World,** a Cinerama extravaganza in which nearly every comic star in Hollywood turned in his least interesting performance.

In the sixties Billy Wilder stopped producing cynical dramas and moved completely into the production of even more cynical comedies. **The Apartment** was the first and probably the best of these, with Jack Lemmon as a rising young executive whose success is aided by a judicious dispensation of the key to his bachelor pad. This pseudo-pimping goes awry when he himself falls in love with Shirley MacLaine, a considerably talented and shamefully underutilized actress. Wilder did later reunite the pair in his de-musicalized version of **Irma la Douce,** but with somewhat less success. His main claim to sixties fame is **Kiss Me, Stupid,** that most tasteless of mid-sixties sex farces. While **Lord Love a Duck** might have been un-American, both the Motion Picture Producers and Distributors of America and the Legion of Decency were convinced that the idea of songwriter Ray Walston promoting his music by having his wife sleep with crooner Dean Martin was plain dirty. This film marked the nadir of Wilder's cynicism, and **The Fortune Cookie,** an otherwise amusing study of lawyer Whiplash Willie Gingrich—Walter Matthau—and one of his fraudulent suits, was actually ruined by the incredibly idealistic surprise ending. Wilder did much to break the ground for the sex-obsessed comedies of the late sixties and early seventies, but he himself floundered aimlessly after the liberalizing of the Production Code, and the tepid **The Private Life of Sherlock Holmes** and **Avanti!** show the strain of having no one left to shock.

In retrospect, of course, one wonders at the furor raised over such films as **Never on Sunday,** the charming Melina Mercouri film whose scandalousness now seems as remote as that of **The Moon Is Blue.** If released at the end of the decade, it would have raised not an eyebrow, but the film was a 1960 release, and the Legion of Decency trotted out its "Condemned" stamp. Such sly romantic comedies were soon to dominate screen humor, however, and beginning in the mid-sixties we can see several very distinct styles on the screen. The first, and mildest, is that of the theatrical tradition of which Neil Simon remains the master. **Barefoot in the Park** (1967) established Simon's reputation and his characteristic Manhattan milieu as well. The film version starred Robert Redford and Jane Fonda (was it that long ago?) as the young couple moving into a Greenwich Village walk-up, and though still dominated by Broadway conventions, the film was a big enough success to establish a long and prosperous marriage between Simon and Hollywood. Among the successful follow-ups were **The Odd Couple,** with Walter Matthau and Jack Lemmon romping through a vehicle that later migrated to television; **Plaza Suite,** starring Matthau again in a romantic triptych set against New York's landmark hotel; and **The Last of the Red Hot Lovers,** this time with Alan Arkin as the hapless hero. Except for Simon's plays, the list of pretested Broadway adaptations is not lengthy in this period, with **The Owl and the Pussycat, Cactus Flower,** and **Forty Carats** being among the more important.

Sharing Simon's New York idiom, but working more in the stand-up comedy tradition, were the films of Mike Nichols and Elaine May. The humor in Nichols's **The Graduate** is largely based on the famous style of their nightclub routines, notably in the first half before the film gets serious. **The Graduate** was enormously influential and its fabulous box-office success spawned a cycle of films on alienated youth of the late sixties, for which we owe not only Dustin Hoffman but Elliott Gould, as well. For a season Gould seemed to be playing in every comedy in town. (He wound up starring in an Ingmar Bergman movie, **The Touch.**) In films like **M*A*S*H, Move,** and **Getting Straight,** he played his familiar curly haired, stubbly chinned type so often and so well that he was driven from the screen for about a year, emerging later disguised as a detective in Robert Altman's classy **The Long Goodbye.** Perhaps Gould was the ideal actor for modern screen comedy, his weathered New York eye taking in the most outrageous occurrences without flinching.

The weird world of Mel Brooks: Zero Mostel and Gene Wilder listen to Kenneth Mars describe his new show, "Springtime for Hitler: A Gay Romp with Adolf and Eva in Berchtesgaden." They produce the show with the idea of putting on a colossal flop, but, of course, it quickly becomes Broadway's biggest hit. What else, with numbers like "Look Out, Here Comes the Master Race." From **The Producers** (1968).

Like **The Graduate, The Heartbreak Kid** shows the traces of Nichols and May's characteristic sixties comedy style. But Elaine May's film examines much more carefully the madness of love and the anguish that it produces. Here Charles Grodin meets Cybill Shepherd on the beach and his marriage begins to evaporate right in the middle of his honeymoon. The casting of Cybill here is inspired (1972).

Nichols's **Carnal Knowledge** had a raw underpinning to its sexual humor, and was notable for the fine performance given by the usually ill-regarded Ann-Margret. Today, however, it seems more important as a test case for the newly reinstituted local censorship boards, back in business thanks to a lamentable 1973 ruling of the U. S. Supreme Court.

Elaine May got off to a good start as a director in **A New Leaf,** but her great success came with **The Heartbreak Kid,** for which Neil Simon wrote the screenplay. A painfully funny tale of a young husband seduced away by the unreal beauty of Cybill Shepherd—while on his honeymoon—this was one of the few comedies of the time able to stand comparison with the best thirties work. One can also see the hand of Elaine May in some of the amusing bits that enliven her screenplay of Otto Preminger's **Such Good Friends,** but she wisely had her name taken off the credits.

Two other skillful films very much in this tradition were **Lovers and Other Strangers** and **Made for Each Other,** both written by Renee Taylor and Joseph Bologna, and sharing with the Nichols and May films a fascination for the delicate pain involved in love and marriage. These films are full of engagements and wedding ceremonies, but the prospects are usually bleak. In **Lovers and Other Strangers** some sound advice is given the younger generation: "Don't look for happiness, Richie, it'll only make you miserable," which pretty well sums up the tone of all these films.

Similar in theme, but concentrating more on the performers than on brittle one-liners was John Cassavetes's slightly bizarre **Minnie and Moskowitz.** The near-improvisatory style of the acting and directing allow the performers (Gena Rowlands and Seymour Cassel) to project a superficial sense of realism which is quite different from the well-made formal structure of a Neil Simon. Its advantages in immediacy are apparent, but occasionally the film tends to ramble self-indulgently, like most of Cassavetes's pioneering work.

At first the sole province of such offbeat New York types as Nichols, Taylor, and Cassavetes, the tragicomic modern-relationship genre was quickly absorbed by the rest of Hollywood. **Pete 'n' Tillie** was somewhat over-tinged with sentimentality, and its idea of the new maturity was to show Walter Matthau playing the piano bare-assed, but the performances of Matthau and Carol Burnett made the film well worth watching. The structure was really that of a fifties family saga well dressed up in seventies garb by director Martin Ritt, a combination that proved quite appealing at the box office.

Another atavistic smash was **A Touch of Class,** sort of a mod-Lubitsch picture, but with a moral. The deft work of Melvin Frank, an old Hollywood craftsman whose credits go back to the Hope and Crosby "Road" pictures, the film was most memorable for giving George Segal and Glenda Jackson a chance to play an updated version of the classic thirties romantic couple. And of course Peter Bogdanovich's **What's Up, Doc?** gave us a somewhat kookier version of this plot, with Barbra Streisand ripping up the scenery, and a great car chase thrown in for good measure. Ryan O'Neal proved himself to be no Cary Grant, however. He was seen to better advantage with his scene-stealing daughter Tatum in the charming **Paper Moon.**

But while most of these films took pains to keep the occasionally zany antics within realistic bounds, a whole underside to this genre had been developing in the hands of Woody Allen. Another recruit from the ranks of New York stand-up comics, Allen made his screen debut in **What's New Pussycat?**, an odd British film at the pinnacle of the swinging-London period. **What's Up, Tiger Lily?** was another slight aberration in his career, actually an old Japanese gangster film which he improved by dubbing in a completely different sound track.

But Allen's real screen image was not formed until **Take the Money and Run, Bananas, Play It Again, Sam,** and **Sleeper.** With this body of work Allen forcefully established himself as the most gifted and inventive comedy mind in American films since the 1930's. The self-deprecating humor, the cracks about analysis or a sexless marriage, the absurd attempts to live up to some fantasy machismo image—each aspect is carefully developed by Allen in all of his films. He is the first comedian to create a definite screen character since Jerry Lewis, and he shares many of Lewis's insecurities and neuroses. But while Lewis had to hide his sexuality behind infantilism, Woody Allen can take advantage of the seventies and turn nearly all his jokes around sex. Like Lewis he does not direct all his own films, but those that are directed by him are wilder and less carefully structured, relying more heavily on surrealist gags and typical Allen one-liners ("I had a date, but she called it off. There's a dock strike."). Practically the only true screen comic of his generation, Allen finds his following enlarged with each carefully heralded release. His fans are so loyal that they even forgive such lapses as **Everything You Always Wanted to Know About Sex,** a rather shaky construction even for Woody, but redeemed by his cameo appearance as a sperm.

And finally, of course, there was the French attitude, perhaps best illustrated in the films of François Truffaut and Eric Rohmer. Truffaut's Antoine Doinel films, with Jean-Pierre Léaud, began very seriously at the start of the new wave in **The Four Hundred Blows.** But as Truffaut's autobiographical character grows up, he runs into the expected romantic problems, first, briefly, in **Love at Twenty,** and then more notably in **Stolen Kisses** and **Bed and Board.** Truffaut's Antoine is so nonpolitical that he almost seems to wave an angry fist in the face of Jean-Luc Godard's activist cinema. In **Stolen Kisses** riots and demonstrations are going on all around him, but he is so self-involved that he remains oblivious. As a private detective he improbably gets tangled up with Delphine Seyrig, but the end of the film finds him on more familiar ground, settling down with Claude Jade (a startling look-alike for Catherine Deneuve). **Bed and Board** continues the story on a lower key, with our hero a happily married bourgeois, troubled only by those extramarital annoyances so common to the French cinema.

Eric Rohmer's romantic fables are far removed from Truffaut's charming rambles, each one a carefully thought out "moral tale" on the virtues and deficits of man's free will. A student of Pascal, Jean-Louis Trintignant found that rolling himself in a blanket protected him from the wiles of Françoise Fabian during **My Night at Maude's,** and the cinema really has no parallel for Jean-Claude Brialy's odd obsession in **Claire's Knee.** Rohmer's series ended with **Chloe in the Afternoon,** but these delightfully discursive Gallic puzzles lead us to expect more from the screen's sole romantic philosopher.

One characteristic genre of sixties comedy that was not romantically based, but existed on the fringes of the spy and detective cycles, was the caper film. These usually involved a group of amateurs (or bumbling semi-professionals) who decide to pull off an inevitably supercomplicated heist of some sort. Although preceded by such fifties films as the French **Rififi,** the British **The Lavender Hill Mob,** and the Italian **Big Deal on Madonna Street** (one of the funniest films ever made), caper films did not begin to flood the market until Jules

Dassin updated his earlier **Rififi** as **Topkapi** (1964). Spurred by the vogue for such comparatively straight James Bond adventures as **Goldfinger,** the series included **How to Steal a Million** (William Wyler), **Who's Minding the Mint?, Dollars, The Hot Rock,** and probably the best of the lot, **The Sting.** As this genre went into the seventies, the schemes became so complicated that they could be justified only by centering on professional con artists like George C. Scott **(The Flim-Flam Man),** Ryan and Tatum O'Neal **(Paper Moon),** and Paul Newman and Robert Redford **(The Sting),** once again driving the amateurs out of the movie-caper business.

But perhaps the most characteristic element of the late sixties humor was a mixture of black comedy and screwball comedy that stemmed from the success of Stanley Kubrick's **Dr. Strangelove** (a film that originally ended with a gigantic pie fight, just too outrageous even for Kubrick, it seems). Sickness, death, war, and nuclear annihilation were the main elements of humor. **The Loved One** was a satire on the Forest Lawn type of mortuary, while **The Hospital** got in a few digs at the medical profession. The same kind of doctor jokes found their way into **M*A*S*H,** with Donald Sutherland and Elliott Gould having a ball while attached to a mobile*army*surgical*hospital during the Korean War. Sort of a bloody Sergeant Bilko. The great black comedy hope of the sixties, Mike Nichols's **Catch-22,** unfortunately got lost in its budget and shooting schedule, and never did find an adequate means of translating Joseph Heller's novel to screen terms. A similar disappointment was Alan Arkin's inauspicious debut as the director of **Little Murders.** This film of Jules Feiffer's nightmare New York is a good example of something coming along exactly one year too late for any sort of success.

An entry in the bad-taste sweepstakes was **Harold and Maude,** with Bud Cort as a young lad who stages mock suicides and tools around Southern California in his hearse. The tasteless slapstick of this school had a sexual parallel in the grotesque **Myra Breckinridge,** in which Mae West, Raquel Welch, and Rex Reed uneasily vied for screen time (although Richard Benjamin's single-handed efforts in **Portnoy's Complaint** deserve at least a footnote in any history of bad-taste humor). **Portnoy's Complaint** seemed like such appallingly bad taste largely because it was, unlike the best-selling novel on which it was based, so relentlessly witless and heavy-handed. Director-adapter Ernest Lehman deserves the blame for this comedy-disaster.

But the blackest period of this cycle seems to have passed, reaching its peak along with the youth and protest films in the early seventies. Contemporary audiences line up for the gentle chicanery of **The Sting,** the neurotic self-deprecation of Woody Allen, or the outright buffoonery of manic Mel Brooks's spoof, **Blazing Saddles.** The comedy film has retreated from the barricades of social comment it had scaled a few brief years ago to a much more subtle form of commentary: that sly exposure of human foibles more typical of the work of Frank Tashlin or Preston Sturges—or even Charlie Chaplin.

Woody Allen's screen image continues to develop in the films he himself has directed. **Bananas** (1971, far l), and **Sleeper** (1974, l), were two of the most successful, and even in this short time span Woody's comedy style can be seen taking a dark turn. **Sleeper** is loaded with bitter observations about the futility of political action, the meaningless qualities of art, and the lack of satisfaction in human relationships. In short, a comedy right on target, aimed at the seventies.

WAR

"Military views" of troops and cavalry on maneuvers were popular in the first Lumière catalogues, but true war films did not arrive until the Spanish-American War of 1898. Albert E. Smith and J. Stuart Blackton of the Vitagraph Company filmed the charge up San Juan Hill while actually on location in Cuba, but had no compunctions about staging the battle of Santiago Bay in a New York bathtub. Smith turned the crank while Mrs. Blackton puffed smoke into the lens and her husband manipulated the bobbing paper cutouts of the battle fleet. Such phony newsreel footage was accepted in all innocence by an undemanding public, and American producers soon offered the Boer War as shot in New Jersey and the Russo-Japanese War restaged at Verbeck's Japanese Gardens in Manlius, New York.

The early story film found war backgrounds effective, though expensive, variations on standard plots. D. W. Griffith's early one-reelers contain a number of Civil War titles that served as sketches for his more important work later on. **The Battle** (1911) is one of the finest of these, a film that won the praise of poet Vachel Lindsay, one of the few supporters of the early films. Thomas Ince produced many films on similar Civil War themes, among them **The Coward** with Charles Ray, but it was Griffith's **The Birth of a Nation** (1915) that first startled movie audiences with the drama of massed columns and the panoramic sweep of smoke-filled battlescapes. Not only were his Civil War sequences staged in a grand manner (with technical assistance from Union and Confederate veterans), but they benefited from Billy Bitzer's careful attempt to reproduce the look of Mathew Brady's Civil War photographs. It was the skill of Griffith's direction and Bitzer's camera work that added life to these huge panoramas, a finesse that was lacking in the equally ambitious **The Crisis,** produced by Selig the following year, where the scope of the battle scenes far outstripped the abilities of the director. But by then the real war had emerged as a topic of more immediate importance. Indeed, Griffith found that war shortages had largely dried up his supplies of horses and gunpowder and the fabric needed to make Ku Klux Klan robes.

After making **Intolerance,** a passionate antiwar statement, he was commissioned by the British government to make the official epic of the war. He combined material shot at the front with staged Hollywood footage for **Hearts of the World,** which turned out to be one of his better films. It cleverly centered on the lives of a few small-town types caught up in the German advance, and Griffith's images of the impact of great forces on little people were never more skillful. Although an antiwar strain permeated most of America's early World War I films, this was soon turned into anti-Hun sentiment as German brutality came to typify war's horrors. Soon the war against the Kaiser was being pictured as a nearly divine crusade. Erich von Stroheim often played the hated enemy whose new order seemed a deadly moral threat to all of Western Civilization. Harassing civilians, forcing his lecherous attentions on palpitating heroines, this new-style villain soon dominated American war films.

Preceding pages:
Warner Baxter and Fredric March
in **The Road to Glory** (1936),
one of the best antiwar films of
the thirties. Howard Hawks directed.
Opposite, top left: D. W. Griffith
on location in France, 1917,
during shooting of battlefront
footage for **Hearts of the World,**
his wartime propaganda feature.
Top right: A realistic trench scene
from King Vidor's **The Big Parade**
(1925), the first cool reappraisal
of America's war experience.
Below: Dolores Del Rio in a
reflective moment from Raoul Walsh's
What Price Glory? (1926).

The fascination with the Great War reached its peak around the time of the introduction of sound. **Lilac Time,** above, was a 1928 Colleen Moore film that still stands as the romantic apotheosis of the air-war cycle. Here Miss Moore rescues Gary Cooper from his downed fighter. Much more grim was **The Dawn Patrol** (opposite), directed by Howard Hawks in 1930, and indicative of the growing pacifist strain in war films. But the greatest of the early antiwar films was Lewis Milestone's **All Quiet on the Western Front** (r), a large-scale epic which also marked a major artistic advance for the early sound film (1930).

In comparison with him, home-grown heroes seemed dull and insipid in such films as **The Heart of Humanity, The Unbeliever,** and **The Hun Within.** The high point of this cycle was reached in 1918 when Carl Laemmle presented Rupert Julian as **The Kaiser, The Beast of Berlin.**

After the Armistice, interest in war films abruptly ceased, for their success had largely been the result of patriotic fervor and audiences were heartily sick of their forced clichés and stereotypical villains. It was not until 1925 that war films returned to the screen in a viable new format. True, films like **The Four Horsemen of the Apocalypse** incorporated a war theme, and Griffith had filmed the Revolution in **America,** but these films were rare examples. King Vidor's **The Big Parade** first established the new pattern with a seemingly dispassionate account of the war in France as seen by three "typical" American recruits, who reacted to it in a much more realistic fashion than the heroes of the earlier films. Its astonishing success (after **The Birth of a Nation** it was the top-grossing silent film) brought on the first peacetime wave of war films. The most important was Raoul Walsh's **What Price Glory?,** an adaptation of a stage play, important not so much for its strong language (which was apparent only to lip-readers) but for its implicit antiwar message. The "glory" was ironically dimmed as each day's heroics filled Flagg and Quirt's trenches with a pile of broken minds and bodies. The film had several sequels, notably Walsh's **The Cockeyed World,** in which friendly enemies Victor McLaglen and Edmund Lowe continued their adventures while battling South American insurgents for Uncle Sam's Marines.

The interwar activities of the U.S. Marines also were featured in Frank Capra's **Flight,** in which air power turns the tide of battle against Central American guerrillas, and George Hill's **Tell It to the Marines,** in which the hero attacks a band of Chinese devils with the cry, "That's for all the punk chop suey I got in Omaha!" Most of the films looked back at the Great War, however. Richard Barthelmess in **The Patent Leather Kid** and Gary Cooper and Colleen Moore in **Lilac Time** presented a nostalgic image of the more romantic aspects of the war, divorced from its grubby realities. One of the more artistic attempts at the war theme was Rex Ingram's **Mare Nostrum,** in which the director of **The Four Horsemen** dealt with Mata Hari-style spy plots in some fabulous Mediterranean locations.

But while many of these films included sops to antiwar sentiment, they chose to investigate the war solely on the grounds of spectacle and romance, something that was especially true of **Wings** and other aviation epics at the end of the twenties. Directed by William Wellman, a veteran of the Lafayette Escadrille who quickly followed up with **The Legion of the Condemned** and **Young Eagles, Wings** gave audiences their first real taste of the speed and excitement of the war in the air. These films saw the war as a conflict between aerial knights with a special chivalric code, and referred to the war itself only as the abstract excuse for their aerial ballets. Life at the front was a

Opposite: In 1937 Jean Renoir's **La Grande Illusion** (top l) marked one of the last efforts of the antiwar cycle. Pierre Fresnay and Erich von Stroheim starred. By 1941 **Sergeant York,** with Gary Cooper, (top r) taught that pacifism should be subordinated to patriotism. More ironic was **Thirty Seconds Over Tokyo** (1944, below), scripted by Dalton Trumbo, author of the antiwar classic, **Johnny Got His Gun.**

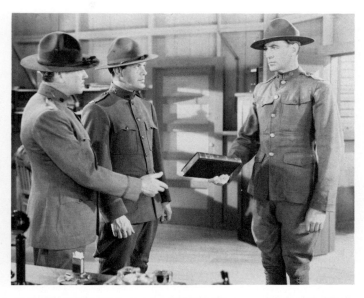

World War II battle action in
full swing. Top: The British
naval classic, **In Which We Serve**
(1942), directed by Noël Coward
and David Lean. Above: John Wayne
in Allan Dwan's **The Sands of Iwo Jima**
(1949). Opposite: John Garfield
in **Pride of the Marines** (1945),
part of the all-ethnic platoon cycle.

European directors returned to antiwar themes in a series of powerful postwar films. From Poland (far l), Andrzej Wajda's **Kanal** (1961). From Italy (l), Vittorio De Sica's **Two Women** (1961), with Eleanora Brown and Sophia Loren. Miss Loren won an Oscar for her role here, although her voice was dubbed in most American prints. From Germany (above), Klaus Hager in Bernhard Wicki's **The Bridge** (1957), a story of children at war.

series of elaborate rituals honoring departed comrades and all-night binges in the local bistro. But Howard Hughes's **Hell's Angels** pointed the way to the more thoughtful attitudes of the thirties. It featured the most impressive special effects yet seen—zeppelin raids on London, midair plane crashes, and daring daylight bombing runs—yet a very downbeat theme emerged from all this spectacle. The idea of dying for your country is at first introduced as a noble concept, but as the film wears on it becomes more and more absurd, the enormity of the carnage underlining the senselessness of these acts. At one climactic point a crew dutifully jumps to its death just to lighten a crippled dirigible. In Great Britain this theme was developed even more strongly in **Tell England,** a chilling re-creation of the Gallipoli invasion, one of England's bloodiest blunders of the war. Spurred by the stage and screen success of **Journey's End,** the thirties swarmed with pacifist works in all media, and the cinema produced its share. **All Quiet on the Western Front** was the most important of these, so effective on the screen that its producer, Carl Laemmle, Jr., was nominated for the Nobel Peace Prize. One of the more imaginative of early sound films, **All Quiet** was recognized as a landmark achievement by critics and audiences alike. But as seen today the film is only a shadow of its former self, having been recut and reissued so many times that even the studio has no remaining copies of the original version. (One may exist, well preserved, in some private collection.)

The antiwar trend moved around the globe, and even such directors as Germany's G. W. Pabst contributed important examples like **Westfront, 1918.** The aerial heroism of just a few years earlier was deflated in **The Eagle and the Hawk,** which starred Fredric March as a nerve-shattered air ace who commits suicide at the front. March returned in Howard Hawks's **The Road to Glory,** where Warner Baxter must send his troop on a suicide mission—a knotty problem, since his aged father is one of the recruits. Hemingway's **A Farewell to Arms** was brilliantly brought to the screen by Frank Borzage, although somewhat romanticized by the screen adaptation and by Charles Lang's lush cinematography. Ernst Lubitsch entered the field with **Broken Lullaby,** the story of a young soldier who pays a visit to the family of the German soldier he killed during the war. By the mid-thirties all war themes were dying out and the genre was only sporadically represented by such films as John Ford's **The Lost Patrol** or William Dieterle's **Blockade,** Hollywood's only attempt to deal with the Spanish Civil War. As the possibility of another war grew more likely, films opposing war became scarcer. The last and greatest of this thirties line stands nearly alone, Jean Renoir's **La Grande Illusion.** Intended to bring the French and German people closer together, to make them realize their common interests and forget the artificial border which separates them, the film was banned in Germany and suppressed in several other countries (not just the expected ones, either).

When World War II actually began, the first combat films were considerably out of touch with reality. In Britain Carol Reed's **Night Train** emerged as an old-fashioned melodrama in the Hitchcock style, while such films as Thorold Dickinson's **Next of Kin** seemed almost defeatist in their view of a vast web of Nazi spies and fifth columnists. In America **I Wanted Wings** and **Dive Bomber** appeared as extensions of the earlier aviation cycle, showing army life as consisting mainly of romantic aerial adventure. But after Pearl Harbor the classic type of war film quickly appeared. The first Hollywood film of the new war was **Wake Island,** with Brian Donlevy holding off the Japs while gaining time for the rest of us to mobilize. A story of heroism in defeat, **Wake Island** realistically ends with the Americans being wiped out, a particularly chilling climax at a time when the war was not going very well. It set the tone for most of the battle-action films to come, a cycle centered mainly on the Pacific theater where most of the American fighting was taking place. **Bataan, Back to Bataan, Guadalcanal Diary,** and **Objective Burma** were among the best of these, with the air war covered in **Thirty Seconds Over Tokyo** and **Air Force,** submarine service in **Destination Tokyo,** and PT-boat squadrons in **They Were Expendable,** probably the finest of all battle-action films. A 1945 release, it shares with **A Walk in the Sun** that same feeling of mature reflection which allows it to concentrate on the people involved instead of merely toeing the line of patriotic propaganda. Films concentrating less on actual combat included **The Story of G.I. Joe,** with Burgess Meredith as war correspondent Ernie Pyle, and **Sergeant York,** the biography of the World War I hero who found fighting his conscience more demanding than fighting the Germans. One of the most interesting films to emerge from the war was Lewis Milestone's **The Purple Heart,** in which Dana Andrews and his bomber crew are captured by the Japanese and tried as war criminals for their raid on Tokyo!

While the war in the Pacific provided most of the battle themes, films on resistance and activities behind the enemy lines centered mostly on the European theater. **The Seventh Cross** dealt with escapees from a prewar German concentration camp, while **Man Hunt** featured Walter Pidgeon and his high-powered rifle on the trail of Adolf Hitler. Franchot Tone ran into General Rommel in **Five Graves to Cairo,** with Erich von Stroheim again playing the enemy Hun, but the classic film of American agents behind the lines was Raoul Walsh's **Desperate Journey,** in which Errol Flynn and his crew try to return to England after being shot down on a bombing run. After making fools of Raymond Massey and the German high command, Flynn steals a plane and flies back across the Channel with the stirring cry, "Now for the Pacific and a crack at those Japs!"

Of course, they were behind our lines as well, even as early as **Confessions of a Nazi Spy,** produced before the war. Spies seemed all over London in **Ministry of Fear** and New York in **The House on 92nd Street,** but most of them were rounded up by the last reel. The activities of local resistance groups were also popular topics, and Bertolt Brecht is supposed to have contributed to the script of Fritz Lang's **Hangmen Also Die,** a story of the Czech

Darryl F. Zanuck saved the Fox Studio in 1962 with **The Longest Day** (top), which he completely supervised in classic Hollywood fashion. Bernhard Wicki was one of the directors. The nostalgic idealization of the war in this film and in others like it was attacked in Richard Lester's surrealistic spoof, **How I Won the War** (1967) with John Lennon.

underground after the assassination of Reinhard Heydrich, the ruthless Nazi overlord. The Yugoslavian underground was idealized in Fox's **Chetniks,** and the Russians in **The North Star** and **Song of Russia,** films which caused their makers considerable embarrassment during the McCarthy era.

Again there was a relieved cessation of war films immediately after the war was over, but Allan Dwan's **The Sands of Iwo Jima** began the nostalgic revival as early as 1949. Although John Wayne doesn't raise the flag on Mount Suribachi in this film, he hands it to the marines who do. The fact that he is shot and killed for his efforts seemed extraordinary enough to win Wayne an Oscar nomination, his first. **Twelve O'Clock High**, which evoked the bygone world of daylight bombing runs, concentrated on the emotional tensions involved. At the same time, **The Desert Fox** turned General Rommel into a hero, probably the sublime example of Hollywood's speed in revising history.

Fritz Lang contributed **An American Guerrilla in the Philippines,** but now Korea provided a new war and a new enemy. Unlike earlier wars, Korea did not induce a great wave of patriotic battle films. Sam Fuller's **The Steel Helmet** and **Fixed Bayonets** were about the best of a meager lot; postwar efforts like **The Naked and the Dead** or **Pork Chop Hill** were able to investigate the activities of men under pressure with a cooler perspective. The fifties provided its share of World War II films as well, the superclassics being David Lean's **The Bridge on the River Kwai** and Fred Zinnemann's **From Here to Eternity** (although a closely related minor film, Walsh's **The Revolt of Mamie Stover,** also bears consideration). An occasional film like **Heaven Knows, Mr. Allison** used the war as the background for a particular dramatic situation, but straight battle films, like Robert Aldrich's brilliant **Attack!,** were more common. There were halfhearted attempts at antiwar themes, such as the film of Erich Maria Remarque's story, **A Time to Love and a Time to Die** (1958), but the Cold War period was not ripe for such efforts. Stanley Kubrick's brilliant **Paths of Glory**—a powerful antiwar story about the French army during World War I—won critical praise but did not have the audience success it deserved. Even such vaunted European antiwar films as Andrzej Wajda's **Kanal** (Polish) or Grigori Chukhrai's **Ballad of a Soldier** (Russian) were far from the polemics of the best thirties films. Perhaps only Bernhard Wicki's **The Bridge** lived up to the earlier standard, the grim, deeply moving story of a group of boys defending a bridge in the last days of the Reich.

In the sixties one of the standard themes of the classic war film vanished completely, the simple story of men under pressure in the most deadly of situations. The resurgence of interest that did occur was limited to large-scale spectacles and antiwar films with a black comedy touch. The giant war films of the sixties were produced on a scale that rivaled the war itself. The D-Day landings were scrupulously restaged with an all-star cast in **The Longest Day** (1962), but its box-office success was not repeated by the tedious 1970 flop **Tora! Tora! Tora!**, the story of the Pearl Harbor attack. A Japanese-American co-

The Vietnam War spawned just one major Hollywood effort, John Wayne's production of **The Green Berets** (1968), adapted from Robin Moore's book. A good director of action films (he also made **The Alamo**), Wayne directed it himself, with some help from Ray Kellogg and Mervyn LeRoy. Army officials were later criticized for the amount of material loaned out for the film. Here, Wayne calls in more advisers.

When Code restrictions were
eased at the close of the sixties,
war films immediately grew much
more graphic. Robert Aldrich's
The Dirty Dozen (1967, above),
with Lee Marvin, set the standard
for them. Right: A great success
with both pro- and antiwar forces,
Franklin Schaffner's **Patton** (1970)
combined an incisive biographical
portrait with spectacular
re-creations of armored clashes.
George C. Scott refused his Oscar.

240

production, it was the most important of a group of films whose production was so international that they often united former enemies. The Italians and the Russians worked together on **Italiano Brava Gente** (starring Peter Falk!), while **The Night of the Generals** was filmed in Poland, **The Battle of Neretva** in Yugoslavia, and **The Bridge at Remagen** in Czechoslovakia. This last film proved co-production a risky undertaking, as the filmmakers had to abandon most of their equipment and flee the country during the Soviet invasion of 1968.

The war film as spectacular caper movie was brightly launched with **The Guns of Navarone** and was inevitably followed by such imitative films as **The Heroes of Telemark** and **Where Eagles Dare.** Robert Aldrich took the caper idea, loaded it down with violence, and produced **The Dirty Dozen,** important as a landmark film in the violence cycle of the late sixties. Although occasional films like John Boorman's **Hell in the Pacific** tried to re-create the classic tensions of the genre, it was swamped by such overproduced spectacles as **PT-109, In Harm's Way,** and **The Battle of the Bulge.** The gigantic war spectacular was so difficult to control that only a few films like **Patton** managed to avoid its booby traps and create a meaningful statement about war and the men who make war. This gigantism even struck overseas where the Soviet's monumental **War and Peace** emerged as the most expensive film ever made,

In 1970 two major antiwar comedies appeared to widely differing receptions. Mike Nichols's **Catch-22** (l), with Alan Arkin, was ignored by audiences and panned by critics. However, **M*A*S*H** (below), made the reputation of director Robert Altman and stars Elliott Gould and Donald Sutherland. Supposedly set in the Korean War, the locale seems more like a creation of Altman's vivid imagination.

coming in for an even one hundred million dollars—not rubles. This remarkable remaking of the Tolstoy classic was directed by Sergei Bondarchuk over a four-year period from 1964 to 1967, and ran almost six hours when it was initially released in two parts.

The Vietnam War produced not a wave of war films (John Wayne's simplistic drivel, **The Green Berets,** was the only visible entry), but the strongest antiwar reaction in thirty years. Period films were found to be a useful vehicle for this expression, so **The Charge of the Light Brigade** exposed the blundering of the Crimean campaign (and the heroics of the Errol Flynn version) and **Oh! What a Lovely War** attacked the carnival-like atmosphere surrounding the legend of World War I. The Vietnam War, it seems interesting to remember, was never attacked directly, only through "interpretations" of films about the Crimean War or Korea. Dalton Trumbo brought his 1939 novel "Johnny Got His Gun" to the screen (an odd antiwar statement from the writer of **Thirty Seconds Over Tokyo**) and Richard Lester directed John Lennon in **How I Won the War.** But neither of these films attracted much of an audience. People lined up instead for films like **M*A*S*H,** which gave them morbid jokes along with a hefty slice of violence and blood, and was set in the rather fuzzy historical context of Korea. It made a terrific program on a double bill with **Patton.**

THE MUSICAL

Preceding pages:
Al Jolson spoke in
The Jazz Singer (1927), but
mostly he just sang. Talkie
revolution was designed to exploit
music, and "all singing, all
dancing" quickly became the rage.
Studios turned out lavish
musical reviews, of which MGM's
Hollywood Revue of 1929,
above, was typical. But vogue
for overstuffed variety shows
was brief. Music had to be
integrated into well-developed
narrative, something Rouben
Mamoulian did in **Applause** (1929, r),
starring Helen Morgan.

Early research in sound film by the major studios was intended not to develop talking pictures but to exploit certain elements of music and sound effects. A canned music-and-effects score was carried on Warner Brothers' **Don Juan** in 1926, and the following year **The Jazz Singer** contained not only songs, but patches of dialogue as well. Musical stories instantly became the dominant screen mode when producers saw that even so poor a film as **The Singing Fool** was outgrossing the top spectacles of the silent screen.

Musical mania also spread to dramatic films, and major silent stars like Mary Pickford and Richard Barthelmess had to "sing" in their first talkie appearances. Dramatic stories set against musical backgrounds, like Universal's **Broadway** or MGM's **The Broadway Melody,** became elaborate excuses for lengthy musical numbers. Revues were borrowed directly from the stage, and Ziegfeld, for one, contributed **Rio Rita, Whoopee,** and **Glorifying the American Girl.** Many of these gaudy productions were filmed in the early Technicolor process, thus giving rise to the "all talking, all singing, all color" catchlines of the ads for early musicals. The revue formula reached its peak when Paul Whiteman and his orchestra were imported for **The King of Jazz.** Soon Hollywood began to develop its patented movie-musical format. Ernst Lubitsch's **The Love Parade,** with Jeanette MacDonald and Maurice Chevalier, and **Monte Carlo,** with MacDonald and Jack Buchanan, first established the light and glossy texture that became the hallmark of the Hollywood musical. In Europe at the same time René Clair was filming **Sous les Toits de Paris** and **À Nous la Liberté,** experiments in the stylized use of music and sound which went even farther than Lubitsch's early work.

But by 1931 the public was sick of musicals and deserted them en masse. They were reacting to such awful junk as **Golden Dawn,** a racist operetta by Otto Harbach and Oscar Hammerstein set in German East Africa and featuring Noah Beery as a native chieftain! Expensive productions like MGM's **The March of Time,** a revue featuring many of the top vaudeville stars, was shelved and never released. Rouben Mamoulian's brilliant **Love Me To-night** vanished into this void in 1932.

In 1933 Warner Brothers decided the time was ripe for a new kind of musical. A strong dramatic story about the birth of a Broadway show, **42nd Street,** was handled in Warners' usual realistic manner, a far cry from the fairy-tale romantic style of many of the earlier musicals. To stage the dance numbers they hired Busby Berkeley, a Broadway dance director who had been brought out to Hollywood to work on **Whoopee** three years before. Now he was given an enormous budget and told to stage numbers like nothing ever seen before. He did. Berkeley's famous Warner musicals of the Dick Powell, Ruby Keeler, and Joan Blondell cycle were masterpieces of artifice, pure filmic creations which laughed at the puny stages supposed to contain them. In numbers like "By a Waterfall" **(Footlight Parade),** "I Only Have Eyes for You" **(Dames),** and "Lullaby of Broadway" **(Gold Diggers of 1933),** Berkeley used his camera

First master of Hollywood
musical was Ernst Lubitsch, who,
in films like **The Love Parade**
(above), developed popular new
operetta style. Maurice Chevalier
and Jeanette MacDonald were
stars of the 1929 hit. In 1933,
Warner Brothers unleashed
Busby Berkeley, who subordinated
his stars to nightmarish
musical numbers like **42nd Street**
routine (r) with Ruby Keeler.

248

and cutting shears to create imaginary spaces and fantasy action of night-marish proportion. After getting the first chorus of the title song out of the way, his stars were quickly disposed of, cut into hundreds of paper dolls, or even pushed out of windows. What Berkeley was really interested in was shooting through dozens of thighs or zeroing in on scores of pretty faces. The dancers in a Berkeley number were quickly reduced to the sum of their parts.

On the heels of the Berkeley films was RKO's musical series with Fred Astaire and Ginger Rogers. Not only could Fred and Ginger sing and dance, they could also act, and the charm of films like **Swing Time** and **Top Hat** emerges just as strongly in the nonmusical episodes. Astaire would not stand for fragmentation in the Berkeley style and insisted on being photographed full length in all his numbers. As a dancer he marked off a given area—whether a ballroom or a bedroom—and devised a dance to fit that particular space, carefully choreographing it for the camera. Astaire's easy elegance was perfectly matched by RKO's production style, with shimmering staircases and floors polished to mirror brilliance that he and Ginger danced on in numbers like "The Continental."

Throughout the thirties Hollywood attempted to borrow musical stars from the stage, and even the opera, in an effort to to add ready-made class to their musical productions. Lawrence Tibbett had a limited success very early on, but not until Grace Moore appeared in **One Night of Love** did the floodgates open for the operatic invasion. Lily Pons, Gladys Swarthout, and Kirsten Flagstad were only a few of the recruits, but their talents were seldom used very intelligently. Flagstad, for example, had to vie for screen time with Shep Fields and his Rippling Rhythm Orchestra in **The Big Broadcast of 1938.** A related phenomenon was one that combined highbrow singing with the vogue for child stars, and used such performers as Deanna Durbin. Her musicals for Universal, like **Three Smart Girls** and **One Hundred Men and a Girl,** kept the doors of that studio open during the lean years of the late thirties. Durbin's first screen appearance was in a 1936 MGM short called **Every Sunday,** in which she was co-featured with the young Judy Garland. One of the many Louis B. Mayer stories has it that when contract renewal time came up, Mayer screened the film, didn't like Garland, and said, "Drop the fat one." Durbin was fired by mistake, and thus wound up at Universal.

At this same time Jeanette MacDonald made a spectacular comeback as a star of the new operetta style. After early success in films like **The Love Parade** and **The Vagabond King,** she had faded in popularity. But with the surge of operatic interest in the mid-thirties she returned to establish her reputation firmly as "the Iron Butterfly." With Chevalier in **The Merry Widow,** with Clark Gable and an earthquake in **San Francisco,** she again became a big box-office attraction. Her popular series with Nelson Eddy included **Naughty Marietta, Rose Marie,** and **Maytime,** in which they sang such classics as "Ah, Sweet Mystery of Life," "The Indian Love Call," and "Tramp! Tramp! Tramp!"

Berkeley's musical constructions were imaginative, dynamic, and dehumanized. Leads as well as chorus line were reduced to bits and pieces of a complex cinematic collage, and new levels of reality were created through camera and cutting tricks. Berkeley thus had no need for really talented singers and dancers, and usually worked with such amiables as Dick Powell and Ruby Keeler, seen here in **Gold Diggers of 1933.**

When given a really fine dancer
like James Cagney (l) in
Footlight Parade (1933), Berkeley
adjusted his style slightly.
But he seemed to prefer
choreographing a hundred pianos
in films like **Gold Diggers of 1933**
(r). Below: Fred Astaire and Ginger
Rogers made dancers once again
the focal point of the musical
number. Astaire insisted on
being photographed full length,
reacting against the
"dancing feet" montages of
the Berkeley films. This is
a rehearsal shot from **Top Hat**
(1935), one of his best.

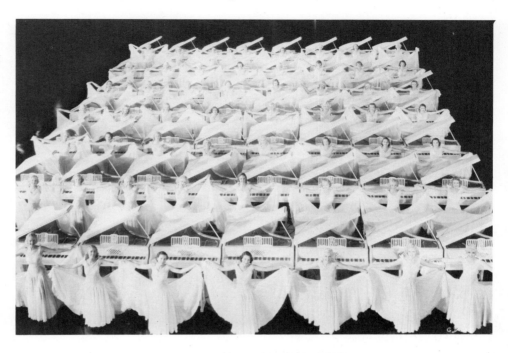

Audiences began to lose interest in such star vehicles by World War II, and a fresh approach seemed needed. At MGM the former lyricist Arthur Freed, who had written such songs as "Singin' in the Rain" and "You Are My Lucky Star," moved into production and began to gather around him a new circle of talent, chosen largely from the New York theater and dance world. Freed had a healthy respect for the story values of the musical, and emphasized them in a revolutionary way. His most important catch was Vincente Minnelli, who had directed Broadway musicals as well as Radio City Music Hall production numbers. Minnelli is the master stylist of the musical, a believer in the power of color, movement, and design to transform even the flimsiest material. He proved this well with **Cabin in the Sky** and **Ziegfeld Follies,** fashioning numbers that dazzled our eyes before our minds had much chance to think about them, the work of a master filmic illusionist. But when given the stronger material more typical of Freed, Minnelli was really at his best, combining the natural joyousness of the musical with a downbeat flavor of his own (which can be seen most clearly in his nonmusicals, films like **The Bad and the Beautiful** and **Lust for Life**). Leaving St. Louis behind is a real tragedy for Judy Garland's family in **Meet Me in St. Louis,** while in **The Band Wagon** Fred Astaire contemplates life in the moody "I'll Go My Way by Myself" number. **An American in Paris** is perhaps the best example of the schizophrenic Minnelli musical, luxurious and exuberant on the outside, but downright depressing on the inside. Minnelli was well suited to Freed's taste for "high class" musicals, and nowhere is this seen better than in the elaborate ballet routines of **Yolanda and the Thief, An American in Paris,** and **The Band Wagon,** expensive and rather overserious attempts to compose a new style of ballet for the cinema. But all this seriousness is balanced off by **The Pirate,** a glistening tribute to show business capped by Gene Kelly and Garland's classic "Be a Clown" routine.

A less serious version of Minnelli's musicals was provided by Stanley Donen, whose **Singin' in the Rain** is a grand show, though it lacks the unifying dramatic vision which Minnelli might have given it. **On the Town** and **Seven Brides for Seven Brothers** are much the same story, lots of sparkle and movement, but lacking something at the core. **Funny Face,** with Astaire and Audrey Hepburn, is a good example of this, although here for once is a film that really does succeed on color, design, and star presence alone.

While one can easily talk about MGM's musicals, Twentieth Century-Fox's contribution defeats analysis and must be seen to be appreciated. Alice Faye singing "This Year's Kisses" in **On the Avenue** or Betty Grable romping through **Pin Up Girl, Moon Over Miami,** or **Springtime in the Rockies** cannot easily be summed up in a paragraph (not to mention Carmen Miranda, who easily requires a volume of her own). Fox emphasized popular stars instead of stories and directors, and sex appeal rather than the broader family appeal of Louis B. Mayer's pictures. Astaire was a better dancer, but by the time of Pearl Harbor Betty Grable was bigger box office.

After Lubitsch, Berkeley, and Astaire, the other musicals of the period seem more prosaic.
Top left: Joan Crawford in **Dancing Lady** (1933). Astaire made his film debut in a small part here.
Right: Deanna Durbin in **One Hundred Men and a Girl** (1937), in which Leopold Stokowski was her co-star.
Below: Nelson Eddy and Jeanette MacDonald in **Maytime** (1937), perhaps the best of their very popular MGM series.

One thing that does unite most of the forties musicals is their use of Technicolor, now developed into a lush and almost overripe process. In Busby Berkeley's **The Gang's All Here,** an otherwise standard Fox wartime musical, he used color to transcend the wildest of his Warner Brothers dreams. Shooting through a Technicolor kaleidoscope, Berkeley broke his dancers into abstract color patterns, not even recognizable as arms or legs. Successfully reissued in the seventies, the film found its strongest support among college students and filmmakers, stunned not only by Berkeley's control of form and color but also by the inane story he was able to append these numbers to.

One trend in the postwar musical, particularly in the fifties, was the biographical film. The thirties had produced **The Great Ziegfeld** with William Powell, as well as Julien Duvivier's delightful biography of Johann Strauss, **The Great Waltz.** And in 1942 James Cagney appeared in perhaps the most admired of all musical biographies, **Yankee Doodle Dandy,** the biography of George M. Cohan. When Cornell Wilde appeared in **A Song to Remember** in 1945, the film's popularity pushed Chopin to the top of the best-seller charts. The lives of classical composers were often filmed in Europe—Mozart, Beethoven, Handel, among others—but Hollywood usually found such material hard to handle. ("Schubert, when are you going to complete your 'Unfinished Symphony' . . .?") Popular composers, singers, and musicians offered the easiest excuse to jam a lot of songs together with a thinly developed, often melodramatic, story line. Tyrone Power had played a fictionalized Irving Berlin in **Alexander's Ragtime Band** before the war, but in the wake of **A Song to Remember,** the full treatment was accorded George Gershwin (**Rhapsody in Blue**) and Cole Porter (**Night and Day**). These were more to the American taste than watching Paul Henreid and Katharine Hepburn as Mr. and Mrs. Robert Schumann in **Song of Love.**

Early Judy Garland (top) in MGM's **The Wizard of Oz** (1939), with Jack Haley, Ray Bolger, Frank Morgan, and Bert Lahr. A delightful, if somewhat garish, version of L. Frank Baum's classic. Right: With Margaret O'Brien in **Meet Me in St. Louis** (1944), an evocation of the ideal family and ideal America. Directed by Vincente Minnelli, this is one of the high points of MGM's golden age.

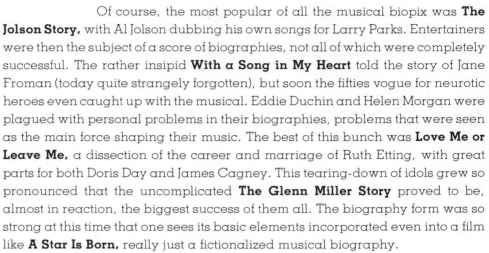

Opposite: The many faces of the Hollywood dance routine. Top: Harriet Hoctor between the lions in MGM's **The Great Ziegfeld** (1936). Below left: Gene Kelly and friends in mid-leap on **Singin' in the Rain** (1952), directed by Kelly and Stanley Donen. Bottom left: Donen's **Seven Brides for Seven Brothers** (1954), with a very energetic Russ Tamblyn. Below right: Betty Grable and Cesar Romero in a graceful moment from **Springtime in the Rockies** (1942). This page: Judy Garland in George Cukor's **A Star Is Born** (1954), the peak of her career.

Of course, the most popular of all the musical biopix was **The Jolson Story,** with Al Jolson dubbing his own songs for Larry Parks. Entertainers were then the subject of a score of biographies, not all of which were completely successful. The rather insipid **With a Song in My Heart** told the story of Jane Froman (today quite strangely forgotten), but soon the fifties vogue for neurotic heroes even caught up with the musical. Eddie Duchin and Helen Morgan were plagued with personal problems in their biographies, problems that were seen as the main force shaping their music. The best of this bunch was **Love Me or Leave Me,** a dissection of the career and marriage of Ruth Etting, with great parts for both Doris Day and James Cagney. This tearing-down of idols grew so pronounced that the uncomplicated **The Glenn Miller Story** proved to be, almost in reaction, the biggest success of them all. The biography form was so strong at this time that one sees its basic elements incorporated even into a film like **A Star Is Born,** really just a fictionalized musical biography.

But Hollywood ran out of life stories by the sixties, and blockbuster stage adaptations took up most of its time and money. The failure of **Star!**, the elaborately mounted biography of Gertrude Lawrence, seemed to show the danger of writing such new material for the screen. Then two films appeared to alter this idea: Ken Russell's **The Music Lovers** revived the classical-composer genre through the judicious use of stylistic pyrotechnics, and Diana Ross made a great personal hit in the Billie Holliday story, **Lady Sings the Blues.** Riding the strong wave of black films, **Lady** took advantage of liberalized contemporary production strictures to get to the heart of Billie Holliday's career, something the well-intentioned but handicapped films of the fifties could never have done.

Although generally shying away from original musical material, there is one new form that has surfaced in the past decade, that of the rock musical. Starting with the Beatles' films **A Hard Day's Night** and **Help!,** they quickly pulled away from the standard Hollywood format and approached that of the revue. Most of the early Liverpool groups were featured in one or two such films, the underground classic being John Boorman's **Catch Us If You Can** with the Dave Clark Five. More recently following the lead of the Beatles' **Let It Be** and the Rolling Stones' **Sympathy for the Devil** (directed by Godard!), the trend has been to pure concert films. The apotheosis of these is the three-hour **Woodstock,** Michael Wadleigh's multi-imaged celebration of the first of the great rock festivals. More important as cinema was Albert and David Maysles' **Gimme Shelter,** an examination of the nature of the documentary film based on the Rolling Stones' infamous Altamont concert. As an offshoot of the current nostalgia revival, it is interesting to note the reappearance of the long-lost fifties rock-'n'-roll films, things like Alan Freed's **Rock Around the Clock** with Bill Haley and The Comets. As timepieces they hold a mirror up to the fifties much as **Mad Dogs and Englishmen** reflects the seventies, and we can hope that future generations will look back as sympathetically.

But dominating the last fifteen years has been the musical epic,

The mid-1960's quickly became the age of the supermusical, but success of a few hits inspired a flock of box-office disasters as well. Right: Julie Andrews in **The Sound of Music** (1965). Left: Barbra Streisand in **Funny Girl** (1968). Below: Audrey Hepburn and Rex Harrison in **My Fair Lady** (1964, l). Breaking away from the confines of the pre-sold Broadway hit were a few films like **Help!** (1965, r), directed by Richard Lester and starring the Beatles.

an elaborately mounted, often overproduced version of some hot Broadway show, the clearest remaining demonstration of Hollywood's faith in the pre-sold property. Sometimes giant originals are tried, but like **Darling Lili** or **Lost Horizon** these seldom succeed. Only **Mary Poppins** has been a notable exception here. **South Pacific** laid the groundwork in the fifties, but not until the early sixties, with films like **West Side Story** and **The Sound of Music**, did the musical epic really arrive. Many of these films were even quite good and deserved all the attention lavished on them: George Cukor's **My Fair Lady,** William Wyler's **Funny Girl,** and Carol Reed's **Oliver!**, for example. Others were just tired and overblown, but it seemed impossible to predict box-office success or failure in advance. No one could tell that **Cabaret** would emerge as a smash hit, while **Man of La Mancha** languished. Millions were spent on titles of marginal interest, like **1776** or **The Boy Friend,** and when these ran out producers reached back for the unfilmed Broadway hits of a generation ago, things like **Finian's Rainbow** and the disastrous **Paint Your Wagon.** Some of these marginal properties did reasonably well, like **Sweet Charity,** but others were hopeless flops. Still, the overwhelming success of a handful of big musicals induced Hollywood to continue this game of Russian roulette. Does a studio head gamble on **Fiddler on the Roof, Camelot, Hello, Dolly!,** or **Mame**? If you land a hit, you're safe until next year; if you're stuck with a flop, the studio gets sold to a conglomerate.

COPS & ROBB

The crime-movie genre goes through especially evident periodic changes. Emphasis sometimes is on the cops, sometimes on the robbers. For example, the early seventies turned the spotlight on police activities in films like **Serpico** and **The French Connection,** although cop films have historically vied with the very different private-eye movies in taking up the side of law and order. On the other hand, there has always been a clear distinction between the organized-crime film **(The Godfather)** and the individual-outlaw film **(Bonnie and Clyde).**

The first "gangster" films were just that, arising out of the growing public consciousness of organized crime which followed the St. Valentine's Day Massacre of 1927. By the end of that year the first two films in the new genre had already appeared: Josef von Sternberg's **Underworld** and James Cruze's **City Gone Wild.** Ben Hecht wrote **Underworld** with, he says, the intention of creating a film full of villains instead of the usual silent-movie heroes. But, while he did write a film about criminals, he romanticized them in the process, thus initiating the first wave of protest against movie glorification of the gangster.

When sound arrived the genre really took off, and the first all-talking film released, **Lights of New York,** was a gangster film. More famous were such early talkies as **Little Caesar, Scarface,** and **The Public Enemy,** a classic trio which established for all time the image of the Hollywood movie gangster. The setting is urban America, the time the Prohibition era, and the heroes maniacal followers of a twisted American dream. When the films begin we see them as cheap hoods, willing to work their way through the hierarchy of organized crime in a murderous Horatio Alger style. The organization is shown as similar to any other big business, with a corporate structure consisting of various officers who run the business—in its classic form bootlegging, but in later films numbers, prostitution, and narcotics. Our heroes succeed in ascending the ladder of success, but as in any good tragedy they are eventually brought down by some inner flaw. The organization continues to function quite well without them, however. These films were invariably noisy, the urban clamor constantly punctuated by the screeching of tires and the rattle of machine guns. This urban-gangster theme was carried on in a large number of early thirties films **(Quick Millions, City Streets)** but had faded by the end of the decade. Raoul Walsh revived it with **The Roaring Twenties** (1939), the first of many late gangster films to hark back to the now notoriously lawless, decade. Perhaps the most notable moment in this excellent film occurs as Cagney lies on the steps of the local cathedral and Priscilla Lane, his moll from Mineola, delivers the ultimate eulogy for the fallen hero: "He used to be a big shot."

Crime as an organized force was pretty well neglected in the next two decades, the main exception being Abraham Polonsky's **Force of Evil,** an unjustly forgotten classic in which John Garfield tries to fix the New York numbers racket. Perhaps prompted by the mid-fifties Kefauver investigations, the organized-crime film returned by the end of the decade with **Al Capone, The Purple Gang, Murder, Inc.,** and the brilliant **The Rise and Fall of Legs Dia-**

Right: James Cagney was the most successful in affecting the smug, sneering mask of the mentally unbalanced killer. Note this perversely satisfied grin in **The Public Enemy** (1931).
Below: Lee Marvin makes a big mistake in scalding Gloria Grahame's face in Fritz Lang's **The Big Heat** (1953).
Bottom: Bogie gets the drop on a down-and-out Cagney, at least temporarily, in the final confrontation scene of Raoul Walsh's **The Roaring Twenties** (1939).

mond by Budd Boetticher. All these films appeared in 1959 and 1960, and most dealt not with the current crime scene (as **Force of Evil** had done), but flashed back safely to the classic gangster period. So did Roger Corman's **The St. Valentine's Day Massacre** (1967), a witty spoof of the conventions of gangster movies more than of gangsterism itself. The series was capped in 1972 by **The Godfather,** the monumental classic of the genre which quickly established itself as one of the most popular films of all time. It took all the conventions of the genre, especially the idea of the big-business nature of organized crime, but added a peculiar feeling of the family epic. Its investigation of the familial side of organized crime was so striking that many critics pointed to the cohesiveness of **The Godfather's** "family" as one of the reasons contemporary audiences found it so fascinating. Still, no one has explained why **The Godfather** was such a staggering success and Martin Ritt's **The Brotherhood,** a similar if less ambitious film made a few years earlier, so dismal a flop.

Opposed to this cycle, in movies as in life, was the lone-outlaw film. Organized crime abhorred the lone gunmen of the thirties as undisciplined and unpredictable. They were outsiders even in the underworld, and the fatalistic films in which they appeared were tinged with a peculiarly existential outlook. Humphrey Bogart as Duke Mantee in **The Petrified Forest** was an early example, but far more interesting was his characterization of the isolated and outmoded outlaw hero of **High Sierra.** The forties produced a few good exam-

Organized crime as a twisted reflection of the American economic system has been the theme of a few of the more thoughtful crime films. Above: Thomas Gomez and Howland Chamberlain in Abraham Polonsky's brilliant numbers-racket exposé, **Force of Evil** (1948). The theme is even more popular today, as proven by Francis Ford Coppola's **The Godfather** (1), with Al Pacino and Marlon Brando, a rare example of a great critical as well as commercial success (1972).

Above: Humphrey Bogart made his
first big impression in **The
Petrified Forest** (1936) as Duke
Mantee, leader of a roving gang
of thirties outlaws. Bogie in
the background, Bette Davis, Joe
Sawyer, Dick Foran, and Leslie
Howard up front. Right: Raoul Walsh
successfully revived the old-time
gangster film in 1949 with
White Heat. James Cagney now
played a completely maniacal
gang leader, and the film was
filled with the Freudian fixations
so dear to postwar screenwriters.
Edmond O'Brien was the Federal
agent who infiltrates the mob.

P-57

ples of this school: **This Gun for Hire, Dillinger,** and Raoul Walsh's **White Heat,** an interesting slant on the lone gangster as psychopath. The setting of these films is usually rural rather than urban, the characters driving around on empty highways and hiding out in small towns or isolated retreats. Their crimes are not bootlegging or protection, but direct and forceful assaults, like bank robbery. **Baby Face Nelson** and **Machine Gun Kelly** provided movie heroes of the late fifties, and by the sixties **In Cold Blood** had added a new wrinkle to the idea.

But the most popular version was that of **Bonnie and Clyde.** Arthur Penn's film wrapped up all the existential threads of the outlaw film and packaged them in a fashionably correct thirties style that became an important new "look." The ads for the film blared: "They're young! They're in love! And they kill people!" as Faye Dunaway and Warren Beatty raced sheriffs and held up banks to the bouncy mountain music of Flatt and Scruggs. Except for the self-conscious artiness of some episodes, like the final slow-motion ambush, the film recalled some of the "on-the-run movies" of the thirties and forties. William K. Howard's **Mary Burns, Fugitive** (1935) with Sylvia Sidney, is the underground classic of the lot, but more important was Fritz Lang's **You Only Live Once.** Here Miss Sidney and Henry Fonda were chased around the country in a far more poetic version of the Bonnie and Clyde story, thoroughly suffused with Lang's Germanic fatalism. And Joseph H. Lewis's **Gun Crazy** (1949) was one of the high points of the genre, the story of a nymphomaniacal sharpshooter and her "gun-crazy" boyfriend who terrorize the countryside with a series of outrageous (and brilliantly staged) holdups and robberies. After **Bonnie and Clyde** a wave of cheap imitations hit the market, the only one of any real merit being Corman's sensational **Bloody Momma,** a family-style **Bonnie and Clyde,** only tawdry.

For many years the villains Ben Hecht spoke of (by convention presented as heroes) completely held center stage in the cops-and-robbers field. But in the mid-thirties a new influence emerged from the popular pulp-novel field, and screen detectives began to give the criminals a run for their money. One of the more popular was Charlie Chan, who made his first screen

Above: The thirties outlaw as
glorified by the sixties cinema:
Warren Beatty and Faye Dunaway
in Arthur Penn's **Bonnie and Clyde**
(1967). Opposite top: **Charlie
Chan in Egypt** (1935), with Stepin
Fetchit, Warner Oland, Thomas
Beck, and Frank Conroy. The
detective was a popular development
in thirties crime films. Below:
The Thin Man (1934), based on
Dashiell Hammett's story, with
Edward Brophy, Myrna
Loy, and William Powell.

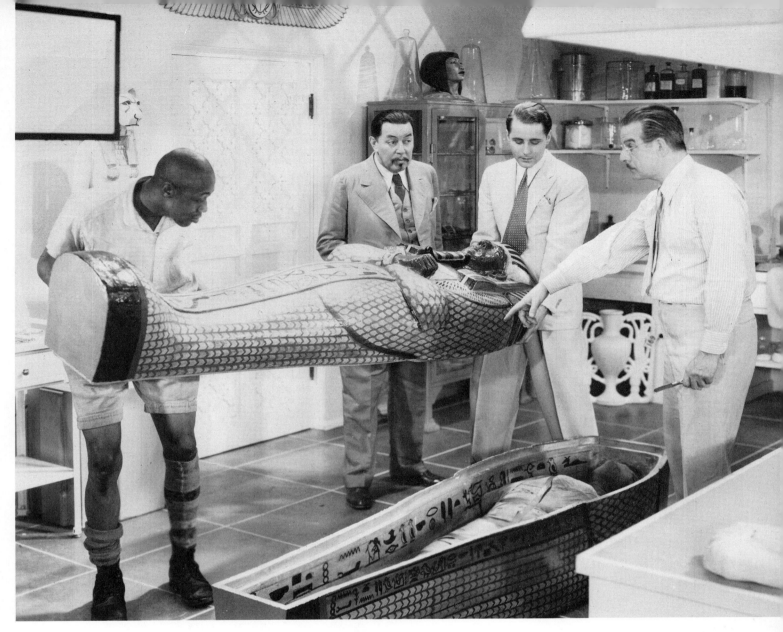

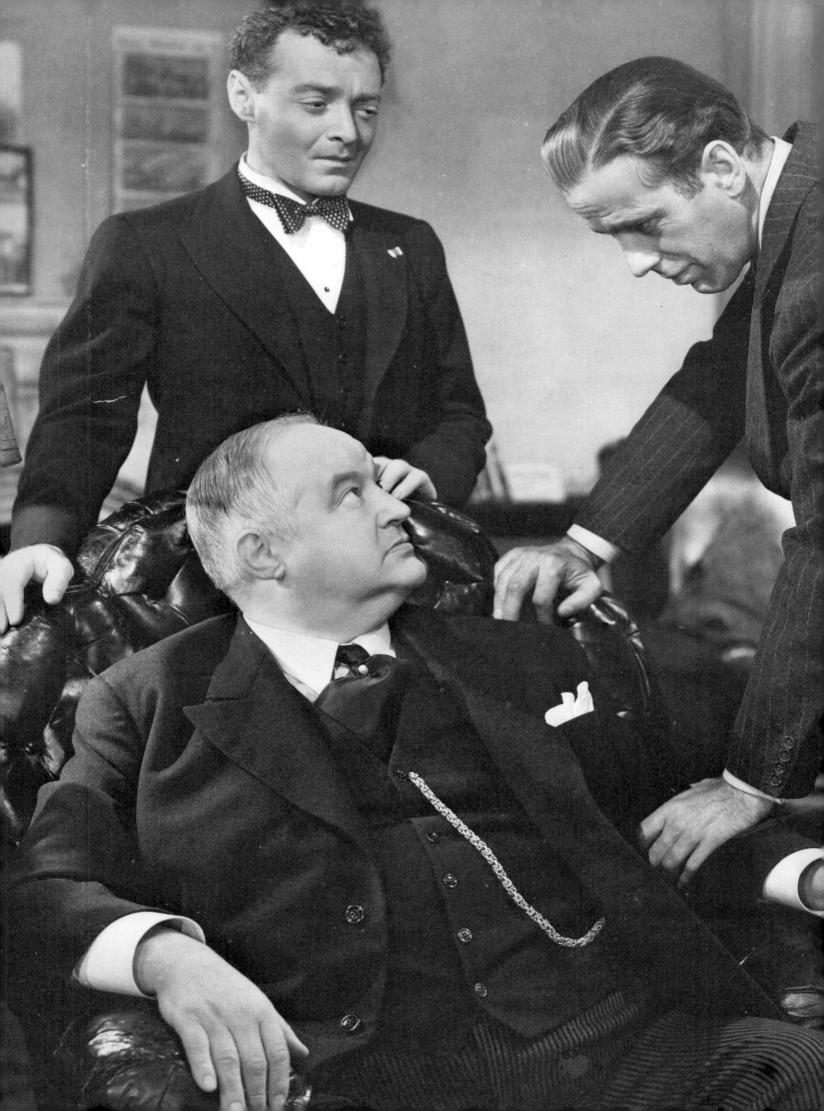

Some screen versions of detective fiction's toughest private eyes. Left: Dashiell Hammett's **The Maltese Falcon** (1941), with Peter Lorre, Sidney Greenstreet, and Humphrey Bogart as Sam Spade. John Huston directed. Below: Raymond Chandler's **The Big Sleep** (1946), with Bogart as Philip Marlowe, Lauren Bacall, and Bob Steele. Howard Hawks directed. Bottom: Mickey Spillane's **Kiss Me Deadly** (1955), with Ralph Meeker as Mike Hammer. Robert Aldrich directed.

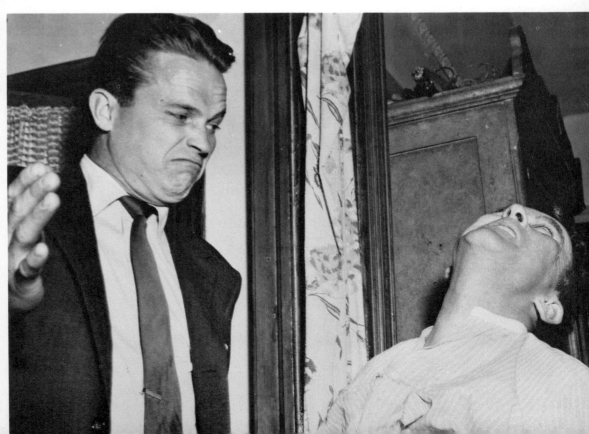

In the postwar period the previously scorned work of police departments suddenly became popular screen material. Many films took advantage of the new trend in location shooting, like Jules Dassin's **The Naked City** (1948, r). The cops began to act tough in William Wyler's **Detective Story** (far r), with Kirk Douglas (1951). The private eye hasn't been on the screen much lately, the few exceptions treating him with considerable lack of reverence. Philip Marlowe returned via Elliott Gould in Robert Altman's **The Long Goodbye** (1973, below), a film that viciously kicked the genre while it was down. And Jean-Luc Godard took a half-serious look at the detective in **Alphaville** (1965). Eddie Constantine reads "The Big Sleep" (opposite, bottom).

PLAY MISTY FOR ME

KWIK LUNCH SANDWICHES

Today the supercop rules the crime film, which has turned into a genre filled with elaborate chases shot against crowded urban cityscapes. Above: Clint Eastwood as **Dirty Harry** (1971), Don Siegel's controversial film, which was labeled "fascist" by its detractors. Opposite: William Friedkin's **The French Connection** (1971) began the current trend of basing a cop movie on the exploits of a real-life cop.

appearance in the silent days, but didn't make a real impression until Warner Oland took over the role in 1931. Chan, with the aid of Number 1 and Number 2 sons (Keye Luke and Sen Yung), unraveled mysteries and nabbed criminals in a decidedly cerebral fashion. **The Thin Man** appeared a few years later and added a little class to the generally inexpensive Chan-type detective film, but followed the principal thirties detective precepts in all important ways. There was as little violence as possible, crimes were solved by brain power, and the police were ineffectual and usually a hindrance, exemplars of the strong-arm method of law enforcement.

This early pattern lasted until Bogart played Sam Spade in **The Maltese Falcon** (1941). Things got considerably tougher here, and a streak of sadism appeared in the methodical beatings so popular in forties detective films. In **The Big Sleep** Bogart was Philip Marlowe, again the lone investigator who uses his wits to solve a mystery so dense that the screenwriters later admitted even they didn't know who was responsible for one of the killings. The

only things the private eye had to rely on were his intelligence, knowledge of crime and criminals, and raw courage. It is interesting to note that the lone-detective film has the same relation to the cop film as the lone-outlaw film has to the organized-crime movie.

In the fifties the concept of the lone fighter for justice began to evaporate. Robert Aldrich's version of Mickey Spillane's **Kiss Me Deadly** saw the lone detective as completely outdated in the new society. Here Mike Hammer tries to use his wits, but the puzzle is too tough for him. He displays contempt for the cops, but they're too smart for him, and eventually his lone-wolf blundering destroys everything he comes in contact with. **Kiss Me Deadly** pretty well killed off the detective-film cycle, although **Gunn,** based on the hit TV series, and **Marlowe** made two not-quite-successful attempts to revive the genre in the late sixties. **Harper,** with Paul Newman playing a Bogart-detective role, was one of the best of the period. In 1973 Robert Altman put Elliott Gould in **The Long Goodbye,** supposedly intended to deflate the detective mystique, something

that had been pretty well flattened when **Kiss Me Deadly** appeared in 1955. It only succeeded in alienating the fans of Raymond Chandler and proving, with its style and wit, why cop films were in the ascendance in the seventies.

During the thirties a policeman was generally portrayed as a dumb flatfoot, incapable of outwitting criminals or of matching wits with private eyes. The FBI was an entirely different matter, however, an elite national police force that was glorified in Warners' **G-Men** in 1935. **T-Men** did the same thing for Treasury agents in 1947, and only then did the law-enforcement spotlight turn to local cops. **The Naked City, Where the Sidewalk Ends, Detective Story,** and **The Big Heat** were all cop-oriented films that examined different aspects of police activity, appropriating many of the elements of the earlier detective films, but expanding them into the more socially conscious position of the policeman as defender of society. A few later fifties films, like **Dragnet** and **The F.B.I. Story,** expanded on this idea, but like most of the other examples of the genre it largely disappeared until the late sixties. Then Peter Yates's **Bullitt** presented a cop just as flashy and independent as the old detective, but backed up by considerably more firepower and the legal approbation of "law and order." **Madigan** and **The Detective** followed almost immediately; then the real blockbusters like **Dirty Harry, The French Connection, The New Centurions, The Seven Ups,** and the 1973 smash hit, **Serpico.** These films sometimes presented the cop as an individual working within the system, sometimes as part of a vast law-enforcement web too powerful for puny individual criminals, but well matched for confrontation with "the mob." Later, corruption within the police department became a key theme, particularly in **Serpico.** In fact, in a manner very reminiscent of a thirties publicity gimmick, it was discovered at the height of the cop-film craze that the heroin so laboriously captured in the real French Connection case had vanished from the vaults of the New York Police Department, adding a bizarre touch of reality to an otherwise very "Hollywood" situation.

Of course, there are a number of important crime films which don't fit easily into these general categories. Stories of plain murder, like **Fallen Angel** and **The Postman Always Rings Twice,** very often involve not professional criminals, but pointedly "average" Americans. Prison pictures are also an important subcategory, like **The Big House, Brute Force,** and **Riot in Cell Block 11.** And the most difficult of all to categorize is the caper film, which mixes the alienation of the lone-outlaw cycle with the planning and organization of the urban-gangster film. John Huston's **The Asphalt Jungle** and Stanley Kubrick's **The Killing** are two of the best examples of these, and it is interesting to note that in recent comic variations of this theme, like Peter Yates's **The Hot Rock,** the criminals are actually allowed to escape with their loot instead of having it blown all over an airport by an inexorably just God. Despite these notable exceptions, the pure, almost ritualistic cops-and-robbers theme continues to dominate the genre. And the contemporary gun-toting supercop seems a likely candidate to dominate movie screens for some time to come.

Al Pacino has become the most ubiquitous star of recent cops-and-robbers films, having been featured in **The Godfather, Serpico,** and **Godfather II.** Here, in **Serpico** (1973), a topical wrinkle was added to the cop cycle by making police corruption a major issue. The production of this film is symptomatic of the moribund state of Hollywood today. Although Sidney Lumet directed, this is really an Italian film, produced by Dino De Laurentiis out of Rome, and shot "on location" in America.

SEX AND THE C

As motion pictures grew up, motion-picture censorship grew up along with them. The "Irwin-Rice Kiss" of 1896 and Fatima's famous shimmy dance initiated the first wave of indignation at the excesses of the new medium. The content of the films was bad, many reformers thought, but the theaters themselves were even worse—dimly lit, reconverted store fronts, where both sexes mingled in the darkness, the only light coming from the sordid activities on the screen. And the sleazy arcades which housed the peep-show Kinetoscopes were no improvement. Neighborhood groups saw the local movie house as next of kin to the pool hall and decided to do something to halt its corrupting influence. Banding together under religious leadership, and with the local police along to lend legal support, pressure groups began to make their complaints known.

The theaters retaliated as best they could by emphasizing the harmless, and often educational, nature of their entertainment. "Electric Theatre, Moral and Refined, Pleasing to the Ladies," their signs said. The reformers and the film people carried on a running battle for some years, and the film had finally achieved a degree of respectability when Hollywood was rocked by scandal. The Fatty Arbuckle case, the William Desmond Taylor murder, and Wallace Reid's narcotics-related death are usually cited as the reformers' three last straws. Hollywood's wild living, and films with titles like **Sex,** had finally gotten to the "better elements" of the public. The movie producers banded together for protection. Will Hays was called in from President Harding's Cabinet to keep an eye on things.

Hays's presence put a damper on protest until the early thirties, but then religious groups began to complain again about the growing wave of sadomasochism in films like **Call Her Savage** and **The Story of Temple Drake.** Under pressure from the newly organized Legion of Decency, and fearing the effect of forty-eight separate state censorship boards tampering with their films, Hollywood in 1934 put teeth into its Production Code. The basic tenet of the Code was to provide "correct standards of life" and suppress anything that might "lower the moral standards of those who see it." It was a rather broad and subjective task, and its interpretation of the "natural law . . . which is written in the hearts of all mankind" was always the Code's main problem.

The Code basically concerned itself with the manner in which crime, brutality, and sex were presented. Crimes could not be shown in detail, thus withholding instruction from incipient criminals. Lawbreakers could not be glorified, and their crimes always had to be punished. The early strictures on brutality were very clear. "Excessive brutality"—including branding, third-degree methods, cruelty to children, and "wholesale slaughter of human beings"—was strictly prohibited, since these "tend to lessen regard for the sacredness of life." Cruelty to animals was also included here, and devices like the "running W," which was used to trip horses for western stunts, were specifically forbidden. Sexual acts were prohibited, and very little could even be suggested. Costuming and dancing were carefully screened for possible nudity

Preceding pages:
A scene from an unknown Edison studio production, circa 1902. Left: Smacking his lips, a lecherous Erich von Stroheim sets his sights on the wife of the American envoy to Monte Carlo (Miss Dupont) in **Foolish Wives** (1922). The escapades of this bogus "count" and his two "cousins" brought forth cries for censorship and suppression. One critic called the film, "an insult to American ideals and womanhood."

287

After the narcotics-related death of her husband,
Mrs. Wallace Reid produced a series of exposés
on dope, prostitution, and other social ills.
Bessie Love (l) was the afflicted heroine of
Human Wreckage (1923). **The Story
of Temple Drake** (1933) was largely responsible
for the application of the strict new
Production Code. The heroine, a daughter
of Southern gentry, becomes masochistically
attached to a hoodlum. Above: Miriam
Hopkins, Jack La Rue, and William Gargan.

or suggestiveness.

The rest of the Code dealt with a variety of other topics which fell outside "the dictates of good taste." Racial and national slurs were prohibited, as were attacks on religion and the flag. Variously banned were dirty words ("broad," "pansy," "S.O.B."), gestures ("finger [the]"), and sounds ("Bronx cheer," "razzberry"). Direct descriptions of the drug trade and the use of drugs were out, as were references to abortion, miscegenation, white slavery, and graphic depiction of surgical operations.

The effect of the Code's enforcement in 1934 was immediate. Directors like Josef von Sternberg and Ernst Lubitsch were forced to alter their approach drastically, not to mention the effect the Code had on Mae West. Betty Boop lengthened her skirts and raised her garter. But within a few years, a slow but steady unraveling of the Code began.

The first crack came in 1939, when Rhett Butler's line, "Frankly my dear, I don't give a damn," was allowed in **Gone With the Wind** only because it was key dialogue from a literary work of, some thought, great merit. Previously both "hell" and "damn" were on the proscribed list. **GWTW** created a considerable stir but was eclipsed by the sensation of Howard Hughes's **The Outlaw,** begun in 1940, but not generally released until 1946. Advertised with lines like "What are the two great reasons for Jane Russell's rise to stardom?", the film ignited such violent protests, especially from women's groups, that it was denied a Code seal—this at a time when theaters were pledged not to show a film without the seal. Hughes had the guts to open it pretty much the way he wanted, but the film suffered innumerable snips later on.

Much less courageous was Darryl F. Zanuck, who withdrew **Forever Amber** from release after it appeared that Catholics in the Philadelphia area were about to boycott all Fox releases. To the already emasculated tale of the seventeenth-century courtesan, the studio added the immortal prologue, "This is the story of Amber St. Claire, slave to ambition, stranger to virtue, fated to find the wealth and power she ruthlessly gained wither to ashes in the fires lit by passion and fed by defiance of the eternal command—the wages of sin is death." **A Streetcar Named Desire** and **From Here to Eternity,** although they compromised with the Code, stretched it to its fullest limits. Then in 1953 Otto Preminger released **The Moon Is Blue,** a light comedy of seduction that was all talk and no action, but had been denied a Code seal. Its success proved that theaters and audiences alike really did not care whether a film carried this stamp of respectability. Preminger went around the Code again in **The Man With the Golden Arm,** in which Frank Sinatra broke the long-standing ban against showing drug addiction.

Such frontal assaults had permanently weakened the Code as the sixties arrived, but the most important censorship question of the time was settled by the Supreme Court. In the 1952 Burstyn vs. Wilson ruling, the Court wrote that the motion picture was an artistic medium and as such was entitled to

Two typical examples of pre-Code behavior. Above: Clara Bow in **Call Her Savage,** directed by John Francis Dillon from a Tiffany Thayer novel, a film with strong sadomasochistic overtones. Below: Charles Laughton as Nero in Cecil B. De Mille's **The Sign of the Cross.** Scantily clad boys in bondage were not uncommon in pre-Code Hollywood. Both films were released late in 1932.

1090-43

Two landmarks in the history of cinema sex during the reign of the Hays Office. Left: Hedy Lamarr in the 1937 Czech import **Ecstasy,** Gustav Machaty's semi-experimental staple of the thirties art-house circuit. Right: Jane Russell was the focal point of Howard Hughes's notorious film **The Outlaw,** which fought a running battle with the censors from the day it began shooting in 1940.

Above: Anna Magnani in Roberto
Rossellini's **The Miracle** (1950),
the centerpiece of a major
Supreme Court decision. Opposite:
Frank Sinatra (top l) in
Otto Preminger's **The Man With the
Golden Arm** (1955). Carroll Baker and
Eli Wallach (top r) in Elia
Kazan's **Baby Doll** (1956). Brigitte
Bardot and Henri Vidal (bottom l)
in Michel Boisrond's **La Parisienne**
(1958). Anne Heywood and Sandy
Dennis (bottom r) in Mark Rydell's
The Fox (1968). Each in its own way was
a step toward liberalization of the Code.

full protection under the constitutional guarantees of free speech. It allowed the
exhibition of Roberto Rossellini's **The Miracle,** which had been banned in New
York as "sacrilegious" but, more importantly, set a precedent for liberalization
for the next twenty years. By the early sixties the remaining taboos were swept
away. **The Pawnbroker** contained the first officially sanctioned female nudity,
while the "approved" language of **Who's Afraid of Virginia Woolf?** forced the
establishment of a new "mature audiences" rating category, with no one under
eighteen admitted. The British **Alfie** dealt explicitly with the abortion issue, and
even more controversial was **Blow-Up.** Because director Michelangelo Antonioni refused to make cuts in two sex scenes, the film was denied a seal. Although
MGM would not handle the film in this manner, it did distribute it through its
subsidiary, Regal Films, and the film was shown intact.

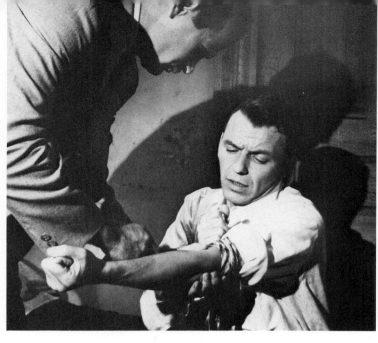

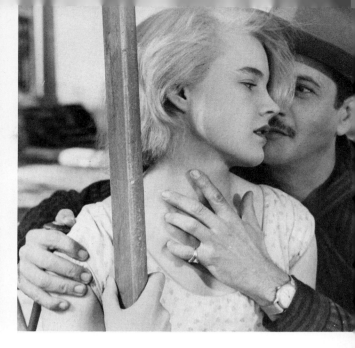

By the mid-sixties the stag film had surfaced as a well-established part of the midtown theater scene. Its underground career dates back to the early silent period, and much of this arcane material survives, mostly in collections like that of the Kinsey Institute. "Exploitation" theaters had always existed, but they seldom if ever showed even soft-core pornography before the fifties. Rather, they specialized in independently produced cheapies that were never even registered for copyright, much less submitted for Code inspection. These films might deal with social problems, like **Child Bride** or even narcotics addiction. **Marijuana, One-Way Ticket to Hell,** and **Reefer Madness** were three classic antidrug exploitation films, although the last has been reissued for somewhat different purposes. **Reefer Madness** was reissued in the early 1970's by pro-marijuana groups in an effort to discredit existing anti-marijuana legisla-

Opposite: Lena Nyman and Borje Ahlstedt in **I Am Curious—Yellow** (1967) by Vilgot Sjoman, another major censorship test case. Right: Brenda Vaccaro and Jon Voight in **Midnight Cowboy** (1969) by John Schlesinger, a landmark in the X-rating game. Below: The old master of the surrealist and erotic, Luis Buñuel, directing Catherine Deneuve in **Belle de Jour** (1968), an elegant and elaborate essay in sexual fantasy.

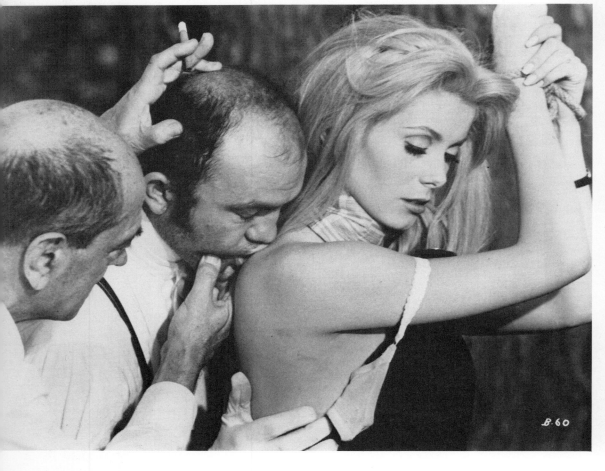

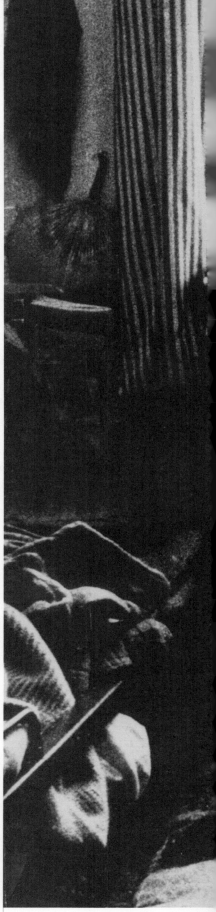

The removal of most censorship restrictions allowed many serious filmmakers the chance to explore previously forbidden territory. Yet it also resulted in an explosion in the previously marginal porno circuit. Left: Dominique Sanda and Stefania Sandrelli in **The Conformist** (1970) by Bernardo Bertolucci. Right: Jon Evans and Erica Gavin in **Vixen!** (1968), one of porn producer Russ Meyer's biggest hits.

tion which dates back to the mid-1930's. Occasionally, some theater would latch onto a European film like **Ecstasy,** which treated audiences to a few brief moments of Hedy Lamarr in the buff (if the print wasn't mutilated). Gradually, a certain type of European film found itself booked into rather unsavory theaters in fringe sections of town. It was often to a fleabag exploitation house that one had to go to see the more amusing French comedies, too risqué for straight houses, and just titillating enough for the underground circuit. It must be kept in mind that as little as twenty years ago films like Max Ophuls' **La Ronde** needed Supreme Court permission to get into the country. In this context, Fernandel in **The Sheep Has Five Legs** seemed pretty hot stuff, indeed.

Once in a while these "art" movie houses might play a travelogue or "nature" film, usually meaning volleyball matches at the nudist colony, but programing was generally pretty timid. Then, in 1959, Russ Meyer released **The Immoral Mr. Teas,** the first official American "nudie." It cost $24,000 and brought in $1 million, starting Meyer on a new career and touching off the explosion of commercial porno films. He soon outgrew the mild voyeurism of **Mr. Teas** and began producing raunchier sexploiters like **Cherry, Harry and Raquel** and the scabrous **Faster Pussycat, Kill, Kill!** Dominating the middle ground of porn, Meyer's films featured fleshy and aggressive heroines who looked as though they belonged in his films.

On the other hand, the Tiffany of the sexploitation market was Radley Metzger's Audubon Films. Expensively produced and lushly photographed, these spend lots of time building mood and even characterization. In **Camille 2000, Thérèse and Isabelle,** and **The Lickerish Quartet,** he paints a sensuous picture of high-class European decadence as a background for his sexual gymnastics. It's been said that Metzger was to the porno film of the sixties what "Playboy" was to the girlie magazine of the fifties. He substituted glamour, class, and good-looking women for the general air of contagion that came before him.

Above left: **A Clockwork Orange** (1971)
was set in a future society gorged
on violence and sex.
Above right: A moment of high
comedy in Robert Altman's **M*A*S*H**
(1970), as Sally Kellerman is exposed
in the shower. A new twist on the
X-rated genre has been provided by
Ralph Bakshi with his adults-only
animation. The success of **Fritz the
Cat** was followed by **Heavy Traffic**,
(below l) in 1973. What Russ Meyer
pioneered was made acceptable by
Radley Metzger, whose **Lickerish
Quartet** (1970), with Frank Wolff and
Silvano Venturelli (below r), was
shown at the Museum of Modern Art.

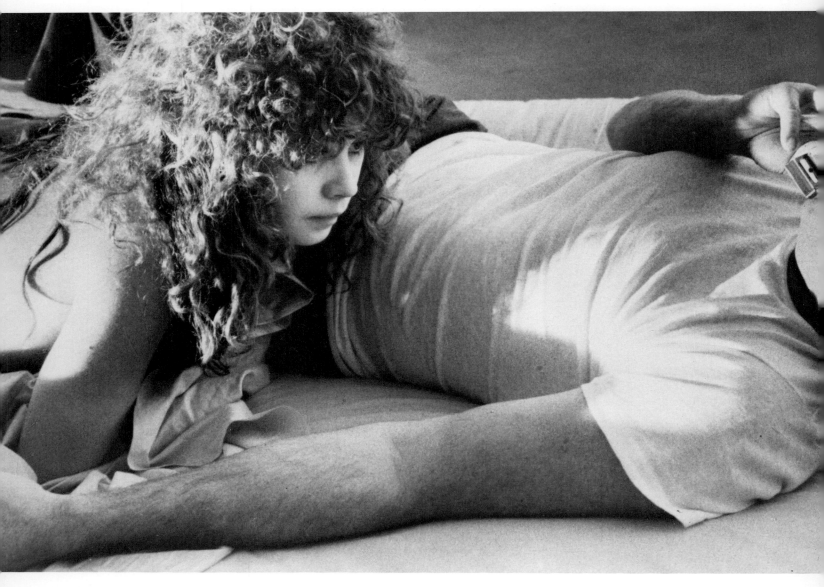

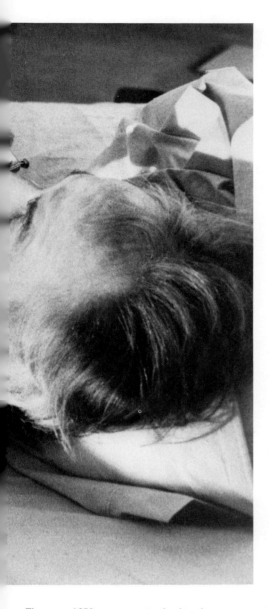

The year 1973 was a watershed in the history of the screen's new-found sexual freedom. Bertolucci's **Last Tango in Paris** (above), with Maria Schneider and Marlon Brando, was called by one critic the greatest event since the premiere of Stravinsky's "The Rite of Spring." And Gerard Damiano's **Deep Throat** (l), with Harry Reems and Linda Lovelace, was one of the year's top grossers. But Supreme Court decisions threw a cloud over these trends.

By the seventies an interesting phenomenon had occurred: The two opposing circuits of straight Hollywood and the exploitation chain seemed to be on a collision course. Commercial films like **The Devils, A Clockwork Orange,** and **Straw Dogs** contained so much sex that a few years earlier they would have seemed rough even for the sexploitation houses. At the same time, Metzger's films were getting so elaborate and artistically pretentious that it was hard to tell them from many European film-festival entries. And Russ Meyer was already in Hollywood, filming **Beyond the Valley of the Dolls** on a million-dollar budget. At the beginning of 1973 **Last Tango in Paris** opened, and many critics viewed it as screen pornography finally raised to the level of art. One major reviewer, Pauline Kael, even saw in its controlled eroticism the greatest cultural event since the premiere of Igor Stravinsky's ballet music "The Rite of Spring." Playing with an X rating that seemed to do it not the slightest bit of harm, **Last Tango** quickly turned into a huge pop success with middle-brow audiences, and "Time" and "Newsweek" both gave it lengthy write-ups.

But screen permissiveness received another jolt in 1973, and from an entirely different direction. The new Burger Court, thanks to the conservative bias of the Nixon appointees, passed up another chance to define obscenity, and ruled instead that obscenity was to be judged by local standards, not national ones. This breathed new life back into local censorship boards, generally liberal in the big Eastern cities, but just itching to use their shears in the rest of the country. The major producers drew back from their increasingly franker productions, and the number of X releases declined noticeably. Stanley Kubrick had already cut **A Clockwork Orange** to an R rating after it played successfully for months as an X picture. Filmmakers were suddenly afraid once more of local reactions and of being saddled with the old problem of designing their films to appeal to the widest common denominator—the television audience. A retreat to the standards of a few years earlier was called for, effectively squelching some of the year's most interesting projects.

But while the producers of serious films shivered in their boots, the porno market was unaffected; indeed, it grew considerably uglier. The relatively mild Metzger and Meyer films had by now been replaced by Gerard Damiano's hard-core **Deep Throat** and **The Devil in Miss Jones,** both multimillion-dollar grossers.

It seemed that porno producers were not worried about a fragmented market, for money would continue to pour in as fast as it could be spent. If local censorship caused any problems, the grosses could be made up in the next town. After being run out of New York, **Deep Throat** comfortably settled on the other side of the Hudson and attracted the same audience. Damiano could work this way, but Paramount and United Artists could not. The Times Square areas across the country moved more heavily into hard-core loops, straight sex without even the glaze of foreplay. There might be no more **Last Tangos,** but plenty of "mixed combos."

BLACK FILMS

The "black film" as a distinctly separate genre has only been recognized for a few years, but its roots date well back into the silent period. Whenever specialized audiences exist in a concentrated geographic area, specialized films inevitably spring into existence to serve them. In the twenties, blacks constituted just such a specialized audience, driven by de jure and de facto segregation to patronize a limited number of theaters which quickly established specialized "black" identities. In certain Southern and rural districts this segregation was enforced by law, while in the growing black metropolitan centers, like New York's Harlem, the neighborhood concentrations alone created a nearly all-black clientele.

By the late teens, black entrepreneurs were providing a special product for this audience, and Noble Johnson, a black actor popular in a series of Universal releases, was soon starring in films intended solely for black audiences. The success of his films brought a clamor for more such material, and several independent producers vied for domination of the growing black theater market throughout the twenties. The most important was Oscar Michaeux, who for over twenty years released the best of the all-black films from his offices in Harlem. Michaeux was a one-man band, arranging for the production and distribution of his films himself, and wielding as much control over his product as any Hollywood studio head. The major difference was in the output involved: Michaeux was only able to release about twenty films.

Nearly all the black films of this period have disappeared, for they were produced by small independent outfits that often faded from existence after a few years, their films vanishing with them. Today they exist only as notations in corporate records or advertisements in black journals of the time. One of the few features to survive is **The Scar of Shame,** directed by Frank Peregini for the Colored Players Film Corporation of Philadelphia in 1927. The film is set in an upper middle-class black milieu and deals with a young violinist attempting to establish himself as a musician. He is hampered in his aspirations by his wife, a woman who is "beneath him" and causes him no end of social and emotional problems. Historians of the black film have pointed out that **The Scar of Shame** shares with many similar films the theme of striving for success in the white man's world in classical bourgeois terms. It also holds to the convention that upwardly mobile and success-oriented blacks are light skinned; less goal-oriented characters are played by darker blacks. One sees this in the contrast between the light-skinned violinist with his classical aspirations and his darker, more sensual wife. (She kills herself at the film's conclusion.) These situations reflect in rather transparent fashion the desire to make it in the white man's world and adopt his values, but in the twenties, before the raising of black consciousness, this was a goal sought by many of the black audience.

When sound came in, the independent black producers were dealt a sudden blow, as zooming production costs outstripped potential profits. Comedies came to dominate a larger share of the market, sound film showing

Preceding pages:
Eugene Jackson and Clarence Muse in Paul Sloan's **Hearts in Dixie** (1929), the first all-black film from a major studio. Opposite: Lucia Lynn Moses (top l) in **The Scar of Shame** (1927), produced by the Colored Players Film Corporation of Philadelphia for black audiences. Top right: Scene from **Spyin' the Spy,** a racist comedy of 1917. Bottom: King Vidor's **Hallelujah** (1929), released right after Sloan's film. This scene seems influenced by Mamoulian's 1927 production of **Porgy** for the Broadway stage.

Two images of black life
on movie screens of the thirties.
Above: Stepin Fetchit and Will
Rogers in John Ford's **Judge Priest**
(1934). Fetchit's exasperatingly
slow performances are still
the cause of heated controversy.
Right: Paul Robeson in **The Emperor
Jones** (1933). This version of
O'Neill's play was filmed
independently at a Long Island
studio, preserving, in somewhat
altered form, Robeson's greatest role.

off the particularly verbal comedy styles of Stepin Fetchit, Mantan Moreland, and Flourney Miller. Many of these black stars went back and forth between Hollywood and the underground black circuit, and it is interesting to note that when they played their comic caricatures in the all-black productions it was with an exaggeration that far surpassed their roles in the Code-supervised Hollywood productions.

Blacks became more evident in the Hollywood films of the thirties, usually in comic or menial capacities. **Hearts in Dixie, Hallelujah,** and **The Green Pastures** provided showcases for a few black talents (especially Rex Ingram, who played De Lawd in **Pastures**), but in general they only dealt with a clichéd image of black life. The dramatic talents of Paul Robeson, for example, were almost wasted by Hollywood. Robeson had appeared in a 1927 film for Oscar Micheaux and then played in **The Emperor Jones,** in Dudley Murphy's film version in 1933. Although the film added much introductory material to O'Neill's play—mainly a lot of crapshooting, fancy Harlem dancing, a knife fight, some Robeson spirituals, and a chain-gang episode—Robeson transcended its limitations and delivered one of the great performances of thirties cinema. Cool and self-assured, he dominates every frame of the film with indisputable star presence. Yet he was forced to go to England to find roles that were not demeaning, and even there, **The Proud Valley** was one of the few films to do him justice.

John Stahl's **Imitation of Life** was practically the only Hollywood film to deal seriously with an important black character. Louise Beavers is Claudette Colbert's partner in a giant pancake corporation, but is constantly troubled by her light-skinned daughter who wants to renounce her race and pass for white. Hattie McDaniel won an Academy Award for her role as Mammy in **Gone With the Wind,** but breathing life into such a stock character was hardly the greatest possible test of her talents. It was only the singing and dancing side of black talent that Hollywood exploited. Dramatic potential was ignored. One thinks of **Showboat,** which featured both Robeson and McDaniel in supporting roles, but the best use it put them to is having Robeson sing "Ol' Man River."

In the forties a similar situation existed, blacks being showcased only in films like **Stormy Weather** and **Cabin in the Sky,** potpourri revues that had no value other than preserving the classic routines of performers like Bill "Bojangles" Robinson, or the early Lena Horne. (Horne was cut out of **Cabin in the Sky** when it played in the South.) The postwar wave of black-interest films like **Pinky** and **Home of the Brave** moved the black man into the position of recognized social problem—well intentioned, but at root still another form of stereotype. The rise of a few actors like Harry Belafonte and Sidney Poitier laid the groundwork for the acceptance of blacks into the mainstream of Hollywood filmmaking. Poitier in **Lilies of the Field** (an Oscar-winning performance), **In the Heat of the Night,** and **To Sir, With Love** became the new image of the black man in Hollywood films. He was well motivated, intelligent, ruggedly handsome, and had mastered the skills and values of white society. In **Guess Who's**

If blacks were used at all in Hollywood films of the thirties, it was usually in some supporting capacity. The 1936 **Showboat** is typical. Paul Robeson and Hattie McDaniel were probably the finest actors in the film, which also featured Irene Dunne, Charles Winninger, and (not seen) Allan Jones and Helen Morgan. Robeson had to go to England for film parts, but these were often poorly scripted and directed.

Over the next decade, Hollywood continued with the pattern of all-black cast or supporting roles only. Opposite: Rex Ingram as De Lawd in Marc Connelly's lavish production of **The Green Pastures** (1936). Left: Hattie McDaniel was awarded an Oscar for her role in **Gone With the Wind** (1939). Below: Lena Horne and Eddie Anderson in **Cabin in the Sky** (1943), the first film of Vincente Minnelli, and probably the best of the all-black musical revues.

Coming to Dinner? he completed the black man's Hollywood odyssey by playing an internationally known doctor who marries into the family of Spencer Tracy and Katharine Hepburn.

But after this, things started to move in quite a different direction. Gordon Parks became the first black director of a major Hollywood film when Warner Brothers released **The Learning Tree** in 1969. A delicate film set in a farming community during the thirties, the film presented a Garden of Eden setting for the moral test of its young black hero, but it found no audience in either the black or white communities. In 1970 two more films were cautiously released, Melvin Van Peebles's **Watermelon Man** and Ossie Davis's **Cotton Comes to Harlem. Watermelon Man** was a fantasy dealing with a white commuter who mysteriously turns black (Godfrey Cambridge), and as a result ends up a violent militant. The advertising campaign of this strange film sold it to white audiences, which were turned off by the savage twist Van Peebles gave the apparently farcical comedy. Much more successful was **Cotton Comes to Harlem,** done in classic detective-film style, but incorporating black characters and values, and featuring unusually interesting Harlem locations. This was the film that established the box-office potential of the genre, and like the earlier films it was intended for white as well as black audiences.

But the black film market as a separate entity was not tapped until Van Peebles's **Sweet Sweetback's Baadasssss Song** emerged as one of the top moneymakers of 1971. The heavy sex and violence of the film, and its cartoon characterization of whites (and some blacks), captivated the imagination of millions of blacks living in the center cities and set the tone for many of the rougher black films to follow. The original **Shaft** (directed by Gordon Parks) attracted a white audience as well as a black audience, but set up the black crime cycle of action, sex, and macho violence—a black version of the James

The revolution:
black filmmakers as well
as black stars.
Opposite: Raymond St. Jacques
and Godfrey Cambridge in Ossie
Davis's **Cotton Comes to Harlem**
(1970). Top: Kyle Johnson
in Gordon Parks's **The Learning
Tree** (1969). Center: Richard
Roundtree in Parks's 1971
production of **Shaft.**
Left: Estelle Parsons and
Godfrey Cambridge in Melvin
Van Peebles' weird
Watermelon Man (1970).

Bond fantasy. While **Shaft** and **Sweetback** were racking up big grosses, producers took note of two of the other black films which didn't do so well. **The Bus Is Coming** was a civil-rights story which came down on the side of nonviolence, and **Man and Boy** was a G-rated western in which Bill Cosby and his son track down the boy's stolen horse. Like **The Learning Tree** before, this kind of material did not go down with the black audience, and by 1972 the black film explosion had solidified into a steady diet of violence and sex. Although they incorporated such varied genres as horror **(Blacula)** and the western **(The Legend of Nigger Charlie),** crime and detective films were the most important. The Shaft series lasted through a few sequels, and a number of other entries were just black adaptations of earlier successes: **Cool Breeze** was a remake of **The Asphalt Jungle** and **Hit Man** was a black version of **Get Carter.** Black stars like Jim Brown **(Slaughter, Black Gunn)** and Fred Williamson **(Hammer, Black Caesar)** added their contributions to this particularly violent cycle. Christopher St. John's **Top of the Heap** was perhaps the best of this lot, about an average black cop and his sometime fantasies, but it was not a great success. A smaller series of actively racist "get whitey" films followed in the wake of **Sweetback:** Oscar Williams's **The Final Comedown** and Ivan Dixon's **The Spook Who Sat by the Door,** a film which actively foments race war. Dixon seems to specialize in the more racially charged black films, his **Trouble Man** with Robert Hooks being the most offensive of the crime cycle.

Much more in the Hollywood tradition were **Sounder** and **Lady Sings the Blues,** both directed by whites and intended for a wider audience, so not strictly a part of the black-film phenomenon. To find a black equivalent of these films we have to look at something like Ossie Davis's **Black Girl,** one of the

The newly established genre of black films quickly split between the fast-buck releases, dubbed blacksploitation in the trade, and the more serious, well-made productions. Cheapies like **The Mack** (1973) raised eyebrows by grossing millions with its glorified story of a pimp (above). In contrast, Motown Records produced **Lady Sings the Blues** (1972), with Diana Ross's highly praised performance as Billie Holiday (r).

As the audience for black films develop, in which direction will it turn? No longer are the sex-drugs-violence entries like **Super Fly** (above), with Ron O'Neal, the instant and immediate successes they once were. On the other hand, material like Martin Ritt's **Sounder** (l) is hard to come by, and still requires a careful promotional effort. Kevin Hooks, Paul Winfield, and Cicely Tyson (not shown) starred.

best films of the whole cycle. The saddest part of the black-film explosion is that films like this languish while racist, sexist drivel like **Super Fly** and **The Mack** —films that glorify a pusher and a pimp—are big box office across the country. But after the appearance of **The Mack** in mid-1973 the general attitude of black films began to change. The cheaper, more purely violent films were driven from the market. They were victims of the surge in popularity of the kung-fu epics, Oriental imports which promised even greater thrills of fantasy violence. Instead, social consciousness is the new thread in the black-film cycle. In **Coffey, Cleopatra Jones,** and particularly Ossie Davis's **Gordon's War,** the heroes are out to rid the community of pushers, dealers, crooked law-enforcement officials, and all the other parasites on the black community. Violence is still the key, but it is now vigilante violence of the law-and-order variety. How long this trend will last is unpredictable.

BIGOTRY IN F

With comparatively few exceptions, the depictions of blacks and other minority groups, including Jews and ethnic groups like the Irish and the Italians, was until fairly recently, a sorry tale of caricature and racial discrimination. In fairness to early movie-industry executives, what was seen on the nation's movie screens from the early 1900's through the 1940's did indeed reflect the prevailing mores and ideologies of the era. But it cannot be forgotten that during this period, especially during the twenties, thirties, and forties, what American audiences saw on movie screens had a profound impact on what they believed. The total impact of movies on American culture and society was far greater before 1950 than it is today in our TV-dominated culture. This, despite the fact that most of today's TV programing is a case of the bland leading the bland.

The first known appearance of Negroes in films (remember it was "niggers" or "Negroes" then, not "blacks") could hardly have been less auspicious. It occurred in a 1902 film, **Off to Bloomingdale Asylum,** by the pioneering French filmmaker Georges Méliès. The description of the short one-reeler from the Méliès catalogue is instructive, and a forerunner of attitudes repeated endlessly in both silent and sound films: "An omnibus drawn by an extraordinary mechanical horse is drawn by four Negroes. The horse kicks and upsets the Negroes, who falling are changed into white clowns. They begin slapping each other's faces and by blows become black again. Kicking each other, they become white once more. Suddenly they are all merged into one gigantic Negro. When he refuses to pay his carfare, the conductor sets fire to the omnibus, and the Negro bursts into a thousand pieces."

The "Negroes" in this early French fantasy were, almost certainly, played by white actors. Until well after the end of World War I, virtually all Negroes in American and foreign films were played by white performers.

D. W. Griffith's 1915 masterpiece **The Birth of a Nation** is the best known of the silent films which caricatured and vilified Negroes. From Griffith's hateful portrayal of Negroes in **The Birth of a Nation,** the attitude of this Southern-born genius had changed, seven years later in **One Exciting Night,** to one of mere contempt. **One Exciting Night** made probably the first and certainly the most noteworthy use of the Negro as comic relief—the role was performed, of course, by a white man, because Griffith would seldom employ a Negro actor in any role, even that of a villain.

Although its place in film history is secure for a variety of other reasons, a large part of the excitement generated by Griffith's **The Birth of a Nation** in 1915 was related to its white supremacist vision of the black man. True, even more objectionable films had been shown previously, like Biograph's **A Nigger in the Woodpile,** or Lubin's **Coon Town Parade,** but it was Griffith's directorial skill which made all the difference. While the earlier films merely reflected current attitudes, Griffith's film had the power to change minds and create entirely new viewpoints. Liberal groups across the country sprang up to attack it. "A deliberate attempt to humiliate ten million American citizens, and to

Preceding pages:
Moneylenders hold the Duchy in pawn. Scene from the chief Nazi anti-Semitic film, **Jud Süss** (1940). For directing this, Veit Harlan was tried after the war for crimes against humanity. Right: D. W. Griffith's **The Birth of a Nation** was greeted with riots and demonstrations in many cities upon its appearance in 1915. In this scene, Gus (played by Walter Long in blackface) is given "a fair trial in the dim halls of the Invisible Empire." Griffith always claimed that his film had been misunderstood.

Top: Blacks were used as comic
relief throughout silent period,
as in this 1918 comedy, **Out West**,
directed by Fatty Arbuckle.
Al St. John and Buster Keaton
can also be seen here. Right: The
Duncan Sisters in **Topsy and Eva**
(1927), another approach at
using blacks for comedy. A spin-off of
Uncle Tom's Cabin, it is particularly
offensive in the way it finds humor
in the very fact of being black.
Opposite: George Siegmann and
James B. Lowe in the 1927
two-million-dollar
version of **Uncle Tom's Cabin**.

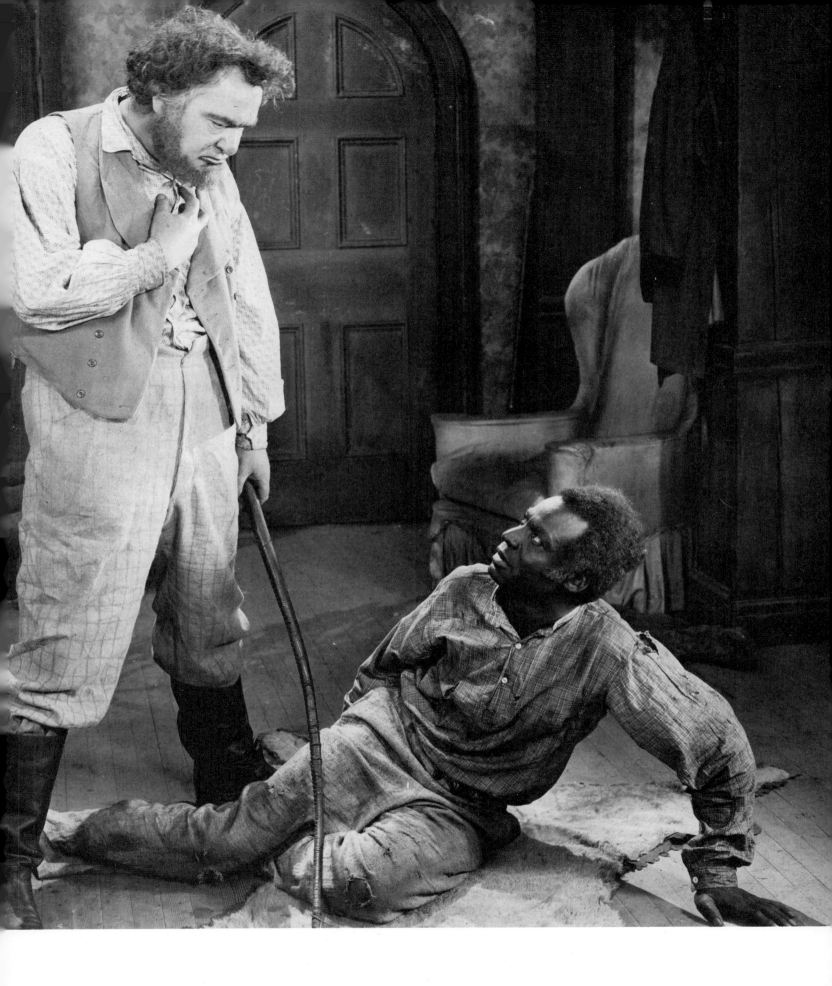

With the coming of sound, blackface and black-stereotype humor were beginning to fade. Above: Colleen Moore in **Synthetic Sin** (1929), one of her lesser efforts. Right: Farina and Jane "cut another melon," according to caption on this 1929 "Our Gang" publicity still. Far right: Moran and Mack, blackface comedians known as "the two black crows," discuss makeup in this posed shot for **Why Bring That Up?** (1929), one of their forgotten Paramount comedies.

portray them as nothing but beasts," was one outraged opinion. The combined protests forced the suppression of the most inflammatory sequences. At one point during **The Birth of a Nation'**s Reconstruction episode, a black accused of attempting to rape Mae Marsh is put to a "fair trial" at the hands of the Ku Klux Klan and murdered. Pressure groups forced the deletion of his castration, presented in the film as justifiable retribution. Another censored episode was the film's "happy ending," in which the solution to America's problems is shown to be shipping all the blacks back to Africa.

In **The Birth of a Nation** the role of Gus, a renegade Negro, is that of a swaggering, hard-swearing, hard-drinking lout in the Southern colored militia who tries to rape the white heroine, eventually driving her to commit suicide. Gus was played by a white actor named Walter Long, who was well known to movie audiences of the period for his normally ferocious-looking countenance. Long was made up to be even more hideous for the prevailing standards of the day, by, among other things, a generous application on the face and hands of what appeared to be black boot polish.

It is true, though, that Griffith toned down the even more militant racism of Thomas Dixon's book "The Clansman," on which he based the film. His blacks are less villains than disobedient children; his is a paternalistic condescension at best. Many of Griffith's defenders argue that the racial attitudes evinced here were shared by all films of the period and that blacks often fared far worse. But this argument does not hold up if we compare the film to, say, the World Film Company version of **Uncle Tom's Cabin,** produced a year earlier. In this film nearly all the black roles were played by black actors, and compassion was shown toward Negroes and their problems that is completely lacking even in Griffith's attitude toward his "good Negroes," like the faithful Mammy. In this **Uncle Tom's Cabin,** blacks are human characters, displaying the human emotions—even in the crude context of the story—which Griffith denies them in **The Birth of a Nation.** It might also be noted that this 1914 version of the often-filmed **Uncle Tom's Cabin** is one of considerable merit, particularly notable for its imaginative use of locations, and deserves rehabilitation as one of the important early feature films.

Because of the outcry concerning **The Birth of a Nation,** blacks did not again receive particularly harsh treatment in the remainder of the silent period. They usually functioned merely as comic relief, but more often than not they simply remained invisible. The one glaring exception was the 1927 **Topsy and Eva,** a spin-off of the Uncle Tom story in which the Duncan Sisters played the leading roles. The role of Topsy the "black imp" was played by Vivian Duncan, a white actress who began her career as a yodeller in San Francisco vaudeville. The same white actress often played both roles of Topsy and Eva in early movie versions of "Uncle Tom's Cabin."

A viewing of a film like **Topsy and Eva** in the 1970's produces a mind-boggling combination of anger, amazement, and bemused laughter. A

The greater realism of talkies
made blackface comedy hard
to sustain, and it gradually
disappeared. In 1931, Laurel and
Hardy mocked the absurdity of
such a disguise in **Pardon Us,**
above. On the other hand, Fannie
Hurst's **Imitation of Life** became
one of first major films to create
a meaningful part for a black
woman. Right: John Stahl's 1934
version, with Louise Beavers and
Claudette Colbert, and (far r)
Douglas Sirk's 1959 remake with
Juanita Moore and Lana Turner. Not
until 1949 and films like
Elia Kazan's **Pinky** (above r),
with Jeanne Crain and
Ethel Waters, was there
any further advance.

publication of the American Film Institute lucidly summarized **Topsy and Eva:**

"Topsy is one of the most damning examples of racist portraiture in the American film: she is ignorant, thieving, superstitious, undisciplined, uneducated, and given over to swearing and biting; she eats bugs picked from flowers and butts heads with a goat. And she is repeatedly characterized as dirty. After she is sold at auction for five cents to Little Eva, Topsy is given her first bath; she fights against the water, and a dog, after sniffing in disgust at her old clothes, takes them out and buries them. The dirt, however, seems to be more symbolic than real, for dirt is somehow equated with being black. ('I won't ask you to make me white as Eva—just a nice light tan will do'), and the color of her skin is understood to be the badness of her character. **Topsy and Eva** has the elements of a Christian parable: Topsy, the bad child, is bad because she is black; she becomes good by following the example of Little Eva, the good white child. The film is about a black character redeemed by becoming white in all things except color. And color is one thing that will never wash away."

The adoption and enforcement of the Production Code in 1934 effectively dampened such insulting racist humor. Under Clause Ten it was clearly stated: "No picture shall be introduced that tends to incite bigotry or hatred among people of differing races, religions or national origins. The use of such offensive words as Chink, Dago, Frog, Greaser, Hunkie, Kike, Nigger, Spic, Wop, and Yid should be avoided." During the 1930's and much of the 1940's the Code was strictly adhered to, and if blacks could not be used in this manner, then they simply would not be used at all. A few early talkies, such as **Hearts in Dixie** and **Hallelujah,** attempted to deal equitably with blacks, but they were not commercially successful with white audiences.

The explicit language of the Code dealing with racial epithets and slurs was a constructive contribution at that time, but it could do nothing about caricatures of minority groups that were found in many films released prior to the enforcement of the Code. The town drunk in westerns for example was usually an Irishman. Another durable cinema cliché, with contributions from such giants as John Ford, was that of the heavy-drinking Irish sergeant (how many times did we see Victor McLaglen or a lesser imitation of him totter through that drunk routine?). Chico Marx was funny and talented, but others who portrayed Italians, usually as either hoodlums or genial organ grinders with a heavy accent, were simply embarrassing. The typical movie "Spaniard" of the twenties through the forties was the dashing, swarthy lover intent, often successfully, on fleecing the naïve American blonde out of her inheritance and chastity, thanks to his prowess on the ballroom dance floor and in the boudoir.

Not until 1949, amid the wave of postwar "liberal" films, did the social problems of black Americans become a fit subject for Hollywood. That year three important films were released: Clarence Brown's **Intruder in the Dust,** based on the Faulkner novel, Stanley Kramer's **Home of the Brave,** and Elia Kazan's **Pinky,** which examined the problems of a young girl "passing" for

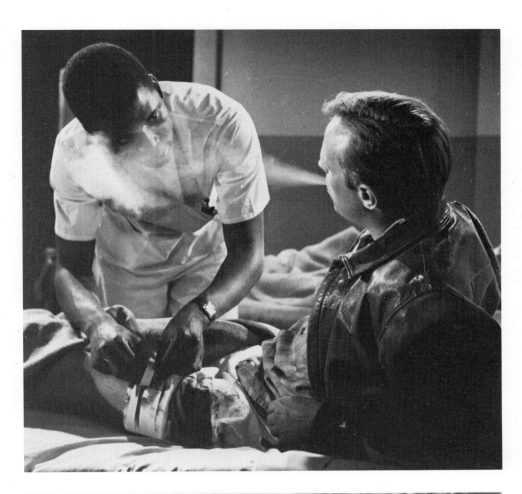

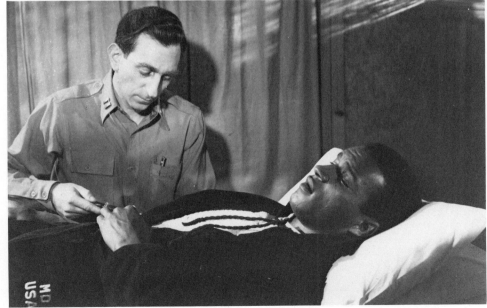

Turning point in Hollywood's view of blacks came shortly after World War II. Juano Hernandez starred in William Faulkner's **Intruder in the Dust** (opposite), directed in 1949 by Clarence Brown. That same year Mark Robson directed **Home of the Brave** for Stanley Kramer (r). Jeff Corey played an army medic who cures James Edwards of a paralysis incurred as the result of bigotry. In 1950, Joseph L. Mankiewicz directed **No Way Out,** Sidney Poitier's first film, with a psychopathically racist performance by Richard Widmark (above).

white. But this brief spurt of interest soon faded, and it was not until the rise of Harry Belafonte **(Island in the Sun)** and, more importantly, Sidney Poitier **(The Defiant Ones)** that Hollywood began to develop black stars and stories especially tailored to their talents.

By the sixties further progress had been made, and in **Nothing But a Man** blacks were shown as ordinary people, not just walking representations of social injustice. Less noted for its impact on the black image, but just as significant, was Sidney Lumet's **The Pawnbroker** (1965). Brock Peters played the nemesis of Jewish refugee Rod Steiger, and it was the first time since silent days that a black had been given the role of a villain. The whole explosion of a new "black film" genre in recent years dates directly from such ground-breaking films as these.

Blacks were not the only abused minority in American films, but at least they had a few defenders. The atrocities heaped on Orientals, Indians, and Mexicans went almost without notice, however. **Broken Blossoms** (1919) told of a delicate but doomed romance of an Oriental and a white girl in London's Limehouse, and D. W. Griffith handled it with care and considerable affection. But he managed to turn completely around a few years later in **Dream Street.** The villain here is a stock Oriental with lecherous designs on the heroine, Carol Dempster. When he gets beaten up for his troubles, Carol warns him curtly, "Now you will leave white girls alone after this." Sessue Hayakawa was an important star in the pre-1920 period, but his success was unique. Orientals were generally considered "mysterious" types, a category which might include either hero or villain. The Fu Manchu series was the most popular incarnation of the yellow peril, with the evil doctor hatching schemes "to wipe the accursed white race from the face of the earth." The negative concept of the Oriental extended to buck-toothed Japanese prison commandants of the war films.

This stock character had improved by the time Hayakawa returned to play him in **The Bridge on the River Kwai** (1957). Still, these films were more than balanced out by the lengthy Oriental detective cycle, a series of Charlie Chan, Mr. Moto, and Mr. Wong films that ran for some twenty years. These detectives used Oriental wisdom, punctuated with Confucian aphorisms, to track down criminals in a very civilized and refined fashion. In fact, the blundering actions of white police inspectors were often amusingly juxtaposed, a standard Sherlock Holmes-Inspector Lestrade technique, but one with obvious racial overtones.

On the ladder of acceptability, Orientals were somewhere between blacks and whites: They couldn't get the girl, but they were often shown as superior to their black sidekicks—Mantan Moreland or Stepin Fetchit in the Chan films, for example.

Indians as stock villains was long an established characteristic of the western genre. But there have occasionally been efforts to rectify this over the years, especially in the silent days, before the stereotypes hardened com-

The Defiant Ones (1958) was taut thriller of two escaped cons on the run. In hands of Stanley Kramer it became parable of racial brotherhood, and one of his better efforts, marked by fine photography and good performances from Sidney Poitier and Tony Curtis. Kramer has been the cinema's specialist in films of social significance, which include **On the Beach, Judgment at Nuremberg,** and **Ship of Fools.**

1919-126

Opposite above: In **To Kill a Mockingbird,** Gregory Peck defended cause of liberalism in small, Depression-era Southern town. The 1962 film was one of the last and best of Hollywood's self-consciously liberal statements. Below: Orientals never had benefit of such efforts, and stereotypes persisted. Here Myrna Loy and Boris Karloff uphold cause of the yellow peril in **The Mask of Fu Manchu** (1932). The Indian has fared somewhat better. Alan Crosland's 1933 **Massacre** (above) exposed brutality on the reservation, and **Broken Arrow** (1950, r) took a serious look at Indian-white relations. James Stewart starred.

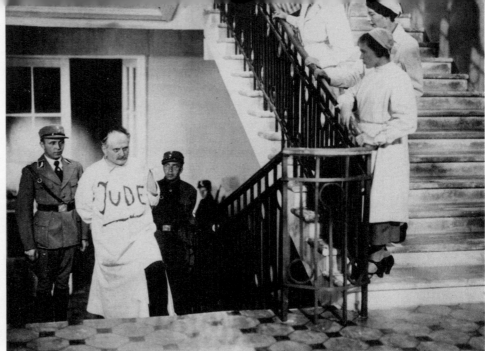

pletely. D. W. Griffith (again) often celebrated the "tragic nobility" of the Indian in his Biograph films, and William S. Hart also showed him as more than just an elemental enemy force. Among the major silent films to deal sympathetically with the Indian was **The Vanishing American** (1925), in which the modern abuses of the reservations were contrasted with the contributions of the Indian to the war effort. Richard Dix starred in this film and in **Redskin,** the story of a Jim Thorpe-type Indian who discovers oil on the reservation and has to outwit crooked Indian agents to keep them from stealing the mineral rights for themselves. In 1933 Richard Barthelmess appeared in **Massacre** as a famous Indian rodeo star who returns to the reservation and battles another group of crooked government officials, eventually going to Washington to get help from the New Deal. All of these films confronted the poverty and degradation which had befallen the Indian while on reservation lands, and while the blame sometimes fell on the easy villains of any western, the crooked sheriff and his friends, one can't help but notice an implicit criticism of government policy.

After a long hiatus the Indian hero returned in Delmer Daves's beautiful **Broken Arrow** (1950), initiating a rehabilitation of Indian attitudes which gained momentum throughout the fifties western cycle. John Ford's **The Searchers** was perhaps the first film to clearly investigate the emotional bases for the racial tensions between Indians and whites, and showed a shocking My Lai-type massacre of an Indian village. **Two Rode Together** was a further exploration of the same theme, the story of an attempt to ransom kidnapped whites who, when found, don't necessarily want to come back. And **Cheyenne Autumn** was Ford's epic of the Indian struggle, a well-researched version of the Cheyenne's doomed flight to escape the U. S. Cavalry. Recently such films as **Soldier Blue, Little Big Man, Tell Them Willie Boy Is Here,** and **A Man Called Horse** have single-handedly attempted to reverse all the wrongs dealt the American Indian through film history—not by showing him in a more reasonable light, but mainly by attacking the actions of the white man. This may expiate a certain amount of guilt, but it is much harder to correct the image of the Indian than to damn the men who perpetrated the Sand Creek massacre. Ford

was working toward this in his last films, but it is a very difficult task, as the Indian caricature is deeply rooted in the genre. One only has to witness the sad fiasco of Carol Reed's **Flap** (1970) to know just how difficult.

Just as deeply rooted is the simplistic, sometimes moronic image of Mexicans, indeed, of all Latin-American "types." The negative attitude westerns have imparted over the years has manifested itself in the current social and political conflicts which Mexican-Americans must cope with on a daily basis in the Southwestern United States. Marlon Brando's **One-Eyed Jacks, The Appaloosa,** and **Viva Zapata!** were rare attempts to portray Mexicans as individual human beings, and Paul Muni in the earlier **Juarez** was as morally uplifting as any filmmaker dared allow. Needless to say, the phony accents, glued-on mustaches, and frequent carnival-style outfits didn't help to humanize them in the eyes of audiences. The Cisco Kid's sidekick Pancho became the prototype for what directors and viewers alike cast as the typical, subservient Latin. Even as recently successful a film as **Butch Cassidy and the Sundance Kid** projected the same attitude toward Latin-Americans.

If Hollywood has been guilty of irresponsible portrayals of numerous ethnic groups, at least one thing is clear: It has never produced an anti-Semitic **Birth of a Nation.** The mild humor of **Abie's Irish Rose** was about as far as Hollywood went in this particular field. Even in **The Cohens and the Kellys** series, it was usually the Kellys who bore the brunt of the worst ethnic slights. In the first of these films (1926), Cohen refers to his neighbor as a "shanty Irisher" and an "Irish bummer," but Kelly only gets to make faces. In the silent period, Universal in particular made several elaborate and quite serious films examining various aspects of Jewish life, usually directed by Edward Sloman, himself a Jewish immigrant from London. In **His People** (1925), Sloman pictured with great care the life of the lower East Side and of a Jew who denies his family when he tries to "pass" in exclusive uptown WASP society, a theme familiar under various immigrant guises. **Surrender** (1927) dealt with the Czarist occupation of a small settlement on the Russo-Austrian border, and featured a lengthy sequence in which the town's chief rabbi is forced to perform the entire Passover ritual under the eyes of the enemy commander (the great Russian actor Ivan Mosjoukine), who has invited himself to dinner. Such a careful examination of ethnic life and ritual has seldom been given to other nationalities, which usually remain on the level of caricature.

But by the talkie era, Hollywood stopped producing such films. Whether or not the market actually dried up is unclear, but at any rate there was no positive image to replace the clearly anti-Semitic one that began emerging from Germany during the thirties. Film historian David Hull finds that while anti-Semitic propaganda was inserted in many Nazi films, they produced few wholly anti-Semitic works. The chief of these was Veit Harlan's notorious **Jud Süss** (1940), the story of a moneylender who gains financial control of the Duchy of Würtemberg, and so oppresses its people that they revolt, killing him and

Opposite left: The documentary can be the most important tool in exposure of prejudice, but getting the public to attend is another matter. Marcel Ophuls' examination of the religious war in Ireland, **A Sense of Loss** (1972), was ignored by audiences. Fiction film has been more successful in attacking prejudice. Opposite, right: The Soviet **Professor Mamlock** (1938) was one of the few prewar films to attack anti-Semitism, while **Crossfire** (above), handled problem in guise of a murder mystery. The 1947 film starred Robert Mitchum, Robert Ryan, and Robert Young.

Recent examinations of anti-Semitism have delved into the deep past, like Vittorio De Sica's **The Garden of the Finzi-Continis** (1971, above), or the Czech **The Shop on Main Street** (1965) with Ida Kaminska (far l). Only Sidney Lumet's **The Pawnbroker** (l) dealt with problem in light of current realities. The 1965 film benefited from Rod Steiger's restrained style.

driving the Jews out of the city. The film ends with the forbidding warning, "May the citizens of other states never forget this lesson!" They didn't, and this vicious piece of work was responsible for Harlan's trial in 1950 on charges of "crimes against humanity." He was acquitted, however, and returned to the film industry to make such tidbits as **The Third Sex**, a homosexual exploitation film.

More insidious, because it was disguised as a fact film, was Franz Hippier's **The Eternal Jew**, a pseudo-documentary history of the Jews. It was described by Hull as "perhaps the most hideous documentary-propaganda film ever made." After the war, these films were scattered over the globe. Many were impounded by the Allied armies, which locked them up in semisecret archives like collections of historical pornography. Unfortunately, the Soviet Union continued to circulate in its territories many Nazi films, particularly the anti-British films which made up the bulk of the propaganda output. And reportedly they prepared new prints of **Jud Süss** with Arabic subtitles for the Near Eastern market.

Since the war, a few films have tried to make amends for these insane works, and audiences have become especially sensitive to caricatures that would have passed unnoticed earlier. David Lean's **Oliver Twist** (1948), for example, was censored because of Alec Guinness's offensive, stereotyped portrayal of Fagin. It had the misfortune to appear right on top of the key "liberal" films of the late forties, Elia Kazan's **Gentleman's Agreement** and Edward Dmytryk's **Crossfire**. These two popular films were the first to confront or even recognize anti-Semitism in American society, although today they might be criticized as naïve. In **Crossfire**, incidentally, the Jewish theme replaced the homosexual theme of the original story, Hollywood seeing all such "social problems" as basically interchangeable. **The Diary of Anne Frank, The Shop on Main Street**, and **The Garden of the Finzi-Continis** were all well received over the years, but they looked backward to what had gone before, providing a valuable lesson, perhaps, but not coming to terms with postwar realities. Audiences felt they could dismiss these aberrations as insane events of long ago, certainly not comparable with our own age. Only a few films, like **The Pawnbroker**, attempted to deal with present-day Jewish problems.

Some critics have recently complained that a new form of anti-Semitism is creeping into American films through screen adaptations of Philip Roth's novels **Goodbye, Columbus** and **Portnoy's Complaint**. Described as a self-deprecating "Jewish anti-Semitism," these films often contain "amusing" Jewish stereotypes worthy of Goebbels and Veit Harlan. It is a further irony that many of the black films—the "blacksploitation" pictures—are dominated by black racism, anti-white inflammatory statements ("kill that white mother-fucker," being a mild example) that are so strong that the excesses of **The Birth of a Nation** pale in comparison.

But whether these films are truly insidious or just in bad taste, one thing is sure: They would never have gotten past the old Production Code.

movies

By the early 1950's television had taken over much of the regular audience of the motion picture. As a result, the Hollywood movie industry changed in several ways. One of the more important was the disappearance of B pictures as television assumed the business of producing second-rate, time-killing entertainment. There was also eventual attrition in children's films and a transference of such forms as the movie serial—cliff-hangers—directly to the home screen. Certain minor film genres disappeared entirely, such as Esther Williams's swimming pictures (gone by the late fifties) and Sonja Henie's ice-skating adventures and romances. Considering the massive coverage of sports events on American television and the development of such elaborately produced specials as Peggy Fleming's visit to the Soviet Union, in which the Olympic champion's skating was skillfully intercut with sequences from the Leningrad Kirov Ballet, it is not surprising that no movie successor to Henie or Williams has appeared on the scene.

Family films like the Andy Hardy series were abandoned with the arrival of TV for good reason. The home screen was deluged with programs like "Bachelor Father," "My Three Sons," "Leave It to Beaver," and such seventies successes as "The Partridge Family" and "Nanny & The Professor," which were aimed primarily at children. By the mid-fifties children no longer insisted on going to the neighborhood movie palaces every Saturday afternoon. The popular Ma and Pa Kettle series, which first appeared in 1949, engendered half a dozen lucrative sequels. But by the late fifties, TV had taken over this home-spun theme and was serving it up with different titles and casts, like the wildly popular "The Beverly Hillbillies." Ann Sothern abandoned Maisie and turned up on television as "Private Secretary."

Television tried nearly every formula that had ever worked for the movie producers. Jeeves was revived on TV and called "Hazel," with Shirley Booth in the title role. The ever-present genial black mammies of Hollywood films surfaced on TV in the "Beulah" series, which at various times featured Ethel Waters, Hattie McDaniel, and Louise Beavers. Francis, the movies' Talking Mule, became "Mr. Ed," the talking horse on TV. Grade B detective series, like Charlie Chan, Ellery Queen, Bulldog Drummond, and Philo Vance, spawned a rash of TV shows working the same turf, beginning in 1950 with "Rocky King, Detective." Others were "Johnny Staccato" (starring John Cassavetes), "Peter Gunn," "Hawaii Five-0," and "Mannix." "Martin Kane, Private Eye" had four different actors playing Kane over a five-year period: William Gargan, Lee Tracy, Lloyd Nolan, and Mark Stevens.

In the early fifties, three durable stars of B westerns all made the transition to TV with their own shows: William Boyd (Hopalong Cassidy), Roy Rogers, and Gene Autry. They succumbed in 1955, with the arrival of slightly more sophisticated TV westerns like "Gunsmoke." The B western was through forever as a significant Hollywood genre, as TV spewed forth endless variations on the theme, including "Wyatt Earp," "Wagon Train," "Have Gun, Will

Travel," "Wanted: Dead or Alive," "Maverick," "Bat Masterson," "The Rifleman," and the worldwide hit, "Bonanza."

It must be remembered that during the peak moviegoing period of the 1940's, about half the population of the country went to the movies once a week. As this vast market eroded and was captured by television, movie studio revenues dropped precipitously. During the 1950's the major Hollywood studios frequently changed direction, trying to recapture the vanished audience. They did not realize until the 1960's that reorganization, resulting in the production of fewer but higher quality releases, was the only workable solution. The impact of TV increased as network television spread inexorably West. Movie attendance on the West Coast did not decline, for example, until the arrival of network TV, several years after movie attendance had collapsed on the East Coast.

During this transitional period Hollywood learned to cater to the audience of young people which remained, and largely gave up producing films designed to attract general audiences. During the fifties the studios attempted to provide something TV could not: vast spectacles for huge movie screens, many featuring visual gimmicks like Cinerama and 3-D.

By the 1960's what was left of the movie industry was still reeling from ten years of competition with network TV. Spectacles had fallen into disfavor, because a number of them had been box-office disappointments, including the much-publicized **Cleopatra.** Spectacles hadn't salvaged the industry, so another tack was tried. Those old staples sex and violence were again resorted to in American-made features destined for movie houses. Generally, films grew more "mature" and less mindless, but they were perhaps even more exploitative in their aim at the narrow audience of teen-agers and young adults.

Opening pages: Nationwide television, emanating from control rooms like this, has won over much of movie audience. Minor film genres, such as Sonja Henie and Esther Williams extravaganzas—**It's a Pleasure** (1945, opposite) and **On an Island With You** (1948, top)—have vanished. Popular Andy Hardy series (**Andy Hardy's Double Life,** 1943, above, with Fay Holden, Mickey Rooney, Sara Haden, and Lewis Stone) sank under TV's tidal wave of domestic shows. Right: Marjorie Main and Percy Kilbride in **Ma and Pa Kettle at Waikiki** (1955), were supplanted by homespun like **The Beverly Hillbillies** (Irene Ryan, far r).

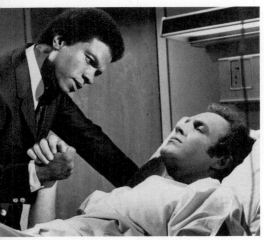

Television at its infrequent
best is often seen in
films made for the home screen.
That Certain Summer (top),
starring Hal Holbrook, with
Scott Jacoby (c) as his
son, and Martin Sheen (r),
dealt sensitively with painful
theme of homosexuality.
Brian's Song, with Billy Dee
Williams as Gale Sayers
and James Caan as Brian Piccolo,
was a sentimental but honest
look at friendship and courage
that sustained Chicago Bears
fullback at the end of his life.

One of television's great successes has been the presentation of news, and this has had a pronounced effect on filmmaking. The disappearance of the movie-house newsreel, including documentary series like "The March of Time," was the first and most obvious result, but later TV journalism redefined for the public its sense of visual realism. Forties films, which earlier had seemed realistic, now appeared theatrical. TV coverage of Vietnam affected viewers' perceptions of the war films produced during this period. TV "realism" can be seen in such pioneering films as Haskell Wexler's fictional documentary, **Medium Cool** (1969), and in such later releases as **The Candidate** (1972). **The Candidate,** which starred Robert Redford, dealt with present-day political campaigning. It not only incorporated TV techniques, but was the product of filmmakers trained in the TV medium as well.

As TV wiped out the B picture, it eliminated one training ground for filmmakers while simultaneously creating a new one. Established movie directors like Arthur Penn, Sidney Lumet, John Frankenheimer, Martin Ritt, and Franklin Schaffner came from a background of live TV drama, while such gifted feature directors as Robert Altman and Sam Peckinpah got their initial experience directing filmed TV series. William Friedkin, who joined the ranks of the top film directors with **The French Connection** (1971), and **The Exorcist** (1973), began his career making TV documentaries for NBC and NETV.

Despite early predictions that there would be a great deal of cross-fertilization between films and TV, with artists switching back and forth from one medium to another, it has not worked out that way for the most gifted and in-demand of the TV-trained directors and writers. Compared to television production, feature films give directors and writers higher budgets, more artistic freedom, greater personal financial rewards, and much longer periods to shoot and edit each film—compelling reasons for not returning to TV filmmaking.

The creative influence of TV affected other areas of film production as well. Technicians were thrown out of work when the number of features made in and around Hollywood declined sharply during the fifties. Many promptly found other film work on the assembly lines of television series, which by the early sixties were almost all being produced on film. The so-called "TV movies" or "world premieres" are, with few exceptions, cheap aberrations, reworkings of stock themes involving doctors, or cops, or the supernatural. They give otherwise vacant studios something to do with their time and facilities.

But each year a few made-for-TV films of superior quality do emerge. There was a period in the sixties when the Hollywood smart money was betting that a number of the best made-for-TV features would find a responsive paying audience in movie theaters after they were shown on television. But it hasn't worked out that way. TV features haven't even had much luck luring paying customers to theaters overseas, where they have not been seen first on local TV. Whatever the considerable merits of the acting and the writing in some of these features, there is generally little of visual interest. There also is a tendency to not try even for the kind of subtlety that is found in films made for

Duel, a movie-of-the-week suspense drama (top), starred Dennis Weaver as target of a crazed truck driver who was determined to kill him. Martin Balsam and Cloris Leachman were middle-aged couple expecting their first child in **A Brand-New Life.** Martin Sheen (tied to post, r) receives last rites from chaplain (Ned Beatty) in **The Execution of Private Slovik,** a drama about the only U.S. soldier executed for desertion in World War II.

theater release. Nonetheless, the outstanding TV films, like **That Certain Summer** (1972), starring Hal Holbrook and directed by Lamont Johnson, have explored painful themes—homosexuality, for example—with sensitivity and compassion. The honor role of made-for-TV features of the seventies would certainly include:

My Sweet Charlie, starring Patty Duke and Al Freeman, Jr., directed by Lamont Johnson, 1970; **Brian's Song,** starring Billy Dee Williams and James Caan, directed by Buzz Kulik, 1971; **Duel,** starring Dennis Weaver, directed by Steven **(Sugarland Express)** Spielberg, 1971; **The Glass House,** Truman Capote's moving prison drama, starring Alan Alda, directed by Tom Gries, 1972; **A Brand-New Life,** starring Cloris Leachman, directed by Sam O'Steen, 1973; **Go Ask Alice,** a story about a middle-class girl hooked on drugs, directed by John Korty, 1973; **Sunshine,** about a young girl dying of cancer, starring Cristina Raines, directed by Joseph Sargeant, 1973; **The Execution of Private Slovik,** starring Martin Sheen, directed by Lamont Johnson, 1974; **The**

Autobiography of Miss Jane Pittman, starring Cicely Tyson, directed by John Korty, 1974.

For various reasons, TV series have not had much luck in producing genuine stars capable of success in the regular film industry. Steve McQueen really built a reputation for himself independently of his early TV work. Superstars like Jackie Gleason, Mary Tyler Moore, and Carol Burnett have been unable to transfer their following to the paying customers.

TV has exerted a certain influence on the actual form of film itself. By the mid-sixties, sale to television was so important that directors were forced, often against their will, to film virtually everything in color. Peter Bogdanovich's **The Last Picture Show** (1971) is an exception to the photograph-in-color rule. It became apparent that the wide-screen films of the fifties were impossibly wide for TV resale, so fewer and fewer films are being shot in very wide anamorphic processes. As the film studios decreased their facilities, they cut stars and directors off their long-term contract lists. This in itself stimulated change in the film industry and allowed for occasional bursts of nonconformist creativity from the packages created by the once-lowly actors and directors.

The ready TV market for old films created a consciousness of the traditions of this unique twentieth-century art form in the minds of filmmakers and audiences alike. Prior to the 1950's, old films could be seen only at a few art theaters in New York or Paris, London or Los Angeles. Thanks to television distribution, however, the old standards of earlier generations are on constant exhibition throughout the country in a range of films that was quite impossible to see before the arrival of TV. This exposure has helped to create a true sense of a classical film tradition. It also made possible the nostalgia wave which influenced other fields of pop culture. TV's insatiable demands for feature films revealed a previously unsuspected earning potential for thousands of old sound films. They were saved and redistributed through and for this market. Unhappily, silent films, which had no discernible earning potential when talking films arrived, often were burned or discarded. Many of the major silents have been lost forever.

There is growing awareness of the aesthetics of TV-movie watching, particularly of how the viewer's perceptions may be altered by the artistic havoc wrought on feature films endlessly interrupted for commercials, by the destruction of whatever mood or suspense has been built up, and by watching a screen less than one percent as large as those for which the films were conceived and photographed. The remarkable cinematography and pictorial composition found in many Ingmar Bergman films, ranging from **The Seventh Seal** to **Cries and Whispers,** have vastly less impact on a TV screen. Movies like Michelangelo Antonioni's **Blow-Up,** whose critical scenes may focus on one small detail on the vast movie-theater screen, are almost unintelligible when viewed on TV. The delicate pastels that engulfed the audience in films like Bo Widerberg's **Elvira Madigan** and Federico Fellini's baroque panoramas are

Cicely Tyson (opposite) won an Emmy for her brilliant performance in title role of the made-for-TV movie, **The Autobiography of Miss Jane Pittman.** This page: Movie movies which have suffered variously from exposure on TV. Composition and directorial style of Ingmar Bergman films, like **The Seventh Seal** (r), are diminished. Welles's mutilated **The Magnificent Ambersons** loses power through further chopping for commercials, but at least it can be seen after decades of premature Hollywood burial.

wasted on television screens.

It may well be that a generation of buffs who do most of their movie-watching on television will profess to have more interest in film than their parents' generation, but at the same time they may have lower standards and make fewer demands on the filmmakers because they have become so used to the distortions and limitations of the twenty-one-inch tube, with its flawed color and cheap, tinny sound system.

What unforeseen effects TV will have on motion pictures in the 1980's? Hard to say. It is possible, however, to hazard a guess concerning the effect of technological change and new, sophisticated TV hardware. With the arrival of widespread urban cable television and its virtually unlimited channel capacity, pay TV, using one system or another, should expand greatly. When over-the-air TV arrived nationwide in the fifties, it decimated movie business. Unlike the earlier experience, the arrival of pay TV on a large scale will be a fantastic boon for motion-picture producers. Selected films will be able to gross millions of dollars overnight through pay-TV hookups and could conceivably earn back their entire production cost in one evening's showing to several million pay-TV homes.

TV will continue to have a profound effect on the future development of the motion-picture industry. Before production begins on a theater release, it is evaluated on the basis of seemingly contradictory criteria. Following the often distorted values of American commercial TV network censors, violence and mayhem have been, and are, perfectly satisfactory for the home screen, while tender caressing or occasional profanity are pretty much taboo. So certain feature films load up on sex and swearing, adhering to the give-'em-what-they-can't-get-on-TV theory, while other features are produced with a careful eye on an eventual sale to network TV. Like it or not, television will continue to be the dominant media for mass audiences, and an overwhelming number of people, in America and overseas, will continue to do most of their moviegoing by way of home-screen TV.

HOW MOVIES

ARE MADE

Moviemaking is a complex and expensive activity involving months of effort from scores of talented people. The photograph on the preceding pages gives a glimpse of the conclusion of Warners' **This Is the Army** (1943), but a lot of hard work prepares the way for climactic moments like this. A screenplay is created by writers like Charles MacArthur and Ben Hecht (r), perhaps at work on something like **The Scoundrel** (1935). Production departments begin to get sets and properties ready for shooting (below: building a spare elephant for Fairbanks' **The Thief of Bagdad,** 1924). And directors prepare and annotate their copies of the script, as in Peter Glenville's copy from **The Comedians** (1967, opposite).

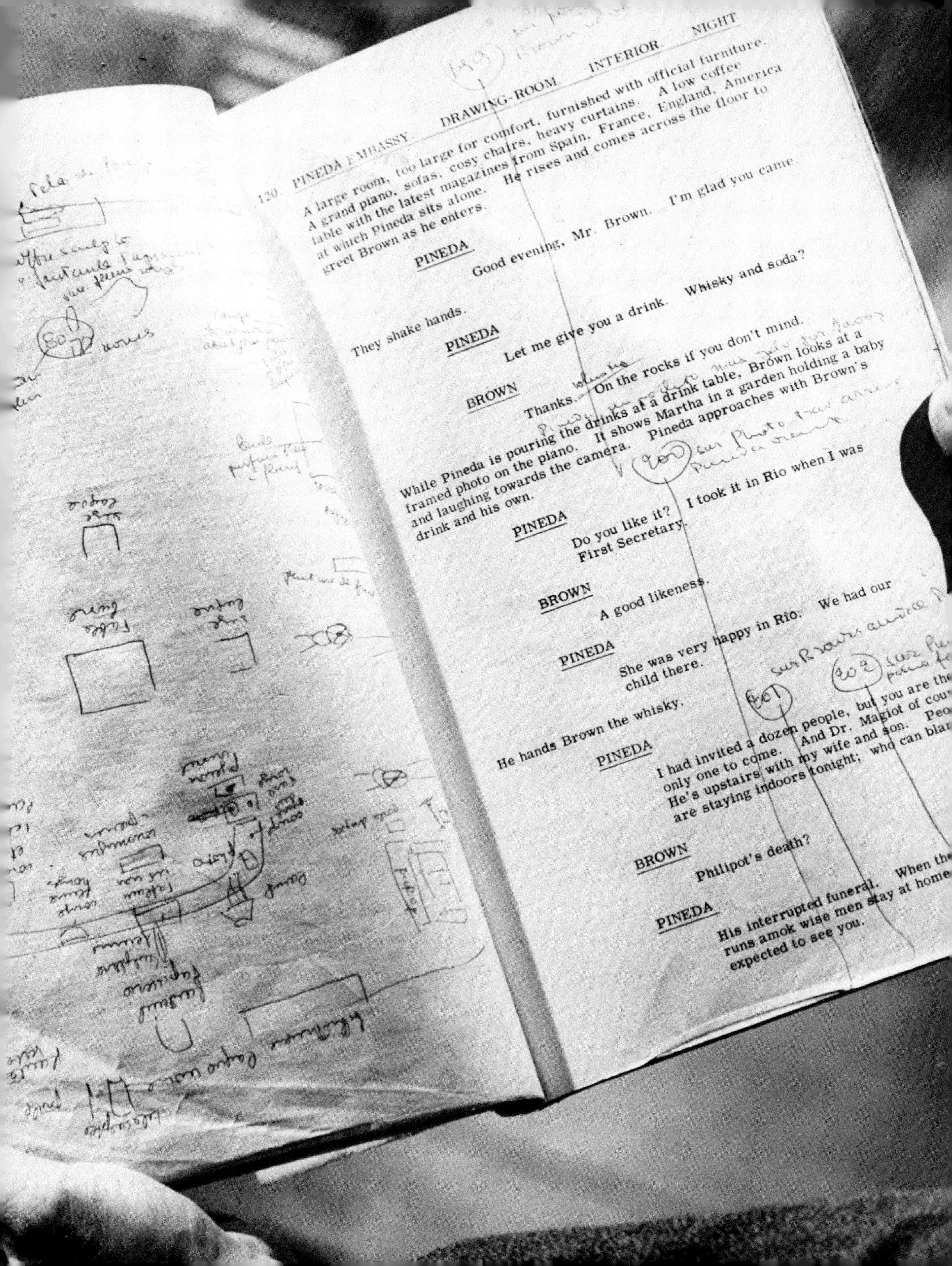

120. PINEDA EMBASSY   DRAWING-ROOM   INTERIOR.   NIGHT

A large room, too large for comfort, furnished with official furniture.
A grand piano, sofas, cosy chairs, heavy curtains.   A low coffee
table with the latest magazines from Spain, France, England, America
at which Pineda sits alone.   He rises and comes across the floor to
greet Brown as he enters.

PINEDA

Good evening, Mr. Brown.   I'm glad you came.

They shake hands.

PINEDA

Let me give you a drink.   Whisky and soda?

BROWN

Thanks.   On the rocks if you don't mind.

While Pineda is pouring the drinks at a drink table, Brown looks at a
framed photo on the piano.   It shows Martha in a garden holding a baby
and laughing towards the camera.   Pineda approaches with Brown's
drink and his own.

PINEDA

Do you like it?   I took it in Rio when I was
First Secretary.

BROWN

A good likeness.

PINEDA

She was very happy in Rio.   We had our
child there.

He hands Brown the whisky.

PINEDA

I had invited a dozen people, but you are the
only one to come.   And Dr. Magiot of cou~
He's upstairs with my wife and son.   Peo
are staying indoors tonight; who can blan

BROWN

Philipot's death?

PINEDA

His interrupted funeral.   When th
runs amok wise men stay at home
expected to see you.

Actual shooting is a chaotic business which only the greatest directors can fully control. Left: Art director Anton Grot, director Mervyn LeRoy, and dance director Busby Berkeley with model and full-scale construction of Grot's helical staircase for **Gold Diggers of 1933.** Below: Cameraman Charles Rosher and director Sidney Franklin shoot Mary Pickford in **The Hoodlum** (1919). The musicians are for getting Mary in the mood. Bottom: A giant crane shot for **Day of the Locust** (1974) and (r) a simple moving camera shot from **Dark Victory** (1939), with Bette Davis and Geraldine Fitzgerald. Director Edmund Goulding shades his eyes.

After shooting is completed the postproduction headaches begin. Lab work must be carefully supervised. Below: Cameraman Ray Rennahan and director Rouben Mamoulian examine a section of the Technicolor feature, **Becky Sharp** (1935). The individual shots are then assembled into cut sequences. The enormous object behind them is a Technicolor camera. Bottom: Jane Loring, a cutter at Paramount in the late twenties. Scoring and dubbing are also part of the editing process. Left: Paul Whiteman and his orchestra record a number for **Rhapsody in Blue** (1945). Robert Alda on screen as Gershwin. Could any director keep a tight enough rein on all this action to call a film his own? To find a few who did, turn the page.

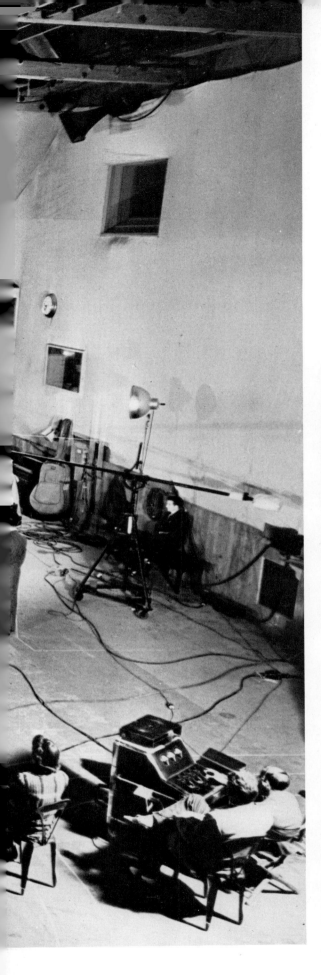

DIRECTORS

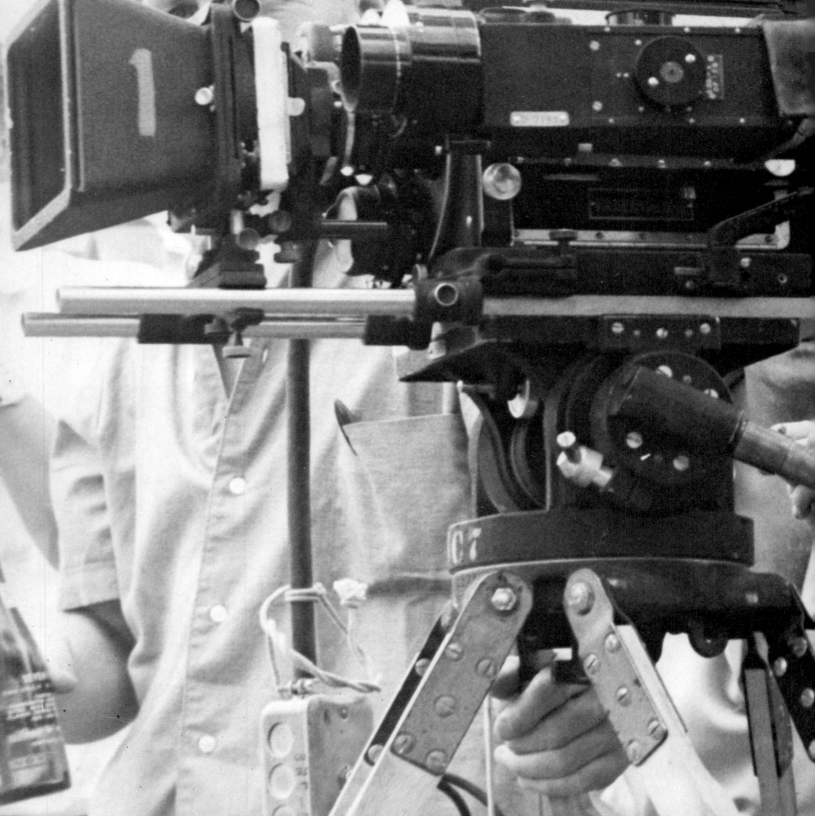

CECIL B. DE MILLE (1881-1959)
Most famous today for his spectacle
and religious films, his early
reputation was built on comedies
and dramas of high life and
wild living. He made a star of
Gloria Swanson and practically
built the Paramount studio.
**The Cheat, Male and Female, The
Ten Commandments, Cleopatra.**

Preceding pages:
HOWARD HAWKS (1896-   )
The master of all film genres,
Hawks has directed many of the
best comedies, westerns, and gangster
and war films. His work is noted
for its strong narrative drive
and his heroes for their allegiance
to stringent moral codes.
**Scarface, Bringing Up Baby, The Big
Sleep, Red River, Rio Bravo.**

D. W. GRIFFITH (1875-1948)
Universally acknowledged as the
creator of film art, he was
the first to unlock the power of
film editing. With his cameraman
Billy Bitzer (l), he pioneered
such photographic advances as
the close-up and camera movement.
**The Birth of a Nation, Intolerance,
Broken Blossoms, Way Down East.**

In the earliest days of the movies, a film was conceived, directed, photographed, and even developed by one man—who often arranged for its exhibition, as well. This was a quite convenient way to handle fifty- or one hundred-foot productions, but as films grew more lengthy and complicated, a primitive division of labor was introduced. Writers thought up material and cameramen saw that it was captured on film, but the supervisory responsibility, developing the script, placing the camera, guiding the actors, overseeing the settings and costumes—in short, creating a unified personal vision—was the responsibility of the director. By the time D. W. Griffith released **The Birth of a Nation,** directors were big news, and the doings of the more flamboyant few were widely publicized in the newspapers and fan magazines. Erich von Stroheim's name was advertised "above the title" on the very first film he directed, in 1919, and by that time a score of directors were well known to the public.

The first critical book on film directors and directing was published more than half a century ago, and the author noted the personal characteristics of Griffith, the two De Mille brothers, Rex Ingram, Ernst Lubitsch, Frank Borzage, and many others. In the mid-twenties, however, the studios cracked down and began to appoint special "producers" to oversee production details, thereby freeing the directors to spend nearly all their time on the set. This was efficient as far as rapid production was concerned, and directors were able to grind out many more pictures a year. Of course, it also forced them to give up their special relationship with each individual production, but this was what the studio heads intended. Directors had become arrogant and extravagant, they thought, and a separation of powers was the best way to keep them in line. Through most of the golden age of Hollywood, responsibility was so split that the average studio release had the personality of a light bulb. Only Charles Chaplin had complete control of his films. Men like Frank Capra, John Ford, and Alfred Hitchcock, once they were well established, could do pretty much what

CHARLES CHAPLIN (1889-   )

The screen idol of millions around the world, Chaplin was not only a fabulous mime but also a director of rare sensitivity. Throughout a fifty-year career he maintained complete control over all aspects of his work, giving his films an unrivaled artistic freedom and unity.
The Kid, The Gold Rush, City Lights, Modern Times, Limelight.

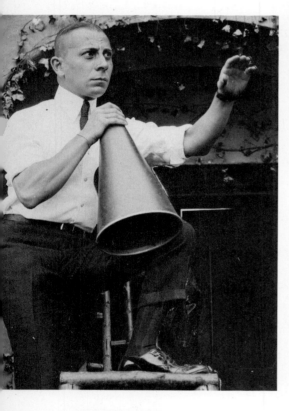

ERICH VON STROHEIM (1885-1957)

While the screen was still dominated by slapstick and melodrama, Stroheim dared to introduce to Hollywood themes of lust, power, and corruption. He insisted that film was an art and made his films uncompromising expressions of his own very personal view of a world in decay.
Foolish Wives, Greed, The Merry Widow, The Wedding March.

they wanted—as long as they could persuade studio heads. Others, like Raoul Walsh and Henry King, were more amenable to accepting assignments that weren't always just what they were looking for. And contract directors like Michael Curtiz and Allan Dwan, who might have handled four or five films a year, considered themselves lucky to get any project of interest. Their triumphs were the occasionally amazing things they did with routine projects.

In those days it was often a producer like Samuel Goldwyn or David O. Selznick who was the real auteur, the one individual ultimately responsible for the creation of any film. And sometimes even the stars had final say. But since 1960, the director has enjoyed a renaissance. For, as the studio machinery fell into ruins, only he could pull all the elements together into something personal. Currently, directors like Stanley Kubrick and Peter Bogdanovich maintain the tightest possible control over all aspects of their productions, and the responsibility for the success or failure of a film is theirs alone. Only a very few directors are more than just names to the audiences who applaud their work, either at East Side theaters or on late-night television. Millions of people know what Alfred Hitchcock looks like, of course, largely due to his hosting of his weekly TV series in the early sixties. But how many other movie masters are recognizable even to movie fans? Very few indeed. So here is a gallery of directors at work, the real creators of the cinema writing the real history of the movies.

ROBERT FLAHERTY (1884-1951) →
An explorer turned filmmaker,
Flaherty produced the first
examples of the documentary film.
His obsessive theme was the
struggle for survival, and he
spent years studying remote
cultures, whose people he idealized
in his controversial, yet
visually striking, film poems.
**Nanook of the North, Moana, Man of
Aran, The Land, Louisiana Story.**

FRITZ LANG (1890-   )
Happiest when working with the
vast technical resources of a
giant studio, Lang was a master of
the German expressionist film
and the equally shadowed and
stylized Hollywood "film noir."
**Dr. Mabuse, Metropolis, M,
Fury, Scarlet Street, The Big Heat.**

F. W. MURNAU (1888-1931)
One of the first to realize that
the moving camera could add a
new feeling of spatial reality
to the screen, Murnau tempered
the distortions of expressionism
into a unique form of stylized
realism. Megaphone in hand, the
director is visited by his friend
and collaborator, Emil Jannings.
**Nosferatu, The Last Laugh, Tartuffe,
Sunrise, City Girl, Tabu.**

THOMAS H. INCE (1882-1924)
Although he soon moved from directing to overseeing the output of an entire studio, Ince so carefully supervised each of his releases that he remains the best example of the producer as auteur. **The Wrath of the Gods, Civilization, The Coward, Hell's Hinges.**

BUSTER KEATON (1895-1966)
A true master of the camera, Keaton made his comedies technically dazzling constructions in which the hero surmounted an array of mechanical obstacles. **Cops, Sherlock Jr., The General, Steamboat Bill, Jr., The Cameraman.**

MACK SENNETT (1880-1960)
The discoverer of Arbuckle, Chaplin, and Langdon, his "fun factory" mass-produced the anarchic visions of his slapstick imagination. Here, his proud mother visits the set. **Fatty and Mabel Adrift, Tillie's Punctured Romance, The Dentist.**

KING VIDOR (1894-   )
A toiler in the studio vineyards who often broke away to produce independent projects of his own, Vidor's films examine the relationship of the individual to the society around him. Here, wearing muffler, he films **The Wedding Night** (1935), with Gary Cooper and Anna Sten. Cameraman Gregg Toland is at lower left. **The Big Parade, The Crowd, Duel in the Sun, The Fountainhead.**

FRANK CAPRA (1897-   )
He created in the thirties a
Populist comedy-drama that pitted the
little guys against the fat plutocrats.
**Mr. Deeds Goes to Town, Meet John
Doe, It Happened One Night.**

←——**ORSON WELLES** (1915-   )
With the help of cameraman Gregg
Toland (in shades), "the boy wonder"
dazzled audiences. But quarrels with
later producers left a trail of
fragmented and unfilmed projects.
**Citizen Kane, The Magnificent Ambersons,
The Lady From Shanghai, Touch of Evil.**

SERGEI M. EISENSTEIN (1898-1948)
A theoretician who developed
the principle of constructive
editing, Eisenstein's career was
sadly blighted in its last years
by pressure from the Soviet government.
**Strike, The Battleship Potemkin, October,
Alexander Nevsky, Ivan the Terrible.**

GEORGE CUKOR (1899-   )
Noted for his fine direction of
actresses, particularly Garbo
and Hepburn, Cukor was imported
from Broadway when talkies
arrived. He quickly developed a
sophisticated film style.
**Camille, Holiday, Born Yesterday,
A Star Is Born, My Fair Lady.**

AKIRA KUROSAWA (1910-   )
The first Japanese director
recognized in the West, his
films examine both traditional
and postwar Japanese society.
**Drunken Angel, Rashomon, Ikïru,
The Seven Samurai, Yojimbo.**

367

JOHN FORD (1895-1973)
America's great narrative film
poet, he examined the fabric
of society through the
fortunes of the social unit, be
it a besieged frontier outpost,
an embattled naval squadron,
or a struggling family.
**Stagecoach, Young Mr. Lincoln,
How Green Was My Valley,
The Searchers.**

BILLY WILDER (1906-   )
The heir to Stroheim's cynicism,
this Viennese émigré lacks any
mitigating romanticism. He is famous
for his black, unrelenting
portraits of a world of weak,
struggling individuals of
notably threadbare morality.
**Double Indemnity, Sunset Boulevard,
Ace in the Hole, Some Like It Hot.**

RAOUL WALSH (1889-   )
His best films are filled with
violent fighting and carousing,
but have reflective sides as well.
**Sadie Thompson, The Bowery, High
Sierra, Gentleman Jim, White Heat.**

ERNST LUBITSCH (1892-1947)
Lubitsch (r) put his sophisticated
"touch" on some of Hollywood's
finest comedies of manners.
**So This Is Paris, Monte Carlo,
Trouble in Paradise, Ninotchka.**

JEAN RENOIR (1894-   )
This French master displays an
unparalleled affection for the
countryside and its people.
**La Grande Illusion, The Rules of the
Game, The Southerner, The Golden Coach.**

PRESTON STURGES (1898-1959)
He gave to his comedies an equal
measure of high-style dialogue
and low-brow slapstick.
**The Lady Eve, Sullivan's Travels,
The Palm Beach Story, Mad Wednesday.**

JOSEF VON STERNBERG (1894-1969)
This creator of an erotic dreamworld was unsurpassed in mastery of light and shadow. **The Blue Angel, Morocco, Shanghai Express, The Devil Is a Woman.**

ALFRED HITCHCOCK (1899-   )
In complete command of the film's tension-producing apparatus, he is a master craftsman of suspense thrillers. **The 39 Steps, Notorious, Rear Window, Vertigo, Psycho, The Birds.**

BUSBY BERKELEY (1895-   )
Basically a director of dance sequences, Berkeley was the first to create abstract musical constructions from rhythms of light, sound, movement, and color. **Gold Diggers** series, **Footlight Parade, Dames, The Gang's All Here.**

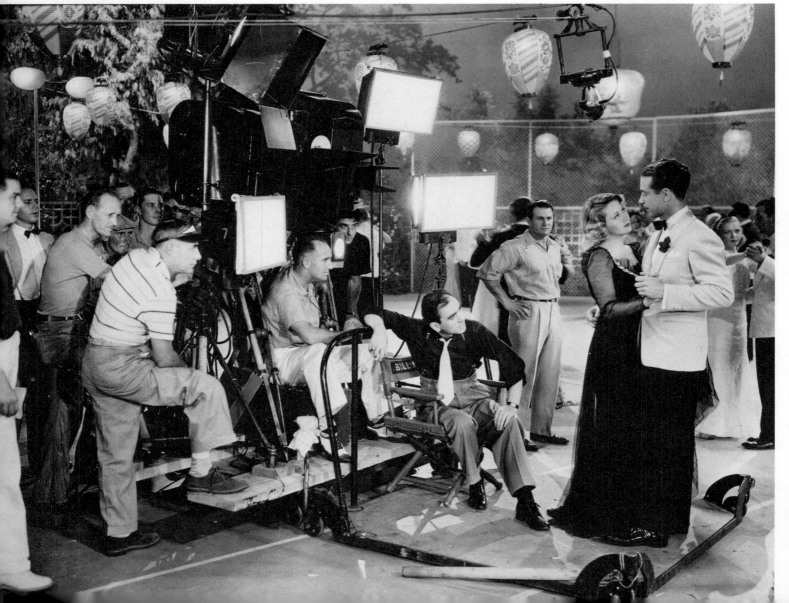

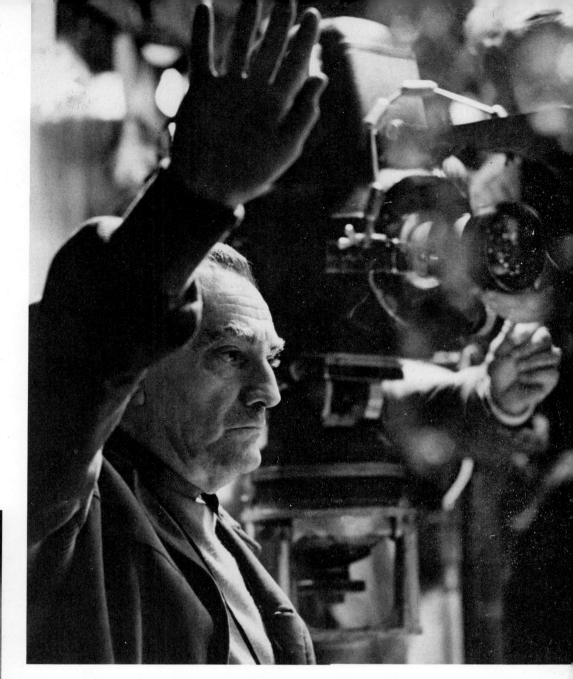

LUCHINO VISCONTI (1906-   )
An aristocrat whose early work
pioneered in neo-realism, the
later films of this great visual
stylist have turned to an
examination of the decay and
corruption among the
upper classes
**Ossessione, La Terra Trema,
Senso, The Damned,
Death in Venice.**

JEAN COCTEAU (1889-1963)
This great French film artist
of poetic sensibility
created a haunting world
of mythic, dreamlike enchantment.
**Blood of a Poet, Beauty and the
Beast, Testament of Orpheus.**

JOHN HUSTON (1906-   )
Many films of this lover of
boxing and race horses have centered
on the exploits of rugged adventurers
on the fringes of organized society.
**The Maltese Falcon, The Treasure of
the Sierra Madre, Moby Dick, Fat City.**

371

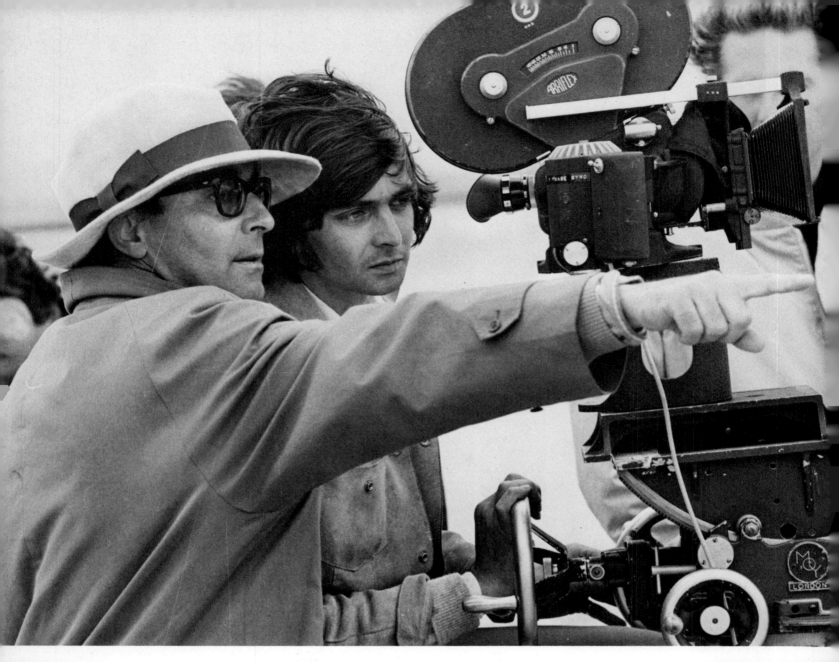

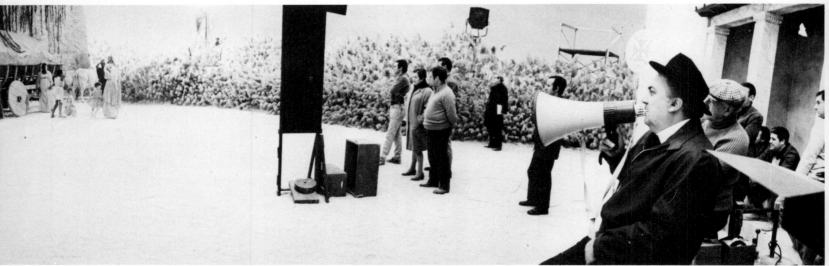

JEAN-LUC GODARD (1930-   )
The most vital and imaginative force to emerge
from the new wave, he revolutionized
film narrative by challenging our perceptions
of film "reality." **Breathless, My Life to Live,
La Chinoise, Weekend.**

FEDERICO FELLINI (1920-   )
Beginning as a neo-realist screenwriter, he
developed by the sixties a stylized film world
of his own imagination—filled with mad
dreams, rampant obsessions, and blazing color.
La Strada, La Dolce Vita, 8½, Juliet of the Spirits.

INGMAR BERGMAN (1918-   )
The most famous of Swedish directors (smiling), he is noted for his complex symbolism and incisive emotional portraits of women under stress. **The Seventh Seal, Wild Strawberries, The Silence, Persona, Cries and Whispers.**

FRANÇOIS TRUFFAUT (1932-   )
This film critic successfully moved from small-scale, new wave efforts to big-budget commercial films without sacrificing either his unique style or peculiarly romantic philosophy. **The Four Hundred Blows, Jules and Jim, Stolen Kisses, The Wild Child, Day for Night.**

MICHELANGELO ANTONIONI (1912-   )
This Italian filmmaker's work has examined every facet of the malaise of modern society. He is master in the stylization of film reality, both in black and white and in color. **L'Avventura, La Notte, Red Desert, Blow-Up, Zabriskie Point, Passenger.**

ROBERT ALTMAN (1924-   )
A willful, independent spirit
with a spotty record of hits and
misses, Altman often examines
the standard genres from
a decidedly unusual angle.
**M*A*S*H, McCabe and Mrs. Miller,
The Long Goodbye, Thieves Like Us.**

WILLIAM FRIEDKIN (1939-   )
This graduate of television
advanced quickly from
canned plays to extremely
popular genre entries.
Here, he wears insulated
clothing on the set
of **The Exorcist.
The Boys in the Band,
The French Connection,
The Exorcist.**

ROMAN POLANSKI (1933-   )
A graduate of the Polish State
Film School, he is obsessed
with themes of sexuality and
death, and is strongly influenced
by Pinter and the surrealists.
**Knife in the Water, Repulsion,
Rosemary's Baby, Chinatown.**

PETER BOGDANOVICH (1939-   )
His work is suffused with
nostalgia and ranges over all
genres and a wide variety of styles.
**The Last Picture Show, What's Up, Doc?,
Paper Moon, Daisy Miller.**

STANLEY KUBRICK (1928-   ) →
A graphic visual style and a
superior filmic imagination enhance his
carefully thought-out, highly personal
projects. **Lolita, Dr. Strangelove,
2001: A Space Odyssey, A Clockwork Orange.**

Picture Credits

BFI	**British Film Institute**
COL	**Columbia Pictures**
JEA	**John E. Allen**
JK	**John Kobal**
MGM	**Metro-Goldwyn-Mayer**
MOMA	**The Museum of Modern Art Film Library**
PARA	**Paramount Pictures**
20th CF	**20th Century-Fox**
UA	**United Artists**
UNI	**Universal Pictures**
WB	**Warner Brothers**

Chapter 1

12-13: JEA. 15, 16, 17: MOMA. 19: PARA (top); MOMA (bottom). 20: Richard Koszarski (top); BFI (bottom). 21: MOMA. 22: JEA (top); PARA (bottom). 23: MOMA. 24-25: Albert Husted Collection. 26-28: MOMA. 29: 20th CF. 30: MOMA. 32: UA. 33, 34: MOMA. 37: PARA. 38-39: PARA (top); MOMA (bottom). 1: UA. 42-43: PARA (top l). 42: Andrew McKay (bottom). 43, 44-45: MOMA. 47: MOMA (top l); UA (bottom l); JEA (top & bottom r). 48: MOMA. 49: JEA (top); MOMA (bottom). 51: COL. 52: MGM. 53: MOMA (top); RKO General (bottom). 54-55: JEA. 56: MOMA (top & bottom l); JEA (bottom r); 20th CF (lower r). 58: JEA (top); RKO General (bottom). 59: MOMA. 60-61: JEA. 62: COL. 63: MOMA (top); J. Arthur Rank; BFI (center); UNI (bottom r). 64: PARA. 65: JEA (top & bottom). 66-67: MOMA (top l); COL (bottom l); JEA (top r); WB (lower r). 68-69: PARA. 71: UA (top); JEA (bottom l); MOMA (bottom r). 72-73: UNI (top l); WB (bottom l). 73, 74: WB. 76: UNI. 77: MGM. 78: MOMA (top); JEA (bottom). 79: UA. 80-81: PARA. 81: COL (top); JEA (bottom). 82: MOMA. 83: WB. 84: MOMA (top); Richard Koszarski (bottom l & bottom r). 86: MGM (top); UA (bottom). 87: MGM. 89: WB. 90-91: PARA (top l); WB (top r); COL (bottom). 92: PARA. 92-93: WB. 94: PARA.

Chapter 2

96-97: JEA. 98-99: MOMA. 100: MOMA (l); JK (top & bottom). 101: MOMA. 102: PARA (l); JEA (top); MOMA (center). 103-104: MOMA. 105: MGM. 106: PARA. 107-108: MOMA. 109: WB (top); JEA (bottom). 110-111: MOMA. 112: MOMA (top l & r, bottom r); PARA (top center); JEA (bottom l); MGM (bottom center). 113: JEA (top l); PARA (top center); COL (top r); MOMA (bottom l); MGM (bottom center). 114: MOMA (top); MGM (bottom). 115-116: MOMA. 117: MOMA (top, bottom l & r); JK (bottom center). 118: COL (top l); MOMA (top r & bottom r); JK (bottom l). 119: JEA. 120: MGM (top l); RKO General (top r); MOMA (bottom l); MOMA (bottom r). 121: JEA. 122: UNI (top l); WB (top center); MOMA (top center); COL (top r); 20th CF (bottom l); UNI (bottom center l); MOMA (bottom center r); WB (bottom r). 123: COL.

Chapter 3

124, 125, 127: MOMA. 128: JEA. 130: MOMA. 132: Andrew McKay (top); MOMA (bottom). 133: 20th CF. 134: MOMA. 135: MOMA (top); UA (bottom). 136: MOMA (top); WB (bottom). 137: MOMA. 138: UA. 139: JEA (top); RKO (center & bottom). 140: COL (top l); WB (top r); PARA (center l); MOMA (bottom l & r). 141: UA. 142: PARA (top l); WB top r); National General (center r); WB (bottom l); 20th CF (bottom r).

Chapter 4

144-145: MGM. 146: BFI. 148: MOMA (top l); JK (top r); WB (bottom). 149: BFI. 150: UNI. 151: Richard Koszarski. 152: MOMA. 153: 20th CF (top); JEA (bottom l); JK (bottom r). 155: Richard Koszarski (top l); UNI (top r); MGM (center l); RKO General (center r); MOMA (bottom l & r). 156: MOMA. 157: JEA (top); MOMA (bottom). 158: PARA (top l); Richard Koszarski (bottom l); UNI (r). 160: 20th CF (top); WB (bottom). 161: MGM. 162: Walter Reade Organization/Continental Releasing Corp. (top l); 20th CF (top r). 163: JEA.

Chapter 5

164-165, 167, 168: MOMA. 170: MOMA (top); Albert Husted Collection (bottom). 172: MOMA (top & bottom r); Albert Husted Collection (bottom l). 173: Albert Husted Collection (top l); MOMA (top r); PARA (bottom). 174: BFI. 175: JK. 176: JK (top); COL (bottom l); JEA (bottom r). 179: JK (top l); MGM (top r); BFI (bottom). 180: PARA (top); MOMA (bottom). 181: MOMA. 182: JEA. 183: UA. 184-185: JEA. 186: JK (top); MOMA (l & center r); MGM (bottom r). 188: COL (top); MOMA (bottom). 189: COL (top). 190: PARA. 191: UA. 192: MOMA. 193: UNI (top); MGM (bottom). 194: MGM. 195: COL. 196: PARA (top); MOMA (bottom). 197: JEA (top); 20th CF (bottom). 199: 20th CF (top); MOMA (bottom l); JEA (bottom r). 200: UNI. 201: MOMA. 202, 204: PARA. 205: MOMA. 207: WB (top); PARA (bottom l); MOMA (bottom r). 208: Richard Koszarski. 209: UNI. 210: UA. 213: PARA (l); Avco-Embassy Pictures Corp. (r). 214: PARA. 215: UA. 216: PARA. 219: MOMA. 220: 20th CF. 222: UA.

Chapter 6

224-225, 226: MOMA. 228: MOMA (top); UNI (bottom). 229: MOMA. 231: BFI (top l); WB (top r); MGM (bottom). 232: BFI (top); MOMA (bottom). 233: MOMA. 234: Andrew McKay (l); Avco-Embassy Pictures Corp. (r). 235: MOMA. 237: 20th CF. 238: WB. 240: MGM. 241, 243: 20th CF.

Chapter 7

244-245: MOMA. 246: MOMA (top); PARA (bottom). 248, 249: JEA. 251: UA. 252: JK. 253: Miles Kreuger (top); JEA (bottom). 254: MOMA (top l); JK (top r); JEA (bottom). 256, 257: JK. 258: MOMA top center and bottom l); 20th CF (bottom r). 259: JEA. 260: COL. 261: JK (top); COL (bottom l); WB (bottom r). 262: COL. 263: Allied Artists.

Chapter 8

264-265: Photoplay. 267: MOMA (top); Andrew McKay (bottom). 268: COL (top); MOMA (bottom). 269: MOMA. 270: PARA. 271, 272: MOMA. 273, 274: WB. 275, 276: MOMA. 277: UA (top); MOMA (bottom). 278: MOMA (top); UA (bottom). 279: PARA (top); Richard Koszarski (bottom). 280: WB. 281: 20th CF. 282: PARA.

Chapter 9

286, 288, 289: MOMA. 291: MOMA (top); JEA (bottom). 292, 293, 294: MOMA. 295: JEA (top l); WB (top r); French Film Office (bottom l); JEA (bottom r). 296: UA (top); MOMA (bottom). 297: Playboy/Hugh M. Hefner Publishing Co. 298: PARA. 299: MOMA. 300: WB (top); American International Pictures (bottom). 301: 20th CF (top); Audubon Films (bottom). 302: UA (top); MOMA (bottom).

Chapter 10

304-305: MOMA. 306: MOMA (top l & r); MGM (bottom). 308: 20th CF. 309, 312: MOMA. 313: MGM (top); JK (bottom). 314: UA. 315: COL. 316: MOMA. 317: WB-Seven Arts (top); MGM, Inc. (center); COL (bottom). 318: Cinerama Releasing Corp. 319: PARA. 320: 20th CF. 321: WB.

Chapter 11

322-323: Carlos Clarens. 325: MOMA. 326: JEA (top); UA (bottom). 327, 328: MOMA. 329: Richard Koszarski. 330: BFI (top); UNI (bottom). 331: JEA (top); UNI (bottom). 334: UA. 336: UNI (top); MGM (bottom). 337: MOMA (top); 20th CF (bottom). 338: Cinema V (l); BFI (r). 339: MOMA. 340: Titanus International (top); BFI (bottom l); JEA (bottom r).

Chapter 12

342-343: David Namias. 344: Stephen Scheuer. 345: Stephen Scheuer (top & bottom r); UNI (bottom l). 346: ABC. 347: ABC (l); NBC (r). 348: Stephen Scheuer. 349: Richard Koszarski (top); RKO General (bottom).

Chapter 13

350-351: JEA. 352: MOMA. 353: MGM. 354: MOMA (top & center); PARA (bottom). 355, 356: JEA. 357: MOMA.

Chapter 14

358-359, 360, 361, 362: MOMA. 363: MOMA (l); PARA (top r); 20th CF (bottom r). 364, 365: MOMA. 366: JEA. 367: COL (top); MOMA (center l & r, bottom). 368: UA (top); MOMA (bottom). 369: MOMA (top l & top r); JK (bottom l); PARA (bottom r). 370: MOMA (top l), UNI (top r); MOMA (bottom). 371: WB (top & bottom r); MOMA (l). 372: MOMA (top); JK (bottom). 373: MOMA (top & bottom l); MGM (bottom r). 374: UA (top); PARA (center l); WB (center r); PARA (bottom). 375: WB.

The author wishes to acknowledge the following for their assistance in providing stills for **The Movie Book**.

John E. Allen; John Kobal; Carlos Clarens; Richard Koszarski; Albert Husted; Andrew McKay; William K. Everson; Judy Johnson; Miles Kreuger; Eileen Bowser, Charles Silver, and Stephen Harvey of The Museum of Modern Art Department of Film; **Film Comment** magazine; Sheila Whitaker of The British Film Institute's Stills Collection; Bill Kenly of Paramount Pictures; and the Publicity Departments of Warner Bros, Columbia Pictures, Universal Pictures, United Artists, Metro-Goldwyn-Mayer, RKO General, Avco-Embassy, National General, Walter Reade, Cinema V, Allied Artists, American International Pictures, Cinerama Releasing Corporation and Audubon Films.

Index

379